Victory

ALSO BY PETER SCHWEIZER

Friendly Spies: How America's Allies Are Using Economic Espionage to Steal Our Secrets

Victory

The Reagan Administration's Secret Strategy
That Hastened the Collapse
of the Soviet Union

Peter Schweizer

THE ATLANTIC MONTHLY PRESS
NEW YORK

Published simultaneously in Canada
Printed in the United States of America

FIRST EDITION

ISBN 0-87113-567-1
Library of Congress Catalog Card Number 94-70867

Design by Laura Hough

The Atlantic Monthly Press
841 Broadway
New York, NY 10003

10 9 8 7 6 5 4 3 2

To My Parents—

Erwin and Kerstin Schweizer

Acknowledgments

I would like to thank those who agreed to speak with me about the subjects raised in this book: Caspar Weinberger, Bill Clark, George Shultz, Donald Regan, Robert McFarlane, John Poindexter, Richard Allen, Herbert Meyer, Henry Rowen, William Schneider, Fred Ikle, Glenn Campbell, Ed Meese, Roger Robinson, John Lenczowski, Stef Halper, Alan Fiers, David Wigg, Dewey Clarridge, Allan Whittaker, Jerrold Post, Yevgenny Novikov, Oleg Kalugin, Mohammad Yousaf, Charles Wick, General Jack Chain, Vincent Cannistraro, Martin Anderson, Oleg Tikov, and Vladimir Kutinov, as well as those who requested anonymity. Several (Caspar Weinberger, John Poindexter, Bill Clark, and Roger Robinson) were also kind enough to review the manuscript.

The Hoover Institution at Stanford University was generous enough to offer me a stimulating yet stable perch from which to write this book. Dr. Tom Henriksen, who possesses a top-rate analytical mind, and Wendy Minkin in particular were helpful in so many ways. Lewis Gann and Peter Robinson offered intellectual assistance during the writing process. Hoover's media fellowship program is a tremendous asset to any writer.

A number of people encouraged me throughout this project. I

am blessed with a wonderful wife, Rochelle, who faithfully helped out as editor, sounding board, research assistant, and cheerleader. This book is in many ways a result of her efforts. My parents—to whom this book is dedicated—have always been supportive, encouraging, and loving. Evelyn Rueb always has a way of putting things into perspective and bringing common sense into my life, and Richard Rueb has become a good friend. Joe and Maria Duffus can always be counted on for some helpful and supportive words.

Good friends make life and work much easier. I am lucky to have many who deserve mention for their support: Ron Robinson, Herman Pirchner, James Taylor, Jim and Karen Melnick, Paul Vivian, Jim and Leslie Lindsay, Bill and Jill Mattox, Dwight and Adrienne Shimoda, Naomi Rueb, Brad and Rita Rueb, David Ridenour, and Dr. Fritz G. A. Kraemer.

A grateful thanks also goes to my agents, Joe and Janis Vallely, as well as to Morgan Entrekin and Colin Dickerman at Atlantic Monthly Press. Morgan has demonstrated many times his ability to publish some of the most fascinating and incisive books on the market today.

The author alone is responsible for the contents of this book. "Seek the truth and the truth shall set you free."

Introduction

"American policy in the 1980s was a catalyst for the collapse of the Soviet Union," says Oleg Kalugin, a former KGB general.[1] Yevgenny Novikov, who served on the senior staff of the Soviet Communist Party Central Committee, says that Reagan administration policies "were a major factor in the demise of the Soviet system."[2] Former Soviet Foreign Minister Aleksandr Bessmertnykh told a conference at Princeton University that programs such as the Strategic Defense Initiative accelerated the decline of the Soviet Union.[3]

The Soviet Union was erased from world maps not because of a reform process or a series of diplomatic arrangements. It was not negotiated out of existence; it simply could not sustain itself. Historians will debate for decades, perhaps centuries, which factors weighed most on the Soviet system. Was it the bankruptcy of the State ideology? Was failure preordained because communism was so contrary to human nature? Did the calcified and rusting Soviet economy finally bear such a burden that it imploded, much like a weak roof collapsing under the burden of heavy snow?

The answer, in short, is all of these explanations and many more. What is clear is that one central, chronic problem for the Kremlin throughout the last decade of its existence was the resource crisis. The

Soviet system had been able to limp along quite well until the 1970s. Yes, there were never-ending food shortages and inefficient factories all along. But by the 1980s, these economic difficulties became intractable. It was Mikhail Gorbachev's attempt to confront this fundamental problem that ushered in perestroika and glasnost. Absent this systemic crisis, Gorbachev never would have begun his walk down the path of change.

Examining the collapse of the Soviet Union outside the context of American policy is a little like investigating a sudden, unexpected, and mysterious death without exploring the possibility of murder or, at the very least, examining the environment surrounding the fatality. Even if the victim had been deathly ill, the coroner is responsible for inspecting everything. What was the cause of death? Was the victim getting the medicines that may have been needed? Are there any unusual circumstances or objects relevant to the death?

The fact that the collapse and funeral of the Soviet Union occurred immediately after the most anticommunist president in American history had served eight years does not prove cause and effect. But it does demand investigation, particularly in light of evidence just beginning to appear. Thus far, the investigation of Reagan policy in relation to the collapse of the Soviet Union has been scant. The focus has been almost exclusively on the policies of Gorbachev. This is somewhat akin to studying the collapse of the South after the Civil War by concentrating on the policies of Gen. Robert E. Lee without at least looking at the strategies employed by Gen. Ulysses S. Grant.

Some believe that little or no connection can be drawn between American policies in the 1980s and the collapse of the Soviet edifice. As Strobe Talbott put it on the talk show *Inside Washington:* "The difference from the Kremlin standpoint . . . between a conservative Republican administration and a liberal Democratic administration was not that great. The Soviet Union collapsed: the Cold War ended almost overwhelmingly because of internal contradictions or pressures within the Soviet Union and the Soviet system itself. And even if Jimmy Carter had been reelected and been followed by Walter Mondale, something like what we have now seen probably would have happened."

Former Soviet officials do not share this view. The fact is that Reagan administration policy vis-à-vis the Soviet Union was in many ways a radical break from the past. There is also irony in this view, in that those who now believe American policy had little effect on internal events in the Soviet Union counseled in the 1970s and 1980s for an accommodating stance toward the Kremlin because it might moderate Soviet behavior. Reagan was called a "reckless cowboy" who might steer us all to the nuclear brink.

The fact the greatest geopolitical event since the end of the Second World War happened after eight years in the presidency of Ronald Reagan has also been described as "dumb luck." It might be wise to recall, however, that when the exploits of a French commander particularly unpopular with his colleagues were dismissed as "luck," Napoleon retorted, "Then get me more 'lucky' generals."

The "resource crisis" that the Soviet leadership faced in the 1980s was not caused by American policy; it was inherent in the system. But what is only now emerging is the fact that the United States had a comprehensive policy to exacerbate this crisis. That policy took many forms: hidden diplomacy, covert operations, a technologically intense and sustained defense buildup, as well as a series of actions designed to throw sand in the gears of the Soviet economy. At the same time, Washington was involved in a number of high-stakes efforts to eat away at the Soviet periphery, in effect to roll back Soviet communism not only in the third world but at the heart of the empire.

Ronald Reagan (to state the obvious) had a passionate dislike for Marxism-Leninism and the Soviet "experiment." He believed that communist regimes were not "just another form of government," as George Kennan put it, but a monstrous aberration. "President Reagan just had an innate sense that the Soviet Union would not, or could not, survive," recalls George Shultz. "That feeling was not based on a detailed learned knowledge of the Soviet Union; it was just instinct."[4] This view is not simply an opinion stated in hindsight but an objective record of fact.

Ronald Reagan, a mooncalf to most American intellectuals, was surprisingly correct in his assessment of the relative health of the Soviet regime. "The years ahead will be great ones for our country, for the cause of freedom and the spread of civilization," he had told students at Notre Dame University in May 1981. "The West will not contain communism, it will transcend communism. We will not bother to denounce it, we'll dismiss it as a sad, bizarre chapter in human history whose last pages are even now being written." In June 1982, he told the British Parliament, "In an ironic sense, Karl Marx was right. We are witnessing today a great revolutionary crisis—a crisis where the demands of the economic order are colliding directly with those of the political order. But the crisis is happening not in the free, non-Marxist West, but in the home of Marxism-Leninism, the Soviet Union. . . . What we see here is a political structure that no longer corresponds to its economic base, a society where production forces are hampered by political ones." He said that Marxism-Leninism would be left on the "ash heap of history" and predicted that Eastern Europe and the Soviet Union itself would experience "repeated explosions against repression." On March 8, 1983, in his famous "evil empire" speech, Reagan again proclaimed, "I believe that communism is another sad, bizarre chapter in human history whose last pages even now are being written."

Now contrast those statements with the views of America's leading intellectuals. Arthur Schlesinger declared after a 1982 visit to Moscow, "I found more goods in the shops, more food in the markets, more cars on the street—more of almost everything, except, for some reason, caviar." With his literary guns directed at the Reagan administration, he summed up that "those in the U.S. who think the Soviet Union is on the verge of economic and social collapse, ready with one small push to go over the brink, are . . . only kidding themselves." Schlesinger compared these Americans with Soviet officials who saw capitalism in its final stages, noting that there were on both sides "wishful thinkers" who "always see other societies as more fragile than they are. Each superpower has economic troubles; neither is on the ropes."

Noted economist John Kenneth Galbraith made a similar assessment in 1984. "The Russian system succeeds because, in contrast to the Western industrial economies, it makes full use of its manpower," he noted. "The Soviet economy has made great national progress in recent years." Distinguished Sovietologist Seweryn Bialer of Columbia University opined in *Foreign Affairs* (1982): "The Soviet Union is not now nor will it be during the next decade in the throes of a true systemic crisis, for it boasts enormous unused reserves of political and social stability that suffice to endure the deepest difficulties." Nobel Laureate Paul Samuelson put it even more strongly in his textbook *Economics* (1981): "It is a vulgar mistake to think that most people in Eastern Europe are miserable." And Professor Lester Thurow at MIT claimed as recently as the late 1980s in his textbook *The Economic Problem:* "Can economic command significantly compress and accelerate the growth process? The remarkable performance of the Soviet Union suggests that it can. In 1920, Russia was but a minor figure in the economic councils of the world. Today it is a country whose economic achievements bear comparison with those of the United States."

Strobe Talbott, in a highly charged article when *Time* magazine proclaimed Mikhail Gorbachev "Man of the Decade," declared that "the doves in the great debate of the past forty years were right all along." He claimed that anticommunists like those in the Reagan administration based their views on a "grotesque exaggeration of what the Soviet Union could do. It was believed to be possessed of immense and malignant strength, including the self-confidence, prowess, and resources for the conduct of all-out war." The record, though, indicates that the opposite was largely true. It was the liberal/left that consistently overestimated the strength of the Soviet regime. As liberal/left economist Robert Heilbroner admitted in *Dissent,* "The farther to the right one looks, the more prescient has been the historic foresight; the farther to the left, the less so."[5]

Ronald Reagan's belief in the fundamental weakness of the Soviet system appeared in more than his speeches; it was translated into policy. The Reagan administration wanted to use Soviet weaknesses to its strategic advantage. Communism was torn by fatal contradictions. It had global and military ambitions but also faced internal economic and resource problems. If pressed hard enough, the Kremlin would be forced to choose between maintaining its global empire and solving its domestic problems.

In early 1982, President Reagan and a few key advisers began mapping out a strategy to attack the fundamental economic and political weaknesses of the Soviet system. "We adopted a comprehensive strategy that included economic warfare, to attack Soviet weaknesses," recalls Caspar Weinberger. "It was a silent campaign, working through allies and using other measures."[6] It was a strategic offensive, designed to shift the focus of the superpower struggle to the Soviet bloc, even the Soviet Union itself.

The goals and means of this offensive were outlined in a series of top-secret national security decision directives (NSDDs) signed by President Reagan in 1982 and 1983. (An NSDD is a formal written order from the president directing his senior advisers and departments on major foreign policy matters. It is usually, as in these instances, classified top secret.) In many respects, these directives represented a fundamental break with American policies of the recent past. Signed by the president in March 1982, NSDD-32 declared that the United States would seek to "neutralize" Soviet control over Eastern Europe and authorized the use of covert action and other means to support anti-Soviet organizations in the region. Approved by Reagan in November 1982, NSDD-66 declared that it would be U.S. policy to disrupt the Soviet economy by attacking a "strategic triad" of critical resources that were deemed essential to Soviet economic survival. Finally, in January 1983, Reagan initialed NSDD-75, which called for the United States not just to coexist with the Soviet system but to change it fundamentally. Several of these orders point to an aggressive American policy to roll back Soviet power and engage in an economic or resource war against the Soviet Union. The administration did not create the Soviet crisis, but it did exacerbate it.

There was a simple division of labor when it came to implementing the strategy. Never one for details, Reagan decided where the tracks should lead, the National Security Council staff built the railroad, and William Casey and Caspar Weinberger made sure the train arrived at its destination.

Because a significant portion of the Reagan strategy made use of covert operations, CIA Director Casey was at the center of carrying out the strategy. He was easily the most powerful CIA director in American history and had personal access to the president. Because of the comprehensive nature of the strategy and the covert methods being used, Casey oftentimes ventured into areas of foreign policy traditionally reserved for other cabinet members. "Bill Casey sort of ran his own State Department and his own Defense Department," recalls Glenn Campbell, the chairman of the President's Intelligence Oversight Board during the 1980s. "He was everywhere, doing everything. 'CIA director' was only a label, not a job description."[7]

Much of what Casey was involved in was shrouded in secrecy—even to some of the president's top aides. "You never knew about Bill

Casey's movements," recalls Richard Allen, who served as Reagan's first national security adviser. "He had that inconspicuous black plane, which had living quarters inside. He flew around the world doing everything imaginable. Even the president didn't know where he was sometimes."[8]

It was Casey who managed several key elements of the Reagan strategy, including covert operations in Poland, Czechoslovakia, and Afghanistan. "He would do whatever he could to cause the Soviets trouble," recalls Donald Regan, a close friend who served Reagan as Treasury secretary and White House chief of staff. "He was always thinking about it. He was obsessed by it."[9]

Casey's obsession was not a recent acquisition. It extended back to his experiences during the Second World War, when he had served in the Office of Strategic Services. For Casey, Soviet communism was not a new threat but part and parcel of the menace posed by Nazi Germany. "He clearly saw this as a continuation of what he had left undone after the Second World War," says Alan Fiers, who served with operations on the Arab peninsula until the mid-1980s before being transferred to Central America. "That's the way he saw the directorship; as a chance to continue on in the fight."[10]

Then there was Caspar Weinberger, a longtime Reagan friend and aide. Weinberger had a strong appreciation for technological innovation and dislike for communism. In his mind, technological innovation was a distinct American advantage that could and should be used to strain the Soviet economy. "Playing to our strength and their weakness, that was the idea," recalls Weinberger. "And that means economics and technology."[11] That meant shifting the emphasis in the East-West military competition from quantity to quality. Weinberger believed that American technological innovation in the military sphere, if allowed to run unhindered, would leave Moscow desperately behind. In top-secret Pentagon documents, Weinberger referred to this as a form of "economic warfare." He understood the technological weaknesses in the Soviet system and wanted to exploit them.

The defense buildup Weinberger orchestrated was not characterized by a simple increase in the budget. How money was spent was as important as how much. What bothered Moscow, according to Gen. Makhmut Akhmetovich Gareev, was a defense buildup "sharply intensifying . . . at a pace and in forms never noted before."[12] Weinberger was also a firm believer in the Soviet Union's inability to muddle along without inputs of credit and technology from the West. At every opportunity he pushed aggressively for restricting transactions between East and West as much as possible.

Casey and Weinberger figure prominently in the strategy if only because they were members of Reagan's first cabinet and stayed with the president well into his second term. Institutionally, it was the Reagan National Security Council that played the sharpest role in formulating the strategy. National Security Adviser William Clark, a longtime Reagan friend who lacked establishment foreign policy credentials but had keen insights, oversaw the drafting of some of the most important elements of the strategy. NSC staffers such as John Poindexter, Robert McFarlane, Roger Robinson, Richard Pipes, Bill Martin, Donald Fortier, and Vincent Cannistraro were pivotal in the formulation of the strategy. McFarlane and Adm. Poindexter, who followed Clark as national security adviser, kept critical elements of the strategy intact and functioning into the second Reagan term.

The strategic offensive was hatched in the early days of the Reagan presidency and waned in early 1987, when the combined weight of Iran-Contra, the loss of key senior officials, and divisions within the administration effectively killed it. The strategy attacked the very heart of the Soviet system and included

- Covert financial, intelligence, and logistical support to the Solidarity movement in Poland that ensured the survival of an opposition movement in the heart of the Soviet empire
- Substantial financial and military support to the Afghan resistance, as well as supplying of mujahedin personnel to take the war into the Soviet Union itself
- A campaign to reduce dramatically Soviet hard currency earnings by driving down the price of oil with Saudi cooperation and limiting natural gas exports to the West
- A sophisticated and detailed psychological operation to fuel indecision and fear among the Soviet leadership
- A comprehensive global campaign, including secret diplomacy, to reduce drastically Soviet access to Western high technology

- A widespread technological disinformation campaign, designed to disrupt the Soviet economy
- An aggressive high-tech defense buildup that by Soviet accounts severely strained the economy and exacerbated the resource crisis

Design and implementation of these policies was in many instances confined to a few individuals on the National Security Council and in the cabinet. "Few of these initiatives were discussed at cabinet meetings," recalls Bill Clark. "The president made his decisions with two or three advisers in the room."[13] Secretary of State George Shultz, for example, learned about the Strategic Defense Initiative only hours before the public did. That the United States was providing covert aid to Solidarity was known by only a few on the NSC. The critical decision to encourage and aid the mujahedin military strikes inside the Soviet Union was never discussed by cabinet members. The president simply discussed it with Clark and Casey, then made his decision.

Much of the literature on American policy and the end of the Cold War—including *The Turn* by Don Oberdorfer and *At the Highest Levels* by Michael Beschloss and Strobe Talbott—deals almost exclusively with the nuances of diplomacy. Such an approach reflects more on the authors than on the Reagan administration. Ronald Reagan, perhaps uniquely among modern-day presidents, did not view arms control agreements and treaties as the measure of his success in foreign affairs. He had little time for most arms control proposals and viewed the East-West struggle as a titanic battle between good and evil.

What follows is not an attempt to go into the already well tilled fields of diplomacy and arms control before the end of the Cold War. Nor is it a history of the U.S.-Soviet relationship during this critical period. Rather, this is an account of a secret offensive on economic, geostrategic, and psychological fronts designed to roll back and weaken Soviet power.

A note of caution, however, is in order. As Ken Auletta has written, "No reporter can with one hundred percent accuracy re-create events that occurred some time before. Memories play tricks on participants, the more so when the outcome has become clear. A reporter tries to guard against inaccuracies by checking with a variety of sources, but it is useful for a reader—and an author—to be humbled by this journalistic limitation."

1. Oleg Kalugin, comments to the author, Hoover Institution.
2. Yevgenny Novikov, interview with the author.
3. Aleksandr Bessmertnykh, comments at Princeton University conference "A Retrospective on the End of the Cold War," February 23, 1993.
4. George Shultz, interview with the author.
5. Robert Heilbroner, *Dissent*, Fall 1990.
6. Caspar Weinberger, interview with the author.
7. Glenn Campbell, interview with the author.
8. Richard Allen, interview with the author.
9. Donald Regan, interview with the author.
10. Alan Fiers, interview with the author.
11. Caspar Weinberger, interview with the author.
12. Makhmut Akhmetovich Gareev, *M. V. Frunze: Military Theorist* (McLean, VA: Pergamon-Brassey's, 1988), p. 395.
13. William Clark, interview with the author.

I

January of 1981 was particularly cold in Washington, DC. There had been freezing snow and rain; the wind was coming off the Potomac River with a startling briskness. Still, there was the eager anticipation in the nation's capital that accompanies any transition in power. Barely two days after his inauguration, Ronald Reagan had summoned William Casey, his CIA director-designate, to the Oval Office. In many respects it was unusual for the director of central intelligence (DCI) to be meeting privately with the president so early in the term of office. There was, after all, a budget to write, and positions left unfilled. The central concern of the new administration was the economy. But Ronald Reagan was not just meeting with his director of central intelligence, he was meeting with a close and trusted adviser.

That trust had manifested itself throughout the long campaign. The Reagan Election Committee was broke and in chaos when Casey took over as campaign chairman in January 1980. "A lot of people forget there wasn't much hope for Ronald Reagan in early 1980," recalls Richard Allen, the Reagan adviser on national security issues. "Bill Casey helped to turn things around."[1] On the campaign trail, Reagan had followed Casey's advice. The president knew he was in the Oval Office in part because of the managerial skill and political acumen Bill

Casey had injected into the campaign. "Ronald Reagan felt indebted to Bill Casey the way any successful leader does to those who helped make their election possible," says Martin Anderson, a Reagan adviser and campaign official.[2] Yet in the weeks after the 1980 election, as the plum cabinet appointments were being handed out, Casey grew increasingly disappointed. He had thought that the level of trust and shared identity between himself and the president would translate into an appointment as secretary of state, the job Casey coveted. But Reagan opted for Alexander Haig, the driven former NATO commander with a sense of drama and a sharp, disciplined mind. Haig was in many ways a Reagan outsider: he had played no role in the campaign and was not a friend or admirer. Yet he had the commodities deemed so important for the job at State: experience and presence.

When the president finally did call Bill Casey, in late November, the job offer was not exactly what the former campaign chairman had in mind. The director of the Central Intelligence Agency typically served more as a servant than as a policy maker. He was rarely part of the team or at the center of power. The DCI usually only offered intelligence estimates and assessments. After Reagan made his pitch, Casey told him, "Let me think about it and get back to you."

The more he thought about it, the more the post of DCI as tradition had defined it was just not enough for Bill Casey. Bursting with schemes and plans, at age sixty-seven, he would in all probability have no other chance to reach the inner circle of national power. So he decided to make the best of it, elbowing his way into the policy-making inner circle.

A few days after the offer, Casey called the president-elect back and said he would accept on three conditions. And, he added, they were not negotiable. First, he wanted full cabinet rank and a seat at the table of any senior foreign policy decision-making body. He didn't want to be out of a single loop.

The second thing Casey demanded was an office in the White House complex. He wanted easy access to White House personnel and the president, not exile in Langley. In politics, as in commercial real estate, location is everything. He could drop by the Oval Office unannounced and informally influence policy. But there was another reason he wanted a place in the White House. Martin Anderson, who served on the President's Foreign Intelligence Advisory Board, watched the whole process and recalls, "Having his own office and secretary up there on the third floor of the Old Executive Office Building [OEOB] meant that Casey could confer easily and secretly with just about anyone on the National Security Council staff. Casey could also use his office for meetings he wished to conceal from his own bureaucracy. The phone calls he made and received at the OEOB were truly private, not tape-recorded and carefully logged as they were at CIA headquarters."[3]

The third and final condition was an "open door": Casey wanted assurances from the president that he would have direct access to the Oval Office whenever he wanted. "He didn't want to have to go through other people to talk to the president," says Herb Meyer, Casey's special assistant at the CIA. "He wanted to be able to phone him or meet him directly, alone."[4]

Reagan agreed immediately to Casey's demands, and born at once was the most powerful director of the CIA in American history. Both formally and informally, Casey was at the epicenter of foreign policy power. The agreement with the president gave him a seat on the cabinet as well as membership in the more exclusive National Security Council. More important still, he would sit on the soon-to-be-created National Security Planning Group (NSPG), the body of real foreign policy power that was limited to the president, vice president, secretaries of state and defense, and the national security adviser. And Bill Casey.

But beyond the formal power he would wield and the sprawling office in the OEOB, Casey had another important commodity that would make him the most powerful DCI in American history: a close relationship with the president. This was the most consequential thing Bill Casey possessed. "They were soul mates," says Herb Meyer. "They were Irish-Americans who lived through the Depression and shared a common worldview. They met twice a week, throughout the Reagan years, often alone. They talked on the phone all the time. National security advisers came and went, but Bill Casey was always there. He was the most powerful CIA director in American history."[5] Casey, Allen, Weinberger, all strongly committed to countering the Soviet challenge, all with access to the president.

✳   ✳   ✳

Casey was met at Langley headquarters and whisked into the back of an unmarked Oldsmobile 98 by the CIA security detail for his late January appointment with the president. Dark blue with tinted windows, the car was bullet proof, bomb proof, and full of well-armed security aides. One man rode shotgun next to the driver and carried a magnum. In the backseat, Casey had at his disposal several phones—to CIA headquarters in Langley, the White House, and a secure phone for whomever he wanted to call. Behind the Olds rolled a backup security vehicle, with four security men, who were packing magnums and also carried Uzi submachine guns concealed in oversize briefcases. Two blocks from Sixteenth and Pennsylvania, the driver called White House Security. Baron (Casey's code name) would be arriving shortly.

Running late for his meeting with the president, Casey hurried up the steps to the back entrance of the White House. He walked with a slight stoop, and his hands and arms moved in random directions with each stride. Under one arm he held some manila envelopes, and he clutched an ink pen in his worn hand. Several aides from the lead car scrambled to keep up. Casey entered the White House quickly, with some security personnel getting their first look at Reagan's chief spy. The strands of white hair on his balding head, the metal glasses, the disarming face of a kindly old man in his retirement years; he just didn't fit the role. But friends and enemies were only temporarily blinded by his kindly looks. As soon as he spoke, his cunning and razor-sharp mind revealed the real William Casey. After conferring briefly with Richard Allen and White House counsel Edwin Meese, he went to meet Reagan.

In the Oval Office, Casey greeted the president with a hearty handshake. They exchanged pleasantries and an Irish joke or two, then quickly got down to business. Reagan, partially deaf in one ear, strained to hear even the most crisp and precise interlocutors that he encountered and often told his aides to speak up. But Casey, with his garbled mumble and muddled syntax, made it even tougher for the president to hear. (Reagan often joked that Bill Casey was the first CIA director who didn't need a scrambler phone.) On the campaign trail Casey had learned an important trick that he would make tremendous use of throughout his service in the administration. He would always seek to be at Reagan's side so he could be heard clearly.

Reagan's hearing problems and Casey's mushy verbal style led to speculation later as to how informed the president really was of what Bill Casey was proposing or doing. One former national security adviser notes, "Sometimes we wondered if the president fully understood what Bill was saying, and, by a nod of the head, what he was committing the country to."[6]

Casey's file folders were bursting with maps, charts, and graphs for the new commander in chief. He also brought raw intelligence and reports concerning the Soviet economy. Mr. President, Casey began, thumbing through the folders, I want to take this time to bring you up to date on the Soviet situation. They're bad off, struggling. He handed the president some raw data on Soviet manufacturing bottlenecks and shortages, as well as anecdotal information pulled from intelligence reports. He also included a chart of the rise and fall of Soviet hard currency earnings. The situation is worse than we imagined, he told Reagan. I want you to see for yourself how sick their economy is and, as a consequence, how vulnerable they are. They are overextended. The economy's in shambles. Poland's in revolt. They're bogged down in Afghanistan. Cuba, Angola, Vietnam: their empire's become a burden. Mr. President, we have a historic opportunity. We can do serious damage to them.

There was a moment of silence, a strategic pause. Casey continued. Mr. President, I want to send to you every week raw intelligence—unfiltered—about what is going on. I'm also putting together a series of studies concerning what we can do, how we can use this to our advantage.

Throughout his tenure as the director of central intelligence, Casey would have raw information brought to the president every Friday. This practice had an enormous effect on Reagan and his views toward the Soviet Union. Seeing raw intelligence on a regular basis was unprecedented for a U.S. president. But it was a critical first step in his understanding the relative weakness of the Soviet Union. When William Clark became national security adviser in 1982, the flow of intelligence was increased further. "The president loved seeing the raw intelligence on the Soviet economy," recalls John Poindexter. "The anecdotal intelligence especially—factories that were shutting down for a lack of spare parts, hard currency shortages, food lines—interested him greatly and helped determine his belief that the Soviet economy was in monumental trouble."[7] Entries in Reagan's private diaries support this view. The March 26, 1981, entry reads: "Briefing on Soviet economy. They are in very bad shape, and if we can cut off their credit they'll have to yell 'uncle' or starve." The intelligence, personally selected by Casey and the NSC staff, was hand delivered to the Oval Office.

After listening to Casey for twenty minutes, the president said, Bill, why don't you raise this at the NSPG? It was at the January 30 NSPG meeting that the subject of a covert, strategic offensive against the Soviet Union was first raised. In addition to the president, members at the time were Vice President Bush, Caspar Weinberger, Alexander Haig, Bill Casey, and Richard Allen. The Soviets were pouring more resources into Afghanistan: 89,000 troops were now there. Soviet forces were still massing around Poland. The prospect of an invasion was growing, and Western Europe seemed uninterested, sending credits to Moscow to build a massive natural gas pipeline.

The entire NSPG was in agreement on the need to expand the defense budget, a trend that had started in the Carter administration after the Soviets moved into Afghanistan. "Everyone agreed that restoring our strength was central," recalls Weinberger. "The real issue was, What were our goals and objectives?"[8]

The meeting was chaired by Allen, who had long viewed U.S. policy vis-à-vis the Soviet Union as strategically flawed. With the discussion about budgetary issues over, Allen began a broad consideration of U.S. objectives. "The discussion was very animated," recalls Weinberger. "It was there that we decided the need to make a stand on Poland. Not only to prevent an invasion but to seek ways to undermine their power in Poland."[9]

The general thrust of U.S. policy toward the Soviet Union had not yet been determined. Secretary of State Haig was eloquently making the case for a "hardheaded détente," which would force the Soviets to negotiate at terms favorable to the United States. By rebuilding the armed forces and negotiating from a "position of strength," argued Haig, U.S. interests would be protected and stability maintained. It was a reassertion of containment, the orthodoxy that had guided American foreign policy since 1947, except perhaps for the few years of the Ford and Carter administrations, when American fortitude, in the shadow of Vietnam, was lacking. Casey, with strong support from Weinberger and

Allen, posited that the threat was much more fundamental, and that therefore a more proactive approach was required. The relative strength of America was not enough, Casey said. What mattered also was the strength and health of the Soviet system: increasing American strength would not alter the threat, it would only deter it. The U.S. goal should be not only to raise American strength in relative terms but also to reduce Soviet power in absolute terms. When a democracy struggles against a totalitarian system, Allen said pointedly, it's at a distinct disadvantage. We need to play to our strengths, not our weaknesses.

The discussion went on for almost twenty minutes and concluded with an animated speech by Casey: Mr. President, for the past thirty years we've been playing this game on our side of the field, refusing to take the game to their half of the field. You don't win games that way. If they are secure at home, it won't matter what we do. Their behavior will only change on the tangent.

The president's own instincts led him to favor a more aggressive U.S. policy. During the campaign, he had made a point of listing the countries that had fallen under Soviet control in the years since Vietnam. Silent for about thirty seconds after Casey's presentation, Reagan finally spoke. "I think Al's ideas are the most likely to get results in the public arena—getting help from our allies and so forth. But Bill's option makes the most sense to me strategically."[10]

The Soviets seemed to understand this division within the administration. As Soviet specialist Seweryn Bialer noted early on, "Soviet analysts do see differences and divisions within the Reagan Administration, although they ascribed little importance to them initially. They distinguish, for example, what may be termed the anti-Soviet position of former Secretary Haig and more generally of the State Department from the anti-Soviet and anti-communist position of the Defense Department and White House. The former are said to espouse policies designed to counteract the expansion of Soviet power by realpolitik. The latter go beyond this position to call for a crusade against the Soviet Union."[11]

The discussion was limited to the conceptual, but it was enough to set the initial course. The president seemed inclined toward a more vigorous policy, one that would not only beat back Soviet probes but actually take the game to them.

At the NSPG meeting, it was also decided that the administration needed to begin a concerted covert effort to play on Soviet psychological vulnerabilities and weaknesses. The Soviets were concerned about Ronald Reagan, whom they characterized as an unpredictable cowboy. Richard Allen had met with Soviet Ambassador Anatoly Dobrynin during the transition. "They thought they had some first-class nut-ball on their hands," recalls Allen. "They were frightened to death."

The new administration saw value in cultivating that image, at least within the Kremlin walls. "It was part of Reagan's strategy to get the Soviets to think he was a little crazy," says Allen. This was a concept proposed by the late strategist Herman Kahn, who had compared the superpower competition to the game of chicken. Neither side wanted a crash, went the theory, but neither wanted to back down when a confrontation arose. Yet ultimately someone would back down, to prevent all-out war. As Kahn so succinctly put it, "No one wants to play chicken with a madman." So the cowboy image had its strategic advantages. Born from the meeting was an informal but very intense psychological operation (PSYOP).[12]

The goal was to shape the Kremlin's thinking by putting it on the psychological defensive and thereby making it less prone to taking risks. This involved a series of military probes on the Soviet periphery. "It was very sensitive," recalls former Undersecretary of Defense Fred Ikle. "Nothing was written down about it, so there would be no paper trail."[13]

"Sometimes we would send bombers over the North Pole, and their radars would click on," recalls Gen. Jack Chain, the former Strategic Air Command commander. "Other times fighter-bombers would probe their Asian or European periphery." During peak times, the operation would include several maneuvers in a week. They would come at irregular intervals to make the effect all the more unsettling. Then, as quickly as the unannounced flights began, they would stop, only to begin again a few weeks later.[14]

"It really got to them," recalls Dr. William Schneider, undersecretary of state for military assistance and technology, who saw classified "after-action reports" that indicated U.S. flight activity. "They didn't know what it all meant. A squadron would fly straight at Soviet airspace, and their radars would light up and units would go on alert.

Then at the last minute the squadron would peel off and return home." The first PSYOP probes began in mid-February and were designed primarily to sow uncertainty and therefore deter a Soviet move into Poland. But the operations would be used throughout the administration as seen fit to send a psychological message to the Kremlin.[15]

Days after his meeting with the NSPG, Casey called together his senior operations directorate. Covert operations would play a critical role in the strategic offensive the administration was planning. Casey wanted to know the agency's covert operations capabilities and explore ways they could be used more effectively. He had requested some memos from his staff on the condition of the directorate. When the reports came in, he found it calcifying through negligence. Quite simply, in his mind covert operations were an underutilized and unappreciated avenue of foreign policy. But this was a controversial view.

Clearly, there were barriers in his own organization. John McMahon was the agency's operations chief, but unlike Casey he was a very cautious man. "John came out of the congressional investigations of the 1970s a wounded man," says Vincent Cannistraro, a former senior agency operations official. "He was very risk averse. He saw problems that would come back to haunt us in almost anything we would do."[16]

The one major covert operation at the time was support for the mujahedin fighting the Soviet invasion of Afghanistan. Set up by Stansfield Turner at the request of President Carter days after the Christmas 1979 invasion, the program had been marginally successful in sustaining the resistance. The CIA was purchasing Egyptian arms and funneling them through Pakistan with the cooperation of the Pakistani ISI. In 1980–81, the value of arms being provided totaled approximately $50 million. The stated U.S. objective in the intelligence finding authorizing the program was to "harass" Soviet forces. Saudi concerns about Soviet adventurism in the region led to some additional contributions. The Saudis agreed to match dollar for dollar the U.S. total.

Washington wanted any weapons going to the resistance to be of Soviet origin, to give U.S. officials plausible deniability if the Soviets complained. Officials in the CIA had come up with the covert Egyptian route for a couple of reasons. Cairo was sympathetic to the struggles of the Muslim brethren in the mountains of Afghanistan. And Egypt had

an abundance of Soviet arms, left over from the close military cooperation it had had with Moscow in the 1960s and early 1970s. In addition,
China was producing its own Soviet-designed weapons and was seen as
a likely candidate to become more involved in the operation.

But while crates of arms were making their way through the
covert pipeline, the quality of those arms left something to be desired.
The CIA was paying for semiadvanced weapons that could hurt the
Soviets—AK-47s, grenade launchers, and mines. However, the mujahedin were being shipped old bolt-action rifles, decomposing ammunition,
and rusting equipment. "The Egyptians were charging top dollar and
selling us crap," recalls one official. "The weapons were just enough to
frighten the Soviets and get a few brave mujahedin killed."[17]

Mujahedin commanders had been complaining for months to
CIA field operatives about the poor quality of armaments. But Langley
had done nothing, fearing that a confrontation with the Egyptians might
lead them to go public with the operation. In his earliest days as DCI,
Casey had reviewed some of the cables running between Cairo and
Langley. He was furious and disgusted.

At the early meeting, McMahon and his aides sat huddled
around the table as the new director listened intently. After a cursory
briefing concerning half a dozen covert operations, the subject turned
to Afghanistan. McMahon told Casey about the quantity of weapons
going to the "muj" (as they were affectionately called at Langley) and
said that the Soviets were paying a price for the occupation. After
McMahon finished, Casey started without delay: "That stuff we're
giving them is pure crap. We need to get them real weapons. You
tell your people in Cairo to correct the problem, or when I'm there
in April I'll raise it with Sadat. I want the Soviets to pay a price."
He then got more animated, leaned forward, and in a burst said,
"Supporting the resistance—this is the kind of thing we should be
doing—only more! I want this sort of activity other places on this
globe, places where we can checkmate them and roll them back. The
captive nations are our best allies. We've got to make the communists feel the heat. We need to bleed them. And to do that, we need
to change some things around here." McMahon left the meeting concerned. The safe operations officer had met "the Crusader."[18]

Throughout his tenure as director, but particularly in the first year, Bill Casey set out to reorganize, revitalize, and reorient the CIA. Under his predecessor, Adm. Stansfield Turner, the CIA had been decimated. The agency Casey inherited had a staff of 14,000 and a budget hovering around $1 billion, but that did not translate into much activity in the field. Turner was a technocrat, a strong believer in satellites and electronic intelligence—and a strong skeptic about the efficacy and desirability of human sources or covert action. During his four years as DCI, the admiral had eliminated some 820 clandestine positions. Morale among agents in the field was low. Despite its public image as an omnipotent force, the CIA in early 1981 was weak and ineffectual. "We didn't have any assets in the places we most needed them," recalls one official. "We couldn't have run a covert operation against the corner 7-Eleven, much less behind the Iron Curtain."[19]

As Adm. John Poindexter recalls, "Sure, in those early years we had a general picture of their military capabilities, but we had no sense of the Soviet policy-making process, no sense of what was going on inside the Politburo. And we had very little ability to engage in covert operations."[20]

Part of the problem, as Casey saw it, was Congress. He told the Senate bluntly during his confirmation hearings on January 13 that he planned to "minimize the restrictions" placed on the CIA. "There is a point at which rigid accountability, detailed accountability can impair performance," he said. And he left few doubters that he felt the country had crossed that Rubicon already. (By summer, he had dramatically reduced the number of CIA staffers assigned to keep Congress informed of agency business.)[21]

Then there was the problem of morale. The CIA had been under assault for years: the Church Commission hearings; the purges under Turner; flaps over the Phoenix Program in Vietnam and botched assassination attempts against Fidel Castro; domestic spying against anti-Vietnam protesters. Bill Casey wanted to put all that behind the agency. "The difficulties of the past decade are behind us," he wrote to his employees in early 1981. "The time has come for the CIA to return to its more traditional low public profile."[22]

The new DCI was surprised when he learned of the limited intelligence sources that he had inherited. "Bill was flabbergasted," recalls his special assistant, Herb Meyer. "After all, we were the leaders of the Free World, and we didn't have one top-notch source in place in the Soviet Union. Given his experience with the OSS [Office of Strategic Services], he accepted no excuses for what had gone on."[23]

The war years had profoundly influenced Bill Casey's views about the game of nations, protracted struggle, economic warfare, and the efficacy of covert operations. In the fall of 1944, Allied armies were preparing to invade Nazi Germany. But the Allies had very little intelligence on what was happening on the ground in Germany. In Italy, France, North Africa, and even Central Europe they had been able to recruit agents who provided valuable information that saved lives and helped the Allies better deal with the German army. Not so in Germany itself. There were no agents providing sensitive military intelligence and no prospects for an intelligence network. Allied commanders approached "Wild Bill" Donovan, director of the OSS, about the problem. To the surprise of many, Donovan turned over this most sensitive and critical intelligence operation to a thirty-two-year-old former navy lieutenant. His name was William Casey.

The navy lieutenant (junior grade) had started out as a consultant to the Board of Economic Warfare in 1943. According to Casey, his job was "pinpointing Hitler's economic jugular and investigating how it could be squeezed by blockade, preemptive buying and other means of economic warfare."[24] Casey found the work somewhat interesting, but he itched for more action. So in 1943 he went to interview with Col. Charles Vanderblue, an official with the OSS. They hit it off, Casey signed on, and barely a year later he was appointed by Donovan to serve as chief of secret intelligence, European Theatre.

Casey's appointment was flattering but his task unenviable. The navy lieutenant relished the opportunity and threw himself into his work. Through creativity (and the fudging of some legal guidelines), Casey set up an intelligence network behind Nazi lines that was one of the great intelligence coups of the war. As author Joseph Persico puts it in his book *Piercing the Reich*, Casey was able to "recruit two hundred crack agents to penetrate the heart of the Nazi Fortress—forge documents, authentic enough to defy the closest scrutiny—manufacture convincing identities to deceive the cunning Gestapo—devise a complex yet infallible network of communications—arrange monitoring, fact gathering, and on the spot analysis."[25]

How he did it proves to what lengths Bill Casey would go to subvert the enemy. Dropping Americans behind Nazi lines wouldn't work, so Casey took volunteers from a group of anti-Nazi POWs. His agents spoke German, they were familiar with Berlin, so the match was natural. The fact that using POWs in such a way was a violation of the Geneva Conventions didn't phase the young spy chief. These were desperate times.

By February 1945, Casey had his first two agents inside Berlin. In March, he had thirty teams. The next month, he had fifty-eight teams in Germany. The methods they used were very creative. Chauffeur, the code name for one Berlin team, used prostitutes as spies.

Casey's war years, immersed in the world of the cloak and dagger, left a lifelong impression on him. The whole experience embedded firmly in his soul lessons about the struggle between foes and the necessity for bold action. And these lessons were as relevant to Soviet communism as they had been to German National Socialism. As he wrote in *The Secret War Against Hitler* (a posthumously published chronicle of his wartime experiences), "I believe that it is important today to understand how clandestine intelligence, covert action, and organized resistance saved blood and treasure in defeating Hitler. These capabilities may be more important than missiles and satellites in meeting crises yet to come, and point for the potential for dissident action against the control centers and lines of communication of a totalitarian power."[26]

His caution aside, Stansfield Turner did leave his heir with some important intelligence assets. The one agent the agency had at the highest levels of the Soviet bloc was Col. Wladyslaw Kuklinski, a member of the Polish General Staff. Courageously, Kuklinski was providing the CIA with a steady flow of intelligence on the Soviets' intentions in Poland. His sensitive reports also included exposing information on the Warsaw Pact's order of battle and operational plans in Europe. Kuklinski was in such a susceptible position as a deep-penetration spy that Turner made certain only the most senior officials saw his reports. Access had been limited to the BIGOT list. In the Carter White House, this list included only the president, Vice President Mondale, and Zbigniew Brzezinski, the national security adviser.

Bill Casey kept the BIGOT list small, and few knew of Kuklinski's exploits. Still, Casey wanted dozens of Kuklinskis throughout the

Soviet bloc. He also wanted the covert operations capability enhanced. So in early March 1981, Casey went on a two-week trip to CIA stations in the Far East. (Throughout his tenure, Casey would spend large amounts of time on the road, more than any previous director.) He wanted to meet with people in the trenches and find out what was going on. This was a spirit the CIA had not seen in quite some time. Under Stansfield Turner, notes his onetime executive assistant William Gates, "The CIA was hunkered down in a defensive crouch."[27]

For Casey, that attitude had to change. As he repeatedly told his aides, "Intelligence work is teeming with risks, and I expect us to live with them. The only thing we should seek to avoid are unnecessary risks."[28]

William Casey arrived in Washington as the most powerful director of central intelligence in American history. By virtue of his relationship with the president and his formal power in the administration, he was a key figure in the emerging U.S. foreign policy. "Bill Casey loved the job; he was perfect for it," according to David Wigg, a longtime Casey business partner and for a while the CIA liaison to the White House. "His effect on policy is hard to underestimate."[29]

So in early 1981, Casey began the redevelopment of the U.S. covert operations capability. It would eventually be put in service under a strategy developed by the NSC that would change the course of the Cold War and hasten the demise of the Soviet Union.

1. Richard Allen, interview with the author.
2. Martin Anderson, interview with the author. See also his *Revolution* (Hoover Institution Press, 1993).
3. Martin Anderson, interview with the author.
4. Herb Meyer, interview with the author.
5. Herb Meyer, interview with the author.
6. Interview with the author.
7. John Poindexter, interview with the author.
8. Caspar Weinberger, interview with the author.
9. Caspar Weinberger, interview with the author.
10. U.S. officials present at the meeting, interviews with the author.
11. The article, which originally appeared in *Foreign Affairs*, is republished in Seweryn Bialer, *The Soviet Paradox* (London: I. B. Taurus, 1986), p. 319.

12. Richard Allen, interview with the author.

13. Fred Ikle, interview with the author.

14. Jack Chain, interview with the author.

15. William Schneider, interview with the author; also Caspar Weinberger, interview with the author.

16. Vincent Cannistraro, interview with the author.

17. Interview with the author.

18. Interview with U.S. intelligence officials; a similar account appears in Joseph Persico, *Casey: The Lives and Secrets of William J. Casey* (New York: Penguin, 1991).

19. Interview with the author.

20. John Poindexter, interview with the author.

21. *The Washington Post*, January 14, 1981; *The Economist*, July 4, 1988.

22. *The Economist*, July 4, 1981.

23. Herb Meyer, interview with the author.

24. William Casey, *The Secret War Against Hitler* (Washington, DC: Regnery, 1988), p. 4.

25. Joseph Persico, *Piercing the Reich* (New York: Ballantine, 1979).

26. Casey, *The Secret War Against Hitler*, p. xiv.

27. Persico, *Casey*, p. 213.

28. U.S. official, interview with the author.

29. David Wigg, interview with the author.

2

With the new administration in the White House, the Kremlin was watching events in Washington very closely. Moscow had been emboldened throughout the 1970s as Soviet world influence grew and American power waned. Leonid Brezhnev had publicly proclaimed in 1979 that the course of events from Vietnam to Iran heralded an era in which "the correlation of forces is shifting against capitalists." America was still tentative in the shadow of Vietnam, but Moscow was bold and aggressive. A series of diplomatic maneuvers had given the Soviets a foothold in North Africa. Now they had potential allies in Central America. And in December 1979, the Kremlin had felt so confident (indeed overconfident) in its ability to dictate events that it had invaded a neighbor—Afghanistan, which had been tottering under the weight of internecine warfare.

Publicly, the election of Ronald Reagan was described by Soviet ideologists such as Mikhail Suslov as evidence that America "was in the throes of a systematic crisis." "Right-wing ideologues bent on war" were a sign of America's "impending fall." But privately, the new administration in Washington aroused fear among the Soviet leadership.

"There was a widespread concern and actual fear of Reagan on the Central Committee," recalls Yevgenny Novikov, then a senior staff member in the International Department of the Central Committee. "He was the last thing they wanted to see in Washington."[1] Oleg Kalugin, then a KGB general and in charge of foreign counterintelligence, concurs: "Reagan and his views disturbed the Soviet government so much they bordered on hysteria. There were cables about an imminent crisis. He was seen as a very serious threat."[2]

The Kremlin was not completely in the dark about what to expect from Reagan. As was the common practice, the KGB and allied intelligence services maintained files on Reagan and his aides during the 1980 election. A 1980 profile by the East German Stasi described Reagan as "a dyed-in-the-wool anticommunist" who had headed "a campaign to drive progressive persons out of the film industry and the unions." It outlined what it saw as Reagan's "virulent anti-Soviet attitudes"; a commitment to "military supremacy"; a desire to "roll back revolutionary gains"; and a commitment to using "economic warfare" against Moscow and its allies. That disquieted the Soviet leadership. The file included a quotation from a speech Reagan had delivered during the presidential campaign: "No one wants to use atomic weapons," he had apparently said. "But the enemy should go to sleep every night in fear that we could use them." The recently launched PSYOP played to this impression.

Beyond the ideological boilerplate, the intelligence profile offered an amazing amount of detailed information on the president-elect's personal life and habits. He likes to delegate much to subordinates; he doesn't drink or smoke; he's uncompromising ideologically; and Nancy, his wife, has a great deal of influence over him. It even scooped Kitty Kelley by almost a decade: the Reagans regularly read their horoscopes, the report noted.[3]

There were also alarming reports concerning the U.S. defense buildup under the direction of Caspar Weinberger. As former Soviet Foreign Minister Aleksandr Bessmertnykh recalls, "The thrust of the reports that were coming to the political leadership was that after a certain period of accommodations [the 1970s] the United States had suddenly with a new president who came to Washington, President Reagan, decided to change the course of defense policy and start an enormous buildup. All the leaks and all the reports that we were getting from our own intelligence in the United States . . . indicated that the

United States was serious about overwhelming the Soviet Union in one basic strategic effort."[4] Meanwhile, the preparations continued.

In early February 1981, Bill Casey sat in his office at CIA headquarters, flipping his tie and looking out on the Potomac River and its border of green trees through a forty-foot-long floor-to-ceiling window. In the office were John Bross, Stanley Sporkin, and two other aides. Casey was discovering that many in the agency bureaucracy did not share his goals or vision for an invigorated, active CIA. His early meetings with John McMahon and his aides from operations had not been all that fruitful. If anything, they had given him the red light. "McMahon was a constant thorn in Bill Casey's side," recalls a senior National Security Council official at the time. "Throughout his tenure, McMahon would sabotage many of Bill's initiatives: ignore his requests, not follow through on directives, fail to write timely reports or memos."[5]

The Directorate of Operations (DO) was dominated by the so-called HYPE—Harvard, Yale, Princeton establishment. They were agents with starched collars, little creativity, and a nervous caution. For an operative to be topflight in Casey's book, he had to break the rules sometimes. That was just the nature of the espionage business. At least that was what the wartime years had taught him. Hence, Casey wanted someone in the deputy director of operations slot who could break the HYPE and would be totally loyal to him: uncompromising, and not a creature of the lethargic operations directorate itself. He also wanted someone easy to control, who knew little about how the agency worked; someone who wouldn't be too independent. In short, he wanted Max Hugel.

When he advanced Hugel's name, both Bross and Sporkin were skeptical. Hugel was a businessman and had been an aide in the Reagan campaign. He had no intelligence experience whatsoever. But that was precisely why Casey wanted him. Hugel was a smooth-talking, supremely loyal deal maker who Casey felt would help him thwart interference from the bureaucracy in running covert operations. "Bill liked Max's toughness," recalls an employee of Operations. "He figured Max would fight with senior officials in DO, so he could pretty much run the operations himself."[6] Hugel, it was hoped, would be adept in helping develop commercial covers for American intelligence agents operating overseas. The gambit just might have worked, but Hugel resigned in July under allegations over business deals. He was replaced by a DO regular.

Bill Casey took several other steps in the early months of 1981 to consolidate control over covert operations and maintain their secrecy. In mid-February, he asked the president for a radical restructuring of the covert operations consultation process. Traditionally, the process included officials from relevant agencies and governmental departments who would meet to review proposed and ongoing covert operations. From the 1960s on, the chairman of the group was the president's national security adviser. Members included the deputy secretary of defense, undersecretary of state for political affairs, chairman of the Joint Chiefs of Staff, and assistant secretaries of state when an operation fell in their regions. Casey proposed that the National Security Planning Group (NSPG) alone review the operations for the executive branch. Any time we try to do something, Casey told the president, "it's going to leak like a sieve. I intend to run covert operations that are truly covert."

Reagan immediately agreed. The new arrangement placed an absolute premium on secrecy. Not only would the NSPG alone discuss proposed operations but members of the group would not be given advance notification that proposed covert operations were going to be discussed. Papers prepared by Casey's aides would be passed out at the end of the meeting and discussed on the spot. Decisions would be made by the NSPG alone—without support staff input. John Lenczowski, director of Soviet and East European Affairs at the NSC, recalls, "We didn't hear much about the stuff going on covertly. Casey was running his operations; there was very little policy discussion. They didn't want any leaks."[7]

It was an extraordinary arrangement for Casey. But it was a reflection of the trust Reagan placed in him, and evidence of just how much power Casey would have in determining covert action policy.

Back at Langley, Casey was shaking up the Directorate of Intelligence (DI) just as he had the DO. He wanted accurate information on Moscow. In late February, he held his first lengthy meetings with the leadership of the DI. Bruce Clarke was running the shop, and Casey was not pleased with what he was producing. Sure, Intelligence was pumping out plenty of reports: national intelligence estimates (NIEs), spot estimates, and economic reports on a variety of international issues, but

Casey found most of them useless. "For Bill, most of the NIEs were completely arcane and irrelevant to the problems we were facing," recalls Henry Rowen, who later headed Casey's National Intelligence Council. "And those that were relevant were still useless—always hedging their bets with conclusions such as 'on the one hand,' but 'on the other.' "[8]

Agency analysts were also too reliant on computer databases and printouts, which were directing thinking rather than serving as a tool. "Facts can confuse. The wrong picture is not worth a thousand words," was one well-worn Casey phrase for the DI. The other: "The most difficult thing to prove is the obvious." Casey told Clarke he wanted the DI turning out more intellectually rigorous projects with some imagination. He also wanted it to focus on more relevant facets of traditional subjects. It wasn't enough to know how much money Moscow was earning from oil exports. Tell me its importance to them, Casey said.

Bringing in new people who shared his worldview—anticommunism, an appreciation for economics and strategy—was another Casey goal. It helped if they had a new perspective for the agency. As he put it in an agency newsletter, the system of intelligence reports had become "slow, cumbersome, and inconsistent with providing the policy maker with a timely, crisp forecast that incorporates clearly defined alternative views."

One of the most important areas of study for Casey was the Soviet economy. True, the Directorate of Intelligence churned out thousands of pages of reports on the subject every year, but little of what it produced was relevant. So he brought in new talent to get pertinent information. If he was going to propose and conduct a strategic offensive against the Soviet economy, he needed his own people in place giving him the necessary information.

Casey managed to lure Henry Rowen, former president of the Rand Corporation, to take over the National Intelligence Council. He brought on as his special assistant Herb Meyer, an editor with *Fortune* magazine. Both, by no coincidence, were experts on the Soviet economy. So, too, was David Wigg, Casey's White House liaison. An economist, he was the first to set up the agency's system for tracking Soviet hard currency flows and foreign earnings. The specialties of the people Casey surrounded himself with left no doubt where his interests were.

Since the 1950s, the CIA had been the primary institution in the

West organizing the study of the Soviet economy. Year after year it reported that the Soviet economy was lumbering along at 3 percent growth per year. But anecdotal information didn't conform to those numbers. Casey believed the Soviets were in trouble, so he asked Meyer to come up with his own assessment.

The basis of CIA estimates was SOVMOD, a computer system that made use of Soviet published statistics, processed through a variety of mathematical calculations. Meyer looked into it and told Casey, "SOVMOD is a fraud."

"The CIA's fairly rosy predictions about the Soviet economy mirrored those of the Kremlin," recalls Meyer. "The reality was food lines were getting longer. There were more stoppages and more shortages. Military spending was increasing dramatically. There was a lot of anecdotal evidence which supported the idea that the Soviet economy wasn't growing."[9]

Casey also had Meyer undertake a series of sensitive studies about the Soviet economy that could be used strategically by U.S. policy makers. These were "vulnerability assessments," top-secret reports pulled by Meyer from raw intelligence that determined in what ways the Soviet Union could be "squeezed." Meyer concluded in one report that Moscow was "terribly vulnerable economically. . . . It should be a matter of high national policy to play to these vulnerabilities."

This process was in many ways a breakthrough at the CIA. Intelligence assessments had always focused on Soviet strengths: their military power, their gold reserves, their foreign assistance to allies. Casey wanted that changed. "Bill felt we had always focused on their strengths in our intelligence efforts," recalls Meyer, "never their weaknesses. If intelligence was going to be a real tool for policy, policy makers needed to know where the Soviets were weak so we could take advantage of it."[10] And the director read many of these reports. According to Meyer, Casey spent one hour nearly every day studying the Soviet economy. "He practically invented the American concept of economic warfare when he served with the Economic Warfare Board during the Second World War. No one should be surprised that he was looking to hurt them."

In addition to relying on his advisers, Casey was constantly on the phone to outsiders—players or analysts—to talk about the Soviet economy. "Bill had a whole world of contacts," says Meyer. "He knew a dozen big bankers and a lot of CEOs. He was working the phones constantly, asking for information, getting their assessment, or asking for a favor."[11]

From the earliest days, the Directorate of Intelligence was resentful of the intrusion by Casey, Rowen, and Meyer. The fast-track, highbrow Soviet section especially resisted efforts to focus on these new areas. So by July, Casey decided to sever the section from the rest of the agency. He had the Soviet intelligence analysts moved from the grounds of the main office campus in Langley to another Washington suburb, Vienna. Casey hoped the transfer would limit the influence of the agency's regular Soviet analysts and allow his team to work more freely.

Another important and neglected area of agency study was the psychological section. The CIA had for years asked psychologists and psychiatrists to write profiles on foreign officials. These were often pulled from biographical reports and the encounters other officials might have with them. But Bill Casey wanted something more relevant for the president. He wanted to know the "psychological dimensions" of the way the Soviet leadership viewed the United States. What frightened them? How was their "ego resilience"? How quickly did they bounce back from challenges? What would shake their confidence? "There were indications early on that the leadership was in trouble," recalls Professor Allan Whittaker, a clinical psychologist who has done work for the agency on the Soviet leadership. "But it wasn't very specific. The hope was that we could get more specific information, and then policy makers could use it."[12] The first areas that Casey wanted the section to explore were the economy, Poland, and Afghanistan.

In March there was another meeting of the NSPG, and Bill Casey was pushing a new idea. Building on the president's commitment to take the strategic offensive, the DCI was encouraged to use covert operations in the developing world. The superpower competition in the third world is taking a lot of our energy, Casey began. The Soviets and their proxies are encroaching on our allies everywhere. They have expanded their power base on almost every continent. We have an opportunity here. There are new insurgencies developing in the third world. These are like the anticolonialism movements of the 1950s and '60s and the communist insurgencies of the 1960s and '70s. Only this time they are fighting communists. We need to be backing these movements with money and political muscle. If we can get the Soviets to expend enough resources, it will create fissures in the system. We need half a dozen Afghanistans.

What Casey was suggesting later became known as the Reagan Doctrine, an effort to finance and support anticommunist insurgencies around the world. Caspar Weinberger, Richard Allen, and Alexander Haig liked the idea, and so did the president. Reagan asked the director to explore the matter in greater detail and identify insurgents who could be supported.

1. Yevgenny Novikov, interview with the author.
2. Oleg Kalugin, comments at the Hoover Institution.
3. File on display at the Reagan Library.
4. Aleksandr Bessmertnykh, comments at Princeton University conference "A Retrospective on the End of the Cold War," May 3, 1993.
5. Interview with the author.
6. Interview with the author.
7. John Lenczowski, interview with the author; The New York Times, June 11, 1984.
8. Henry Rowen, interview with the author.
9. Herb Meyer, interview with the author.
10. Herb Meyer, interview with the author.
11. Herb Meyer, interview with the author.
12. Allan Whittaker, interview with the author.

3

In early April 1981, William Casey was off for a three-week tour of the Middle East and Europe. It was usually during darkness that his aircraft arrived in sensitive spots like the Middle East. The huge black C-141 Starlifter taxied up to a secluded part of the airport terminal. No U.S. embassy diplomatic personnel were ever present, either at the plane's arrival or at its departure.

The aircraft always flew nonstop from Washington to its destination. If necessary, a KC-10 tanker aircraft based overseas would intercept for midair refueling. The crew wore civilian clothes, as did all the passengers. The plane had no external markings, to prevent identification. Inside, the transporter had been transformed into a flying hotel and communications center. Up front, the VIP area was luxuriously appointed with couches, easy chairs, bed, and washing facilities. The rear portion contained the ultrasophisticated communications that allowed the DCI to speak securely to Washington or anywhere else. He could communicate with a CIA station halfway around the world, or even agents in the field outfitted with special equipment. The aircraft was protected by the latest electronic jamming equipment and radar to counter the threat of incoming missiles. The U.S. crew was heavily armed and stayed on board twenty-four hours a day. No other personnel could enter the aircraft. When on the ground, it was protected by armed guards.

On his transoceanic flight, Casey was getting updates on a wide array of issues. The situation in Poland was shifting quickly. He spoke with Caspar Weinberger about the mujahedin and U.S. military assistance plans for the Middle East. He was also getting advice on dealing with the Saudis, with whom he would be speaking shortly. But first there was the matter of Egypt, and the poor quality of arms going to the muj.

Cairo was dirty and crowded. The mood was tense. Casey was in the country for two days to meet with Anwar Sadat and an assortment of military and intelligence officials. The Egyptian president and his guest covered a lot of ground, but Casey was there to tell Sadat in no uncertain terms that the current arrangement for supplying the mujahedin was unacceptable. This stuff is garbage, he told Sadat. The Saudis were also paying for arms and would not be happy to learn how Cairo was spending their money, since the Saudi king was at the same time providing substantial funds to support Sadat's government.

Weinberger was an old hand when it came to the Saudis. He had spent years at Bechtel handling many delicate issues with them. He was considered a good friend and was welcomed by the royal family whenever they met. Casey, with the support of the president, wanted to talk with them about upping the ante in Afghanistan. Weinberger reminded Casey that the royal family was very anti-Soviet and felt vulnerable to Soviet designs in the Gulf.

Vice President George Bush was also close to the Saudis, particularly the director of Saudi intelligence and Casey's host, Prince Turki al-Faisl. During his brief stint as CIA director, Bush had worked with Turki, and the two had gotten along splendidly. When Bush returned to private life in the late 1970s, he maintained his relations with the Saudi intelligence chief. Bush liked him and was involved in the oil business, so it only made sense. He had given Casey some insights into Turki before his trip, and the vice president's assessment seemed quite accurate. Bush sent the prince a note shortly before Casey left Washington, saying that Casey would be a good friend of the Saudis and was sympathetic to their geostrategic position. Saudi Arabia is 865,000 square miles of desolation. With sandy, barren soil, the secret to Saudi wealth lies deep underground.

Saudi Arabia and its oil wealth were of critical importance to the West. But the country was also quite vulnerable. It had barely 9 million people and was surrounded by enemies with large, well-equipped armies. The royal family was insulated from the rest of Saudi society. Just north, Iran and Iraq were fighting a bloody war. The Ayatollah Khomeini had already made provocative statements to his radical followers about the corrupt nature of the House of Saud. Should the Iranians overrun Iraqi lines, Riyadh feared it might be next.

The ayatollah's radical Islamic ideology was also attractive to numerous people in Saudi society who were unhappy with the country's political and economic order. Security had been stepped up after the bloody incident at Mecca in 1979, but more trouble was expected. In a very real sense, the biggest security concern for the Saudis was not the state of Israel, the avowed enemy, but Muslim brethren across the Gulf in Iran.

The Saudis also faced another threat right on their border. A radical pro-Marxist government had come to power in South Yemen, which borders Saudi Arabia on the east. The kingdom felt that South Yemen had two powerful incentives to seek the overthrow of the royal family. Along with its ideological fervor, South Yemen coveted Saudi oil resources, which it lacked. There was no defined border between the two countries. Aden had welcomed Soviet military advisers, which clearly troubled the Saudis. As one member of the Saudi royal family told *The New York Times:* "The Soviet military presence in Cuba is not nearly so serious a threat to Western security as the military presence of the Russians in the Gulf and in the Horn of Africa."[1]

The Soviet invasion of Afghanistan was also widely interpreted in Saudi ruling circles as a move toward the Persian Gulf, with the end hope of capturing rich oil fields on the Arab peninsula. The head of Saudi Arabian intelligence put Soviet objectives in the region in very clear terms: "The answer is simple: our oil. . . . At this moment we do not expect an invasion, but we do expect the Soviets to use their power to maneuver themselves into a position to make arrangements for a guaranteed oil supply."[2]

Within the borders of the kingdom, several groups and organizations were hatching conspiratorial plans against the royal family. Organizations such as the Union of Democratic Youth, Socialist Workers Party, and the Shiite-dominated IRO (Organization of the Islamic Revolution for the Liberation of the Arabian Peninsula) were getting backing from Syria and Iran.

To Casey, the Saudis' concern about Soviet intentions presented a chance to make Saudi Arabia a powerful ally of the United States. Oil was the mother's milk of industry, and the West needed stable, secure access to reserves if there was going to be any economic recovery. In the 1970s, when Arab oil producers had been aggressively aligned against the West, the price of oil had gone through the roof. And while the virtual monopoly on oil production that OPEC enjoyed in the '70s was gone, the organization still touted power and influence. Weinberger had expressed the view that a lot had changed in the past two years to make the Saudis much more amenable to the United States. Bringing oil prices down was an important goal of the new administration. It would help the U.S. economy enormously.

The giant black bird taxied off the runway into a secluded hangar at the north end of the strip. There the plane was greeted with an attachment of U.S. embassy security personnel and two people from the CIA station.

The CIA station in Saudi Arabia was small and demoralized. Not only had the Turner years meant cutbacks and restrictions but the Iranian revolution had forced caution. When radical students had stormed the U.S. embassy in Tehran, CIA officials there had been taken by surprise. As a consequence, thousands of pages of CIA reports and cables were in the hands of extremists. No doubt some of the cables contained information about the station in Riyadh.

For Casey this was a get-acquainted session. He wanted to meet those foot soldiers out in the field, find out how good they were, and discover what made them tick. But it was also an opportunity for the station to meet the new director, whose reputation had preceded him. The Saudi station had been long neglected, in Casey's eyes. While the State and Commerce departments had upped their presence in the 1970s because of Riyadh's central importance in world oil production, the agency did not follow suit. Casey made rebuilding the Saudi station one of his most important tasks. It would be critical if the administration's objectives were to succeed. The Saudis, with their mix of wealth, secrecy, and avowed anticommunism, would be a critical component of the strategic offensive against the Soviet bloc. "Saudi Arabia was one of the most important American allies for us in the 1980s," recalls Alan Fiers, who ran operations for the agency on the Arab peninsula at the time. "They were seen as a linchpin, and we had an unabridged relationship with them. They were critical for a whole host of important objectives."[3]

Station briefers told Casey that in the next several weeks Kuwait was expected to cozy up to Moscow. The emir of the tiny oil-producing kingdom was running scared. This wealthy country had a ringside seat for the Iran-Iraq War raging along its border. Even worse, it had no military to speak of. The turmoil in the region created by the Iranian revolution, the Soviet invasion of Afghanistan, and the presence of hundreds of radical Palestinians in Kuwait City, emboldened by radical Islam, all served to unhinge the government. At the end of April, Sheik Sabah, the Kuwaiti foreign minister, was going to visit Moscow for consultations on Gulf issues. Sources in Kuwait were hinting that Sabah was going to declare that the Gulf area was threatened not by the Soviet Union but by the United States. Kuwait was appeasing Moscow because of its vulnerability. Sabah was actively courting the Saudis to say the same and work with Kuwait to prevent the deployment of U.S. forces in the region. Would Saudi Arabia be tempted by his proposal?

The Saudis were not sympathetic to the idea—they knew who posed the threat, the briefers told Casey. The Reagan administration was proposing the sale of AWACS and advanced fighter aircraft to the Saudis to strengthen their military capability, but they were still concerned about America's reliability. Weinberger had basically told Casey the same thing.

The Saudi king and Prince Turki were basically pro-Western. While they regularly voiced their opposition to U.S. support for Israel, they detested even more the anti-Muslim propaganda and oppression that Moscow was so aggressively pursuing in Soviet Central Asia and now Afghanistan. Casey was one of the first senior cabinet officials to come to Saudi Arabia. And his anticommunist inclinations were already well known in Saudi diplomatic circles.

That afternoon a motorcade pulled up in back of the U.S. embassy. Prince Turki al-Faisl had arrived with a dozen security officials to pick up the new DCI personally. The two chiefs exchanged handshakes and greetings, then got into the backseat of the limousine. The motorcade raced off. Casey's Saudi hosts were kind, generous, and very warm.

Turki was an engaging man, with a keen mind and a strong affection for Western sensibilities. A devout Muslim, he was peculiarly Western in his outlook. He despised Marxists and atheists. He got along surprisingly well with Casey, the equally devout Catholic. Turki saw to it that the director could attend a private and secret Catholic mass whenever he came to Riyadh. It was an extraordinary gesture, given that Bibles were not even allowed in the country. For the rather cosmopolitan Turki, Bill Casey was a man of a different faith who shared his convictions about the Soviet Union.

They entered a secure facility outside of Riyadh. It was ornate with date trees and other exotic plants, offering some color and greenery in an otherwise pale desert. They moved into a small conference room. The prince and Casey went first, followed by their aides. On the walls were some Arabic rugs. Casey asked a few quick questions about them. In the 1970s, he had been involved in an export-import business that brought Bosnian rugs into the States and sold them to dealers.

The most immediate concern for Prince Turki was the "encirclement of Saudi Arabia by the Soviet Union." There were an estimated 1,500 Soviet military advisers in South Yemen; 500 in North Yemen; 2,500 in Syria; 1,000 in Ethiopia; and 1,000 in Iraq. With the Soviets' almost 100,000 troops in Afghanistan, Turki expected a thrust to the Persian Gulf shortly. The Soviets can easily take over the soft underbelly of Baristan-Baluchistan, then head straight for the warm waters of the Persian Gulf, he told Casey.

Both the president and I understand what the communists are up to, Casey concurred. He quoted then Foreign Minister Molotov when he told Hitler's Moscow ambassador in 1939, "The area south of Bantum and Baku in the general direction of the Persian Gulf is recognized as the center of the aspirations of the Soviet Union." That's still the case today, said Casey. Nothing has changed.

He continued, We should never have let the shah down. We'd be in better shape if he was still in power. He informed the prince of Washington's plans to extend a large amount of aid to Pakistan shortly to deal with the Soviet threat. He also told the prince that he was going to push for a large increase in U.S. aid to the mujahedin. We want to make them bleed in Afghanistan, punish them badly, said Casey. We very much thank you for your support for the Afghan project. He went on to describe his conversations in Cairo about the quality of arms. I want to expand the operation, he said. More arms, better arms.

Turki offered the program his full support and agreed to continue to match the U.S. contribution dollar for dollar. He also revealed that the king saw Central Asia as a weak point in the Soviet empire. The Saudis were going to boost their religious and anticommunist radio broadcasts into Afghanistan and Soviet Central Asia. The king is committed to helping our Moscow brothers under the Russian yoke, he proclaimed. He told the director that Saudi Arabia was going to institute a widespread program to smuggle copies of the Koran into Afghanistan and eventually into Soviet Central Asia. It was, in Turki's words, a way to fight the Soviets in the spiritual realm, "where God is with us." Casey liked the idea and suggested others tracts—on Russian atrocities committed in Soviet Central Asia after the revolution and the Second World War.

The threats around Saudi Arabia were real, said Turki, and the kingdom intended to expand its already massive arms-purchasing program overseas. For several years, the Saudis had been asking the United States for advanced aircraft. Both Iraq and Iran are violating our airspace weekly, said Turki. We do not have an adequate capability to defend ourselves in the air. He pulled out a list of known violations of Saudi airspace.

Turki knew full well that Casey was not just the DCI but also on the cabinet, the National Security Council, and the National Security Planning Group. He tried to enlist his support in efforts to obtain military hardware from Washington. The president understands your predicament, said Casey, and so do I. We intend to dramatically change the arms sales policy of the previous administration. My recommendation to the president will be that we provide what is needed, in keeping with the security needs of your country. The prince was pleased. Casey also agreed to share more intelligence than his predecessor had. Then, as he often did for his foreign counterparts, Casey pulled out some reports.

He had brought some raw intelligence on South Yemen. It was a present the prince had never received—transcripts of secret National Security Agency (NSA) intercepts. South Yemeni officials had been receiving communiqués about a band of Saudi separatists who wanted help to overthrow the royal family. The Yemenis had agreed to work with the squad, and they were being trained at a desert compound outside the capital. Casey gave the intelligence on the operation to the prince, as a gift. No strings attached.

He then pulled out some other papers and slid them across the table. They were copies of CIA top-secret reports on Soviet oil production. They weren't anything fancy, and the prince probably had better intelligence on world oil production than anyone in the agency did. But they were a useful prop that would prove Casey's point. Moscow is financing its world empire through oil exports, Casey began. He had taken his coat off to get down to business. Turki was eyeing the reports. They made a killing in the 1970s when the price went through the roof. Every time the price goes up one dollar a barrel, it means $1 billion a year hard currency for Moscow. We can't afford to have that happen again.

What Casey was trying to do was send the prince a message. No single world oil producer had a greater effect on world oil prices than Saudi Arabia. At the time, it accounted for 40 percent of OPEC's production. It also, unlike other producers, had ready easy access to huge oil reserves. That meant it had production flexibility that would allow it to greatly influence world oil prices. There was an oil glut of 2 to 3 million barrels a day on world markets. A majority of OPEC countries were pushing for the Saudis to raise oil prices from $32 to $36 a barrel while cutting exports.

By raising the issues of oil pricing and the U.S.-Saudi security relationship in the same conversation, Casey was in effect saying that the two were related. It was an element of the Reagan strategy. "We wanted lower oil prices," recalls Weinberger. "That's one of the reasons we were selling them arms."[4]

The prince thanked Casey for the reports and mentioned in general terms that Riyadh had already announced a more moderate oil-pricing policy. It serves our interests to have the U.S. economy recover, for you to be robust, strong, said Turki. We will not be pushing for higher prices. Riyadh would resist any pressure to cut production and increase prices, he assured his guest.

After three hours, the meeting broke up. It had gone very well; both men were pleased. Turki had found someone who seemed sympathetic to all his requests and concerns. Casey had found someone who shared his anticommunist impulses and was willing to work with an America that had so recently proved unreliable. Most important perhaps, one of the cornerstones of the secret war against the Soviet Union had begun to be constructed. Saudi Arabia, vulnerable and fearing for its survival, was looking to the United States for security protection. The United States would willingly offer it, in return for Riyadh's serving Washington's interests in world oil markets.[5]

That evening the black unmarked plane took off from a military air base in Riyadh without fanfare. It headed west, for Tel Aviv. As the plane streaked across the sky at 40,000 feet, Casey was talking with his aides about Poland. Moscow is scared of the Poles, he told them. They're never going to stay out of there if Solidarity survives. What can we do to keep the movement going?

Under Jimmy Carter, the United States had launched a minor program to support Solidarity with literature and other materials, such as printing presses. National Security Adviser Zbigniew Brzezinski, himself a Pole, was the catalyst behind the program. But it was all pretty minor stuff and extremely limited in scope. Funds were being used to print and sell pro-Solidarity T-shirts, to pay printers and sign plasterers, and to put together and distribute pro-Solidarity materials. All the activity was taking place outside of Poland. It was considered too risky to do anything in the country. Solidarity was 100 percent made in Poland. Any traceable aid would taint the movement as an arm of the CIA. Besides, the agency didn't have real covert contacts in Solidarity.

Casey was looking at the updated intel on Poland put together in a briefing book by the Directorate of Intelligence. Events were moving quickly. In Casey's mind, there was little question that a crackdown would come. He often predicted it with his aides. The Polish government was weakening in the face of Solidarity demands, and Moscow was desperately trying to stave off the collapse of Polish communism. In early March, senior Polish officials had been summoned to the Kremlin to get guidance from the Politburo. Polish Party leader Stanislaw Kania, Prime Minister Wojciech Jaruzelski, and two Politburo members met in private on March 5 with Leonid Brezhnev, KGB chief Yuri Andropov, Defense Minister Dimitri Ustinov, Foreign Minister Andrei Gromyko, and five other senior Communist Party officials. The meeting ended with a statement issued through the Polish News Agency.

The parties had agreed on the need for unspecified "urgent action" to counter the threat against socialist Poland. Most telling, the statement noted Moscow's anxiety that its empire might unravel: events in Poland should be of concern to the "entire socialist community," it read. "Imperialist and internal reactionary forces were hoping that the economic and political crisis in Poland would lead to a change in the alignment of forces in the world, a weakening of the socialist community, of the international communist movement and the entire liberation movement," the report continued. "For these reasons, it is particularly urgent to give a firm and resolute rebuff to all kinds of dangerous attempts."

It concluded, "The socialist community is indissolvable. Its defense is a matter not only for every single state but for the entire socialist community as well. . . . The Soviet people believe Poland has been and will be an infallible link in the socialist community."

There was also a constant drumbeat of propaganda from Moscow that seemed to be laying the justification for a crackdown or invasion. Sensationalist articles were coming out in the Soviet press daily and growing in intensity. *Krasnaya Zvezda*, the defense ministry newspaper, was accusing NATO of trying to "woo" Poland into the Western alliance. The paper accused Solidarity of "antisocialist escalation." It said, "The situation is not developing satisfactorily. There is no sign that the government is reasserting control." In February, *Literaturaya Gazeta* accused the West of fomenting the unrest and giving orders to Solidarity. Voice of America and Radio Free Europe were being used to communicate "orders" to Solidarity activists "as to when, where, and how to fan up strikes under the slogans of Solidarity." It was the same old propaganda boilerplate, but it had a deeper meaning. By pointing to a foreign "threat," Moscow could justify military intervention.

Caspar Weinberger, immersed in the details of the Pentagon budget, was keeping close watch on the situation in Poland. The secret military probes were continuing, as well as a series of AWACS flights, which were tracking troop movements. The president was issuing warnings to Moscow that military action would invite an American response. He was vague about what form the response might take.

When his plane touched down in Tel Aviv in the morning on April 13, Casey was met by a security detail that immediately sped off to Mossad headquarters. Security was tight, and as usual there were no diplomatic officials there to greet him. They would draw too much attention.

At Mossad headquarters, Casey met with Maj. Gen. Yitzhak Hoffi, the chief of the Israeli agency. Several deputies were also present. The Mossad was one of the most respected and efficient intelligence agencies in the world. Not only did it have enormous capabilities in the Middle East but it also had developed quite a network in Central Europe. With the cooperation of émigrés from Poland, the Soviet Union, and Hungary, the Mossad ran a "ratline" from Albania to Poland, then east into the heart of Russia. Made up mostly of Jewish dissidents and religious figures, the ratline was activated when the Israelis needed particular information or a conduit for smuggling people or items in and out of the Soviet bloc.

Since the earliest days of the Jewish State, the ratline had been a remarkable success. In 1956, it was the ratline that smuggled out of Moscow Nikita Khrushchev's historic and secret de-Stalinization speech at the Twentieth All-Union Party Congress. (Rumor had it the ratline was given the document by a member of the Party Congress.) With his ever-present concern about human sources, Casey wanted to be plugged into the ratline. The first subject of discussion was the situation in the Middle East. The director assured his hosts that the new administration in Washington was firmly committed to the defense of Israel. He further told them that they could look for a new, invigorated CIA. The agency had worked with the Mossad effectively in the past, but in the late 1970s it had increasingly come to be seen as unreliable. Casey emphasized that he was going to turn the agency around. And he wanted close cooperation with the Mossad.

Major General Hoffi said he appreciated the sentiments. The Mossad, too, wanted greater cooperation. It was strapped for cash, and its resources were strained. Perhaps the two services could cooperate and compensate for each other's weaknesses.

For their part, the Israelis needed two things. They were desperate for more access to U.S. satellite intelligence, particularly as it related to Iraq and Syria. The United States had the world's best satellite photos of both countries, including images of the Iraqi nuclear program that concerned Tel Aviv. In addition, the Mossad needed funds to sustain its intelligence operations overseas. Both are easy for me to give you, Casey said, without even hesitating. Here's what I need.

He raised the subject of Poland. He was trying to rebuild U.S. human intelligence assets overseas. He had some sources in Poland, but no access to the opposition. In particular, he was interested in Solidarity and the other dissident movements in Poland. Casey wanted to know, Is the ratline still active? His host nodded yes. For financial assistance to sustain it, Casey could have access to the ratline. They shook hands. The deal was done.

It was the evening of April 26. Again, the black unmarked plane was flying off into the night. This time it was headed north; Casey would meet the next day with agents in the Rome station. He had met the station chief in early February in Paris when the European chiefs had been brought together to meet the new DCI. This time it would be more straightforward business. While he was interested in seeing the station at work, Casey was interested most of all in two subjects: terrorism and Poland. The first would be raised because the Rome station was large and tasked with tracking terrorist movements in Southern Europe and the Middle East. The Red Brigades in Italy were very active, and there were many terrorist organizations that used Athens and Rome as entryways to the continent. Terrorist International is what one agency wit called the Italian capital.

The subject of Poland brought Bill Casey to Rome because it was there that one of the key players in the unfolding Polish drama lived. It was Ronald Reagan who had suggested that the United States approach the Polish pontiff about cooperation in the region. Richard Allen recalls sitting with the president watching news reports about John Paul's visit to his homeland in 1979. "He [Reagan] said then and there that the pope was the key figure in determining the fate of Poland. He was overcome by the outpouring of emotion that emanated from the millions who came to see him. There were tears in his [Reagan's] eyes."[6]

Karol Wojtyla was born in 1920 near Krakow. His studies in philosophy at Jagellonian University were interrupted in 1939 by the German invasion of Poland. The university was closed down, and his professors thrown in jail. Consequently the young student was forced to work by day as a common laborer. But by night he participated in clandestine church activities. In October 1942, he joined the underground seminary organized by Cardinal Adam Saphieha, the archbishop of Krakow. Thus, he was accustomed to resistance of totalitarian forces. The pope's personal history greatly impressed the Reagan Administration. He had shown an abiding interest in Poland even after his appointment in 1978. And he was willing to act on his beliefs. Rumor had it that in December 1980 the pope had sent a letter to Leonid Brezhnev warning that if the Soviet premier did invade Poland, John Paul would return and take an active role in rallying the people to resist the occupation.

The pontiff was a strong and vocal critic of Marxism everywhere. In March 1980 he gave a strangely worded speech in Mexico warning against the dangers of liberation theology, a branch of radical Catholic thinking that tied Christianity with Marxism-Leninism. The pope's speech positioned the Vatican firmly against procommunist priests in places such as Nicaragua and El Salvador—all of Latin America for that matter. His views made him unpopular in that church of communism the Kremlin. Not only was he now the one individual with the highest moral authority in Poland but he was also popular among Lithuanians, in whose tongue he was fluent. Seemingly mindful of their plight, the pope had appointed the imprisoned Lithuanian archbishop cardinal in pectore (secret) in 1979. Word of the appointment spread like wildfire in Lithuania and emboldened the underground church.

The Soviet press wrote about the pope as a threat to be managed or contained. His views and faith were an "infection." "For the present leadership in the Vatican, the Ukraine is an object of particular solicitude. It is trying to use the still considerable active nucleus of the Catholic church as a basis for extending religious influence over the population of the republic."[7]

A Ukrainian pamphlet titled "In the Service of the Neofascists" used these vehement words: "Revanchists and enemies of democracy and socialism look with hope upon the new Pope . . . for he has made it his goal to unite Catholics all over the planet into a single anti-communist force. It is dictated not by anxiety for mankind and its future but by the desire for religious authority over the planet."[8]

The CIA personnel in Rome gave Casey a briefing on terrorism. They also passed to him information that might prove critical, especially to the situation in Poland. Lech Walesa, the Solidarity leader, had made a historic visit to Rome in January 1981 and met with the pope. His host was Luigi Scricciollo, a spokesman for the Italian labor confederation. The Italian labor official had taken a trip to Poland in 1980 to advise Walesa on the setting up of Solidarity and had helped provide typewriters, printers, and copy machines for Solidarity activists. But Scricciollo was actually working for the other side. According to Italian counterintelligence officials, he was a source for Bulgarian intelligence, his case officer an official at the Bulgarian embassy. Such a source could pass vital information to the Soviet bloc. He was on the inside and trusted. Walesa was vulnerable.

Casey had requested that the Rome station set up a private meeting with Agostino Cardinal Casaroli, the secretary of state at the Vatican. Casaroli was a dedicated church leader who had been a close adviser to four popes. He had served with great distinction and favored closer normalized relations with the communist governments of Eastern Europe. It was ostpolitik: forging in a slow but deliberate manner state-to-state relations between the Vatican and the Communist bloc.

Casaroli claimed he had a conflict in his schedule and could not meet the director. Casey figured the refusal was a reflection of the secretary's foreign policy. Casaroli had met recently with leftist rebel leaders from El Salvador and Marxist Palestinian leaders. There had been no direct request from the president for a meeting, so Casaroli could gracefully decline. He did offer to dispatch an aide to meet the DCI, but complete discretion would be required. Public disclosure of the meeting would play into Soviet hands by fueling speculation that the Church and the CIA were plotting the overthrow of Poland. Casey, never too concerned about protocol, agreed.

Casaroli suggested some church offices next to a cathedral in

Rome. His aide would arrive through the front entrance of the church. The director would enter through the rear. They would meet in an administrative office in the back.

The arrangement went like clockwork. Casaroli's aide came dressed in his church garb. With a cherublike face and active eyes, he greeted Casey warmly and apologized for Casaroli's inability to meet with Casey; he appeared uneasy himself. After all, Vatican officials were not often seen in the company of the director of the CIA. Casey tried to ease his anxiety by making it clear early on that he just wanted insights into the situation in Poland.

A bit relieved, the aide spent the next hour and forty-five minutes giving Bill Casey his views on that subject. Cardinal Stefan Wyszynski was dying of terminal cancer. A central player in Polish church and political affairs, Cardinal Wyszynski possessed great skills that had maintained a stability which had allowed Solidarity to thrive and grow. He was keeping Polish government authorities in check by threatening widespread unrest if a crackdown came. At the same time, he was asking the more radical elements of Solidarity for restraint, lest the government be provoked into violent action or invite their Soviet brethren to intervene. Adam Michnik, the Jewish dissident, declared that because of Cardinal Wyszynski, "the . . . Church has become the most formidable opponent of the totalitarian system." His loss, the Vatican official told Casey, would be enormous. Nevertheless, the Church would continue to support Solidarity and oppose repression.

The pope was convinced that repression would come sooner or later. What mattered was the form it would take and how prepared the Church and opposition would be. The food crisis was spreading, and strikes would continue to grow. The Church hoped to facilitate the process of reform without inviting a clampdown, but, minus Wyszynski, this would not be as easy.

After nearly two hours, Casey thanked the aide and asked him if Casaroli might be available the next time the director came to Rome. No, said the aide flatly. The cardinal thinks it best not to cooperate on these matters, or we might inflame the situation. It was an abrupt turndown, but it would not matter. The fact was, they were already helping with important intelligence. Casey had learned more about the internal situation in Poland in this one meeting than he had from all the briefers in Langley.[9]

And what he heard confirmed what his instincts were telling him, and what President Reagan was willing to commit to. "Although there weren't any hard signed agreements, clearly in terms of gathering intelligence and sharing it, the Vatican was very helpful," recalls Adm. John Poindexter.[10] And events would soon unfold bringing the Vatican into an even closer relationship with the United States, particularly where their interests coincided in Poland. Within a few weeks of Casey's departure from Rome, there would be an assassination attempt on the pope. The president, Caspar Weinberger, and Bill Casey would see a veiled Soviet hand behind the whole thing. So would the pontiff.

1. "Saudis, Stressing Regional Stability, See Soviet Threat," *The New York Times*, February 8, 1980, sec. A, p. 6.
2. Ibid.
3. Alan Fiers, interview with the author.
4. Caspar Weinberger, interview with the author.
5. U.S. official, interview with the author.
6. Richard Allen, interview with the author.
7. From *Voproy Nauchrovd Ateizma*, cited in "Increasing Activity of the Ukrainian Catholic Church in Western Ukraine," RFE/RL Research Report, 119/83, March 16, 1983.
8. N. O. Safronova, *Uniats'ka Tserkva i fashizm* (Lvov, 1981).
9. U.S. official, interview with the author.
10. John Poindexter, interview with the author.

4

In May 1981, there was a major KGB conference in Moscow. Senior intelligence officials from all the directorates were assembled. Such meetings were held regularly to permit party leaders to lay out policies and make major announcements about international challenges that faced the Soviet state. Both Chairman of the Party Leonid Brezhnev and Yuri Andropov, the KGB chief, made secret speeches. And while they touched on issues as diverse as Latin America, Afghanistan, and China, the number-one topic was the new administration in Washington.

With slow, deliberate steps, the weary general secretary ascended the podium first. He looked weak, the survivor of decades at the highest levels of the Politburo. Rumors were circulating already about his impending death. Speaking from a prepared text and looking through his thick reading glasses, the dying patron of the Party began: the new administration in Washington was "exhibiting extreme revanchism" and was working to "dangerously destabilize the world situation." Reagan was committed to "a further expansion of the arms race and . . . working to undermine the Soviet economy." The new president had "failed to recognize that the correlation of forces are now against capitalism." He wanted to "erase the gains of international socialism through provocations . . . [and] economic warfare."

During the forty-five-minute address, Brezhnev paused often to find his place in the text. After the final words rolled from his lips, he was visibly exhausted. He was led quietly back to his residence.

Minutes later Yuri Vladimirovich Andropov strode up to the stage. Though not much younger than the general secretary, he seemed a different physical specimen. He was commanding, powerful, assertive. He also painted a more ominous picture of the United States.

He too fired a barrage at the new administration. Andropov described how he had expected the anti-Soviet rhetoric of the campaign to cease after Reagan entered the Oval Office. But it was continuing. He told the assembled what Reagan had said during his first press conference from the White House: "They [the Soviets] reserve unto themselves the right to commit any crime, to cheat in order to attain that. . . . So far, detente's been a one-way street that the Soviet Union has used to pursue its own aims."

For Andropov, the Reagan comments were crystal clear. These were "dangerous times," in which the West was engaged in a constellation of "provocations against socialism." What was more, Washington was preparing for a "nuclear first strike." Not since the Cuban missile crisis had Soviet officials used such aggressive language, or painted such a frightening picture.

Andropov may not have been correct in his statement that Washington was preparing for a nuclear first strike against Moscow. But "economic warfare" was very much on the minds of officials like William Casey and Caspar Weinberger. Everywhere they went they were pushing for a cutoff of Soviet access to Western trade, technology, and credits. And when they couldn't make it policy, they were trying to persuade.

On May 9, Casey was in the southern West Virginia resort town of Hot Springs, delivering a speech before the Business Council. The Soviet economy was "showing increasing weakness," and there was "growing internal discontent" in the country. Although he didn't say explicitly that the United States should exploit it, he certainly implied that.

In private, with leading U.S. business executives, Casey was reeling off statistics about how poorly the Soviets were doing. Bad business investment, he said. Wouldn't go near the place if I wanted to turn a profit. He was trying particularly to persuade bankers to stop making loans to the Soviets. Over the course of his tenure, Casey would make dozens of speeches, many of them to business organizations. He was constantly pushing his line—business with Moscow was a bad idea. At times he even phoned company executives directly, giving them the hard sell, or sharing sensitive, secret information to convince them that a given project would be contrary to American interests. Sometimes it worked, other times he failed.

The largest and most critical economic venture for the Soviets was the energy project known as Urengoi 6. It was slated to be the most substantial deal in East-West trade history. And both Casey and Weinberger were "obsessed by it." The project was a natural gas pipeline running 3,600 miles from Northern Siberia's Urengoi gas field to the Soviet-Czech border. There it would be attached to a West European gas grid that would dispense 1.37 trillion cubic feet of gas a year to a French, Italian, and West German consortium. It was originally configured to be a two-strand line, providing Moscow with as much as $30 billion per year in hard currency earnings. To a country with annual hard currency earnings at the time running at about $32 billion a year, it represented vital economic life support. "For Moscow, the pipeline was critical to its economic livelihood. It is hard to overestimate the value that Moscow placed on this project," recalls former senior staff member of the Communist Party Central Committee Yevgenny Novikov.[1]

"It was a cash cow, plain and simple," says former Undersecretary of Defense Fred Ikle.[2]

Strapped for foreign exchange and without the technology to build and operate the pipeline efficiently, the Kremlin, in 1979, looked to the West for help. The Europeans, anxious to develop an alternative to Middle Eastern oil, jumped at the opportunity when Moscow offered them twenty-five years of gas at guaranteed prices. In exchange, the Kremlin received a financial dream. As in the past, West European banks agreed to finance the purchase of pipe-laying and other equipment as well as construction at below-market interest rates—guaranteed by their respective governments. At the same time, other West European companies offered to sell the same sophisticated equipment in exchange for future shipments of natural gas. As it had the 1,700-mile Orenburg pipeline project, Moscow was using Urengoi 6 to raise credits in the West, in effect, double-financing at least portions of the project.

This double-financing scheme—like the critical security risks associated with the new Siberian gas pipeline—was first uncovered by Roger Robinson, a Chase Manhattan vice president with responsibility for Chase's loan portfolio in the Soviet Union, Eastern Europe, and Yugoslavia. At the time of the construction of the Orenburg pipeline in the late 1970s, he was having dinner with the Soviet gas minister. "I asked the Soviet minister whether or not he supported borrowing money on the Eurodollar market to finance the project," recalls Robinson. "He laughed and said, 'I would never take out such loans, the gas deliveries to Europe pay for everything.' The Soviet Foreign Trade Bank apparently had failed to brief him adequately on its ongoing plan to double-finance the bulk of the project, which further analysis proved to be the case. All the key Western imports were being financed through so-called compensation arrangements or straight barter—gas for pipe, gas for compressors, turbines, et cetera. And yet at the same time, the Moscow-dominated International Investment Bank was raising some $2.2 billion on Western credit markets in four jumbo syndications. Ironically, the loan documentation made clear that the proceeds were ostensibly to finance the purchase of pipe, compressors, turbines, et cetera. The arrogance was quite stunning."[3]

Robinson discreetly informed the CIA of his findings, but nothing was happening. A memo on the subject was forwarded to Bill Casey in early February by Sumner Benson, a senior analyst at the agency. He, too, had been very concerned about the pipeline project. It would make Western Europe highly vulnerable to political threats of a Soviet shutoff of gas. Austria, Berlin, and Bavaria would be 90 to 100 percent dependent on Soviet gas deliveries. And they were not being very open with their own publics about this fact. One American banker recalls a private session in 1980 with then West German Minister of Economics Otto von Lambsdorff. He admitted to one of the participants that German dependence on Soviet gas could well reach 60 percent, not the ceiling of 30 percent cited in public. "But don't worry," Lambsdorff said, "the German public will not be informed of the true figure."[4]

The economic boon to Moscow would be enormous. Benson had written in a 1980 classified report, "The energy trade has helped the Soviet Union to pursue its military build-up even while facing persistent serious economic problems." His concerns fell on deaf ears during the Carter administration, which seemed preoccupied more with securing diverse sources of energy for the West than with putting the clamps on the Soviets. But now Benson had people who were more sympathetic, most important the president, Casey, and Weinberger.

In early May 1981, soon after receipt of a draft article by Roger Robinson, Weinberger and Casey were meeting at the Pentagon on a variety of topics, including the situation in Poland and the defense budget. However, the subject of the pipeline continued to emerge. "We really felt we had to stop it, or at the very least delay it," recalls Weinberger. "It would give them a large strategic advantage, and an enormous cash flow."[5]

There was not a consensus in the administration on the topic. Secretary of State Alexander Haig was resisting efforts to pressure the Europeans to drop the deal. It's too late to squelch it, he said. Under pressure from Weinberger, he had dispatched Myer Rashish, undersecretary of state for economic affairs, on a tour of European capitals to argue for pipeline alternatives, such as U.S. coal, synthetic fuels, and Norwegian natural gas. But the Europeans apparently weren't buying them. As far as Haig was concerned, that was the end of the matter. But for Casey and Weinberger, the pipeline was too important to let it pass without a fight to the finish. The United States was the leader of the Free World, not just a partner. So Casey and Weinberger put their analysts to work searching for viable alternatives to the deal.

At the Department of Defense, the effort would be overseen by Assistant Secretary Richard Perle, the wily defense intellectual who wanted to take a tough anti-Soviet line on everything. He brought Benson on staff and began hiring consultants to come up with alternatives to the pipeline deal. Some of the ideas were frankly absurd: one consultant claimed that the Dutch were sitting on huge reserves and that Europe could be self-sufficient in natural gas. Another suggested a trans-Africa pipeline from Algeria. Still another proposed a pipeline from Iran-Turkey-Greece. At the agency, Casey put analysts to work on various aspects of the proposal. The Office of Soviet Analysis focused primarily on the benefits to the Soviets of hard currency and favorable credit and on their ability to build the pipeline without outside help. Energy analysts were tasked with coming up with possible alternatives.

In late May, the National Security Planning Group was meeting in the White House. President Reagan had recovered strongly from the assassination attempt at the end of March and was again focusing on Soviet economic prospects. He had seen the Robinson publication in draft. Although there were several items on the agenda, most were related to the Ottawa Summit in July. It would be the president's first summit with foreign heads of state. Most important, it was with America's closest allies and economic partners, the G-7 countries. It was clear that the president needed to put in a good performance. The West was split over a variety of contentious issues, not the least of which was the Soviet natural gas pipeline. And the NSPG was of the unanimous opinion that Washington needed to reassert its leadership role in light of the myriad challenges facing the West.

Weinberger, with backing from Casey and Richard Allen, was aggressively pushing for a U.S. confrontation at the summit. Mr. President, he began, we must stop this project. The potential benefits for them could be enormous. He summarized what the Soviets would gain from the deal, which Reagan already knew. He then pushed for a policy: "I believe we must impose sanctions immediately to stop this thing from being built."

Al Haig quickly jumped in. Mr. President, the Europeans are not going to get out of this deal. It's too late, they are in too deep. Raising it at Ottawa in a public way will only antagonize Western leaders before we even have a chance of working with them. Let me talk with the foreign ministers privately and see if they will consider an alternative to the pipeline.

As was his way, Reagan retired to the Oval Office with the advice of both. Two days later it was announced that he would not openly challenge Western leaders or push for sanctions. Haig would raise the matter privately with foreign ministers. But Casey and Weinberger would soon get another chance.

At the same time, Casey and Weinberger were working in tandem on another front. Moscow was trying to get its hands on Western technology any way it could to help ease industrial bottlenecks and enhance its military potential. And it was largely succeeding. The Soviets were buying some kinds of equipment and stealing others. The Soviet Military Industrial Commission was in charge of the massive effort. An estimated 100,000 people were working in the USSR just translating technical documents. "Soviet access to Western technology was a lifeline for them, no question about it," says William Schneider, the former undersecretary of state for military assistance and technology. "It was greatly relieving their industrial problems." Cutting off that "lifeline" was an early and important objective.[6]

Technology transfer was of enormous economic benefit to the Soviets. Intelligence indicated, according to Stef Halper, executive director of the Interagency Committee on Technology Transfer, that "the Soviets had made a strategic decision to avoid the expenditure of funds for research and development and acquired Western technology through theft and illegal purchases. They had established a large staff for the purpose of gathering the technical needs from their productive communities, and then made their decisions about how they would prioritize what they stole." Technology transfer was perhaps saving the country tens of billions of dollars a year in research and development.[7]

Moscow wasn't stealing just anything it could get its hands on. Specialists were identifying technologies that would relieve bottlenecks in both civilian and military sectors. Rather than focus on protecting every technology, Casey and Weinberger pushed to zero in on those same critical technologies. "They focused on bottlenecks and so did we," says Halper. "They looked for technologies that could stimulate their growth in a number of different ways."[8] For Casey this was nothing new. During the Second World War he had done the same thing—trying to identify Hitler's economic vulnerabilities and bottlenecks. "You could say—with his experience during the war—Bill Casey, to a certain extent, invented the field of American economic warfare," says Casey's special assistant, Herb Meyer.[9] At the Department of Defense, it was again Richard Perle who led the way. At CIA, Casey had ambitious plans. He wanted an office devoted to tracking the Soviet technology base and monitoring imports.

In the late 1970s, the agency under Stansfield Turner had created the secret K Project, designed to stop the flow of technology to the Soviets. Casey had a full review done and found the project completely lacking. There was very little staff committed to the problem, and it had very little direction in terms of which technologies were deemed vital and necessary to halt.

In early spring 1981, a steady flow of sensitive intelligence on the Soviet high-technology espionage effort began to cross Casey's desk. The French counterintelligence service, the DST, had a source in the KGB. Code named FAREWELL, he was in Directorate T, the scientific and technical branch of the intelligence service's elite First Chief Directorate. He proved a remarkable conduit for information. What he provided revealed that the Soviets were counting on the illicit purchase or theft of Western technology to shore up deficiencies in the industrial and military sectors of the economy. In all, FAREWELL passed along more than 4,000 documents on how the KGB was seeking specific items, and how Soviet "companies" and the Soviet Military Industrial Commission were set up and agents dispatched abroad to buy or steal embargoed scientific material.

The United States had always been mindful of Soviet efforts on this front but had not before known of their truly massive scale. FAREWELL never asked the French for money. Eighteen months later, in November 1982, just as suddenly as FAREWELL had approached the DST, his contact stopped. It was later discovered that he had apparently been involved in a fight with his wife. When a member of the Moscow militia approached his car, he panicked and shot him. FAREWELL was sent to prison and later executed.

The information was a bonanza to Casey, and as he received it he passed on excerpts to Weinberger, Haig, and the president. "Reagan was really intrigued by the stuff," recalls one NSC staffer. "Whenever he saw it he said, 'We need to stop this.' "[10]

FAREWELL's and other intelligence was painting a picture of just how important technology transfer was to the viability of the Soviet technology, military base, and economy. Documents revealed that from 1976 to 1980, for example, the Ministry of the Aviation Industry alone saved $800 million in research and development costs through the illegal acquisition of Western technology. That represented over 100,000 man-years of scientific research.

The program was managed by the most powerful organization in Soviet defense production—the Military Industrial Commission (VPK) and the Presidium of the Council of Ministers. The Ministry of Foreign Trade assisted. Together they drew up target lists of Western technologies they wanted to acquire to improve the technical level of manufacturing. The VPK controlled a national fund, equivalent to $1.4 billion, for acquisitions. Much of this money was in valuable hard currency, obtained by exporting to the West. It was to be used overseas for purchases and to support intelligence operations abroad.

Casey and Weinberger first brought the information FAREWELL was providing to the Oval Office in early June 1981. Casey showed the president on charts what the Soviets were acquiring and how much it was worth. Mr. President, he said, the VPK is getting about 50 percent of what they ask for. We need to get that number down. It's too easy for them, and our security is threatened.

While the Soviets were using flat-out theft to procure Western technologies, they were also purchasing equipment from unscrupulous businessmen who would buy sensitive Western products and resell them to Moscow. They were obtaining 100 million computer circuits a year. They were purchasing manufacturing cells, complete production lines. By the late 1970s, Moscow was diverting billions of dollars' worth of high-tech items. Most of the diversion was arranged in Europe. Mr. President, chimed in Weinberger, the neutrals—Sweden, Switzerland, and Austria—are leaking like sieves.

Reagan nodded in agreement and asked what they had in mind. The two had come to discuss expanding the powers of the Coordinating Committee for Multilateral Export Controls (COCOM). (This committee coordinates trade controls over the export of strategic items to communist bloc countries. It is composed of all NATO countries, except Iceland, and Japan.) Casey and Weinberger looked at each other, and the defense secretary began, We want to expand the list of technologies on the COCOM lists. There are many technologies that need to be restricted and aren't. We also want to pressure our allies, but especially the neutrals. The 1979 Export Control Act gives us a lever. We can severely limit distribution licenses for sensitive technologies to those who ship high-technology exports to the Soviet bloc. It's on the books but hasn't been used. Section 6 of the Export Administration and Control Act gave the president an enormous tool to stop not only U.S. exports but those of other countries as well. It gave him the power to halt or limit the export "of any goods, technology or other information subject to the jurisdiction of the United States or exported by a person subject to the jurisdiction of the United States." That meant not only U.S. companies but American subsidiaries overseas, and equipment provided by any foreign company using American technology under a licensing agreement.

Reagan liked the idea and nodded in agreement. OK, let's do it. Let's stop this as best we can.

By early summer, Weinberger had dispatched Richard Perle to begin the first in a round of secret trips to European capitals to pressure allies to restrict technology exports to the Soviet bloc. Their area of most intense interest was the neutrals—Sweden, Switzerland, and Austria. The message: tighten your export controls or risk losing access to licensed U.S. technologies.

One of the key areas in which a technology shutoff could have a dramatic effect on Moscow was the oil and gas industry. In early June, Casey received a study that he had ordered by energy analysts at Langley. It painted a picture of a Soviet energy sector with promise but in great need of a technological infusion from the West. The Soviet Union had estimated oil reserves between 6 and 12 billion tons. But the oil was increasingly inaccessible using current Soviet methods. Maintaining output and exploiting new reserves would require Western technology. Many of the most accessible fields in Volga-Urals, European Russia, the Caucasus, and Central Asia were in steep decline. Moscow was expending more money every year to keep the fields viable, the report said. During the early 1970s, Moscow had invested $4.6 billion per year in maintaining its oil industry. By 1976–78, the price tag was over $6.0 billion. And by the early 1980s, it was running $9.0 billion per year. The Soviet Oil Ministry wanted to alleviate these problems by making large purchases of Western technology. In particular, the report noted that Moscow would need:

- **rotary drills.** The Soviets would have to drill deeper in existing wells and through harder rocks to sustain production. This would force them to shift from their domestic turbo drills to American rotary drills.

- **exploration technologies.** The Kremlin had already publicly announced plans to step up exploratory drilling two and a half times by 1985.
- **offshore technology.** The Oil Ministry foresaw great promise in offshore wells, particularly in the ice-free regions of the Barents Sea, but current yields were dismal. They were hoping to get their hands on the British technology and know-how that was proving so successful in the North Sea.

The report concluded by noting what the administration wanted to hear most: the United States had a near monopoly on many of these oil-drilling technologies. The next few years were critical. If Moscow could be denied access to these technologies, it would cost them billions. So Caspar Weinberger, Bill Casey, and the NSC staff under Richard Allen were pushing for an aggressive crackdown on illegal high-tech exports to the Kremlin. In October 1981, the U.S. Customs Service began Operation Exodus, a program to disrupt sales of American technology to Moscow. A quiet command post in the customs building in Washington coordinated the effort.

Energy was an important battleground in the Cold War calculus. The emerging fight in the energy market was a zero-sum game. The only question was who would win. And more than any other country, Saudi Arabia, the world's most important producer, could determine the winners and losers. So the Saudis became a focal point of administration policy.

A classified State Department study, drawn up by David Long, painted a picture of Saudi Arabia as an unstable country, run by a royal family vulnerable to a wide array of threats. The study noted, "Partly as a result of Iranian agitation, there is a good likelihood that at least some Shias will, for the first time, begin to associate their grievances with the U.S. and, by extension, with ARAMCO as well as with the Saudi regime. Anti-regime and anti-American literature has recently begun to appear at ARAMCO and elsewhere in the Eastern Province, and there are reports of Shia dissident organizations being established."

Early on in the administration, there was a commitment to

shoring up the Saudis, in effect serving as their protector in exchange for oil policies that benefited the U.S. economy and cost Moscow dearly. One of the first and most visible examples of this effort involved the fight over the sale of advance fighters and AWACS in 1981.

1. Yevgenny Novikov, interview with the author.
2. Fred Ikle, interview with the author.
3. Roger Robinson, interview with the author.
4. Otto von Lambsdorff, interview with the author.
5. Caspar Weinberger, interview with the author.
6. William Schneider, interview with the author.
7. Stef Halper, interview with the author.
8. Stef Halper, interview with the author.
9. Herb Meyer, interview with the author.
10. Interview with the author.

5

On June 8, 1981, at 4:30 in the afternoon, William Casey received a call at home. The Israelis had bombed the Osirak nuclear reactor in Iraq. After he received the news, Casey jumped back on the phone. He ordered an American KH-11 Big Bird photo reconnaissance satellite diverted from its regular orbit over the Soviet Union to get pictures of the damage in Iraq. Within six hours, Israeli intelligence was receiving KH-11 photos directly from the satellite. Their mission, they found out courtesy of Bill Casey, had been a success.

Two days later, the director was on a secure line to Maj. Gen. Yitzhak Hoffi, head of Israeli intelligence. Casey commended Hoffi on the precision of the attack. Hoffi thanked Casey for his help in targeting the facility. Glad to do it, General, Casey said in response. Now perhaps there is something you can do for me.

Casey reiterated to Hoffi the importance of selling AWACS to the Saudis. He had proven his commitment to the security of Israel. Now Tel Aviv needed to help Washington out. It was too much to expect Israel to support the sale of the AWACS, but couldn't it mute its criticism?

Hoffi said that he still had great reservations about the sale but would press the government to turn down its volume of criticism. Casey said he would appreciate it and asked Hoffi to call him any time he needed more satellite photos.

In the months ahead, the volume and sharpness of criticism coming from Tel Aviv about the AWACS deal did decline substantially. But that wasn't going to be enough. The administration, particularly Caspar Weinberger, Bill Casey, and the president, would have to lobby hard to secure the deal.

Prince Bandar bin Sultan was in Washington, DC, that summer to steer the sale through Congress. Weinberger would work with him and forge a close personal relationship. Casey had met him a few times on the dinner party circuit. He was pro-Western and had a very promising future. The son of the defense minister, Bandar was close to Crown Prince Fahd, the man who really ran Saudia Arabia. He was positioned to rise within Saudi ruling circles upon the death of King Khalid. Weinberger knew that Bandar could work in common purpose with the United States on a number of international issues. Charles Cogan, then a Middle East operative for the CIA, was suggesting that Casey forge a close working relationship with the prince.

In late July, the DCI met with the prince and Saud, a son of Fahd. The two foreign guests had an eight-room private suite at the Fairfax Hotel (now the Ritz-Carlton) in downtown Washington. Just west of Dupont Circle, it was popular with the Saudis. The employees seemed discreet, and the atmosphere was both elegant and cosmopolitan.

Bandar was good looking, debonair, and had a good sense of humor. He was extremely charismatic and liked Western tastes and fashions. (A Big Mac is a prince favorite.) He had been a fighter pilot in the Saudi air force and was vehemently anticommunist. Casey and the prince hit it off right away.

The meeting lasted almost two and a half hours. They talked mostly about the AWACS fight. Casey hinted that Israeli opposition would be muted, but he couldn't go into details. Bandar and Saud were skeptical. There had been American promises before, but they had usually been done in by Congress, lobbied by pro-Israel organizations. The director offered to make some calls to friends in the business community to help lobby for AWACS.

Casey was also interested in broadening the relationship between Washington and the royal family. He shared a new bit of information that might interest them. Libya and South Yemen had just signed a cooperative agreement, which would raise a good deal of concern in Saudi circles, given that the two radical states were known to support the overthrow of the Saudi royal family. Casey offered electronic intercepts and other critical information relating to the deal. He promised to be more forthcoming in sharing intelligence with the House of Saud than his predecessor. A regular CIA briefing for Bandar was immediately arranged. The setup was actually quite remarkable. When Prince Bandar wanted a briefing, the analysts came to him.[1] The administration also offered to be of assistance in a pesky problem the Saudis were facing on Capitol Hill.

Every year the Treasury Department compiled a list that estimated the level of foreign investment in the United States. This covered all countries, including Saudi Arabia. The classified versions of these reports contained detailed information on Saudi investments in the country. Congressman Benjamin Rosenthal, chairman of the House Subcommittee on Commerce, Consumer and Monetary Affairs, was making a bit of a crusade out of getting the extent of Saudi investment in the United States on the public record. Stansfield Turner and Bill Casey had both provided some information to Rosenthal from the CIA's Office of Economic Research that related to Saudi financial practices in the States, but key materials had been kept sealed. These included classified documents such as "OPEC: Official Foreign Assets," "Kuwait and Saudi Arabia: Facing Limits on U.S. Equity Purchases," and "Problems with Growing Arab Wealth."

Bandar wanted the administration's assurance that these documents would not see the light of day. If such information is made public, we will see it as a grave threat to our relationship, he told Casey. And we will be compelled to pull back some of our investments in America.

This was an early test case of the budding U.S.-Saudi relationship. If the administration could not be counted on to keep information private, the Saudis were unlikely to trust the president and his advisers. But there were also financial interests at stake. The Saudis had some $75 billion invested in the United States, not a small amount. We will do whatever we have to, Casey told Bandar. Don't worry.

The two then discussed internal measures to keep the royal family secure. The Saudis were establishing a National Information

Center (Markaz al-Ma'lumat al-Watani) within the Ministry of the Interior. It was an internal security organization being developed with the cooperation of French intelligence. A central computer with a data bank connected the security services in the capital with terminals in all airports, seaports, and other major towns and provinces. Casey said the administration was prepared to help train personnel to man the system. Bandar liked the idea.

Casey then turned to what he wanted. The Soviets were trying to increase their exports of oil to the West and were having some success. He wanted what the Saudis could offer—the best information on Soviet oil exports available. He wanted to know what sorts of deals they were brokering, what sorts of contracts they were negotiating, and the attitudes of other oil producers to the Soviet export drive. The prince said it would not be a problem. Soon after, with raised glasses, the prince offered a toast: "To a new and vibrant friendship."

Casey left early that evening having solidified his relationship with the Saudi royal family. He was rapidly becoming one of their best friends in Washington.

In early August, disturbing news was coming out of Poland, the brightest flash point of the Soviet empire. Colonel Kuklinski, a member of the Polish General Staff, had passed along to his handlers, through a complicated series of drops and signs, plans about the impending declaration of martial law. He had supplied copies of Polish leaflets printed in Moscow that ordered citizens to remain calm and listed martial law regulations. He had also relayed information on Polish implementation plans. The intelligence Kuklinski was funneling westward had always checked out. But was this information for real? Many in the administration had their doubts. It seemed all too easy—getting a copy of a leaflet. The Poles had to know there was a leak. Perhaps they were providing disinformation or trying to set Kuklinski up? Because of doubts, and the still disorganized state of the NSC staff, the information was never fully debated.

The White House was, however, maintaining a keen interest in Solidarity. The president, in broad language, had encouraged his aides to come up with creative ways the administration might aid the movement. Richard Pipes on the National Security Council was pushing for a strong U.S. diplomatic position in the hope of deterring a Soviet invasion. But the U.S. ability to initiate rather than react to events was very limited.

The Israeli ratline into Poland had not yielded any valuable intelligence assets. Casey was desperate for an approach to Solidarity. The assassination attempt on the pope and the fact that a Bulgarian agent had penetrated Lech Walesa's circle of friends in the West led to speculation that the labor leader might be a target for the next assassin's bullet. United States embassy officials were being watched at every turn, making an approach through ordinary channels foolhardy. Solidarity was riddled with government spies. If the CIA tried to tip off Solidarity by using the information Kuklinski had provided, the Polish mole might be exposed. Casey recalled that Winston Churchill had faced a similar dilemma during the Second World War. He decided not to defend the cathedral at Coventry against a Nazi air raid in order to protect the Ultra secret: that the Allies had broken the German code. If the agency were going to warn Solidarity, only the ratline could work.

The president had made an early vow to keep the Soviets out of Poland. And he was committed to keeping it. Under the guidance of Weinberger, the United States was continuing to fly aggressive formations toward Soviet airspace. In late August and the first half of September, there were eleven such flights. They included, at times, SAC bombers launched from bases in the Midwest and fighter-bombers launched from air bases in West Germany. The latter in particular were designed to raise questions in Soviet minds about the possibility of an American military response. The squadron would leave their air base and fly only a few thousand feet above the Baltic along Poland's northern coast. Soviet air defense units would track them and send reports back to the Soviet General Staff. At the last moment before entering Soviet airspace, the aircraft would turn and come back to base.

Back in March, Weinberger had verbally dueled with Soviet Ambassador Anatoly Dobrynin at a private birthday dinner for PepsiCo CEO Donald Kendall. Dobrynin inquired about talking with the secretary of defense, and Kendall brought the men together. The Soviet ambassador proved to be quite inquisitive.

"In what direction do you see our two countries moving?" he asked. "Why is there so much rhetoric in the air right now?"

"I think that part of it is because people in Washington feel it is important that the Soviets and the world know that the United States has changed," Weinberger said, "and that we have and will acquire much greater strength as well as greater firmness and resolve during this administration, and that there is also great concern here about the Soviet actions in Afghanistan and Poland."

Dobrynin was quick to fire back. "I assure you that my country knows very well how much the United States has changed. I tell them, I am a good reporter. But don't you think it is important that our two countries talk to each other and not just exchange statements?"

"Yes," said Weinberger, growing impatient, "if the atmosphere and circumstances are such that there is some prospect of effective talks, and some possibility of successful conclusion to such talks. If the Soviets went into Poland, it would be a clear signal that such talks would be useless."[2]

Moscow, for its part, was giving no indications that it was about to back down in Poland. The Soviet army had been conducting low-level exercises along its western border for months. Recalls one former Soviet intelligence officer, "Our hopes were that we could scare the Poles into submission."[3] Soviet aircraft were performing combat overflights in the region of Torun and other parts of the country. Military helicopters and cargo planes were being transported into Poland, evidence that military operations might be imminent. Aside from terrorizing the Poles, the operations were a safety menace: Soviet pilots were ignoring Polish air traffic controllers.

The highest circles of the Warsaw Pact were leaning toward using military force as early as 1980. According to the minutes of an emergency Warsaw Pact meeting convened by Leonid Brezhnev, several leaders recognized the Polish union as a threat to the whole Soviet system. Erich Honecker wrote an appeal to Brezhnev before the summit in late 1980: "According to information that we are receiving through various channels, counterrevolutionary forces are on a constant offensive in Poland. Any hesitation will mean death—the death of socialist Poland. Yesterday our collective measures might have been premature. Today they are necessary, but tomorrow they will be too late."

Brezhnev seemed sympathetic to Honecker's concerns. According to the minutes of the meeting, the Soviet leader said, "The situation in Poland and the danger that is emanating from Poland are not simply Polish matters, they affect us all." The political earthquake in Moscow just might shake the foundations of the entire empire. But Brezhnev was uncertain about Washington. Just what would the new cowboy in the White House do?

Over at the National Security Council, there was some recognition of exactly how high the stakes were in Poland. Richard Pipes, the director of Soviet East European Affairs, had put together a two-page memo for the president. It was broad and theoretical but reinforced in Reagan just what sort of threat Solidarity posed to the Kremlin, and therefore how important it was to keep the labor movement alive. Next to the Soviet Union itself, Poland was "the single most important state in the Warsaw Pact," Pipes had written. The Kremlin saw Solidarity as an "infection" that needed to be cleansed from the socialist body. Failure to do so put the Soviet bloc "at risk" for "instability" across the entire empire. Already the "virus" was "spreading." In the Baltics there were tremors similar to those that had preceded the formation of Solidarity. Solidarity activists were communicating with their Catholic brethren in Lithuania, and their views were being received favorably. In September 1981, Solidarity activists even went public with a proclamation of support for any independent unions established within the Soviet bloc. Union leader Andrzej Gwiazda had forwarded a resolution at the union's convention in Gdansk that read: "We support those of you who have decided to enter the difficult road of struggle for free and independent unions." Poland's communist government issued a swift denunciation of the resolution, noting quite accurately, "The appeal sets Solidarity against the socialist world."[4]

The Pipes memo was forwarded to all the senior members of the NSC—Reagan, Allen, Bush, Haig, Weinberger, and Casey. It had a galvanizing effect. "More than ever," recalls Weinberger, "we knew Solidarity needed to survive."[5]

The Kremlin wanted to force Poland back into the fold, while the Reagan administration saw the fissure in the Soviet bloc as something to be exploited. The stakes were enormously high, but neither superpower wanted to risk global war by too aggressively pursuing its aims. This would instead be a shadow struggle, fought between the lines of war and peace.

Poland was economically unstable and heavily in debt. A rationing system for meat started in March had since been expanded to include everything from diapers to detergents. It was failing to ensure sufficient food for the populace. More strikes were the result, further exacerbating the economic crisis. Financially the country was a basket case. In 1981, Poland needed to borrow between $11.0 and $12.0 billion. It would require $3.5 to $4.0 billion in new hard currency loans to finance debt service, and $7.0 to $8.0 billion more would be needed to roll over the third of the debt that would come due by the end of the year. Without credits from Western markets, Warsaw would default on its loans.

All the while, the Kremlin was watching events with uncertainty. In late August, the Soviet Politburo made a public appeal to the Polish government to revive its economy "without running into excessive debt with the capitalist states."[6] Moscow had sent $4.5 billion in aid to Warsaw from August 1980 to August 1981 and had increased deliveries of essentials such as oil, gas, and cotton. Although funds were already scarce, the risk of Poland's sliding into anarchy was just too great for the Kremlin to sit idly by.

In Washington, President Reagan instructed the cabinet to use any leverage possible to preserve Solidarity and advance reform in Poland. In early July 1981, a steering committee of eleven banks had reached agreement concerning the stance American financial institutions should take in negotiating with 400 international banks over how to deal with Poland's indebtedness. A resolute position was adopted. In effect, the proposal called for Warsaw to pay at once approximately $2.7 billion in loans to banks around the world. Bill Casey and Donald Regan had called some bankers to whom they were close, encouraging them to get behind a hard-line American position. At consultative meetings on bank loans to Poland in Paris on August 7, U.S. representatives met with government officials from Britain, West Germany, and France. The meeting was informal, and no communiqué was published.

But the United States had taken a hard position promoting reform, requiring some sort of economic and political change in Poland as a precondition for more loans.

The Reagan administration was also trying to acquire leverage by providing food aid directly to Warsaw. The United States was hoping that the desperate Warsaw government, beset by economic maladies, might be lured away from Moscow with promises of trade and aid from the West. By July, the administration agreed to $740 million in aid to Warsaw. "Our clear hope was to promote reform and Solidarity," recalls Robert McFarlane.[7]

But as the administration was working aboveboard to promote Solidarity and reform in Poland, Bill Casey was working under the deck of the ship of state to establish some sort of covert relationship with the opposition. American labor was his first attempt at a route to the Polish unions. The AFL-CIO was providing advice, training, and financial support to Solidarity. In 1980 alone it had sent something like $150,000. At the same time it was providing printing presses, typewriters, and, through West European unions, technical assistance and expertise. Casey was quite impressed with the operation. So in mid-September 1981, he called Irving Brown, a senior official in the AFL-CIO International Department.

Brown was tough, uncompromising, and a little rough around the edges. He was a former AFL representative in Europe, where he had served as a channel for U.S. covert aid to the noncommunists in the 1948 Italian elections. He had also fought communists in his own union and was a big supporter of Lech Walesa.

It's great what you're doing in Poland. Keep it up. It's driving the communists crazy, said Casey in rapid-fire succession, his hands as usual waving in the air. I see reports all the time about you guys and how they want to get you.

After twenty minutes of swapping stories, Casey got down to business. He wanted to make contact with Solidarity, specifically with senior leaders who were involved in decision making. He wanted intelligence on the internal situation. We get garbage or nothing out of Poland, he told Brown, obviously failing to mention Kuklinski.

What do you need me for? Brown asked.

Casey wanted to set up briefings with the AFL-CIO to get

intelligence on the internal situation in Poland. They were on the ground and knew what was happening. They were living this stuff. Brown said he would be glad to help. The relationship grew in both scope and depth. Until 1986, Brown would meet with Casey or a deputy, and with John Poindexter of the NSC staff. "I used to meet with Brown every so often to find out what intelligence he had as to what was happening and also make sure that he understood U.S. policy," recalls Poindexter. "And in his meetings with labor leaders in Europe, he would convey our policy and collect information. We asked him to do one or two minor things for us, but it was mostly just sharing information."[8]

Casey then asked a more direct question. He wanted agents in Poland, especially those who could provide liaisons with Solidarity. Could Brown "cooperate"? The labor leader didn't even have to think. The answer is no, he said immediately. Such cooperation would compromise the integrity of the union if it ever became public, he said. It would give credence to the charge the Soviets were always making—that AFL-CIO really meant CIA.

The situation was frustrating for Casey. His key asset in Poland, Colonel Kuklinski, was providing critical information on the impending martial law. But the situation was getting too hot for the colonel, and his enemies were getting too close. On November 2, he had been summoned to meet with the deputy chief of the general staff of Polish Army Division General Jerzy Skalski, who was supervising the planning of martial law. General Skalski had informed Kuklinski and two other aides, General Szklarski and Colonel Puchala, and Colonel Witt that "the Americans know the latest version of our plans." All eyes had turned to Kuklinski. Through quick thinking and calmness, the colonel had managed to talk his way out of it—temporarily. But he felt they were on to him. So he gave an emergency signal to his CIA contacts and was spirited out of the country. Gone was the best line of information the administration had in Poland.

On a hot day in mid-September, Caspar Weinberger, Ed Meese, Pentagon aide Frank Carlucci, and Richard Allen were at the White House discussing procurement plans with the president. "We were outside because of the warm weather," recalls Meese. "Cap brought a stack of documents." The Weinberger Pentagon was growing at a feverish pace, its budget rising 13 percent in 1981 alone. Procurement budgets were increasing by about 25 percent per year. The president had campaigned on the need to rebuild defenses, and Weinberger was organizing the buildup.

The secretary of defense brought a list of primary objectives. There was a special focus on high-tech weapon systems. Weinberger wanted a heavy investment in "emerging technologies," wonder weapons that made use of the microchip, lasers, and advanced technologies. We need to play to our strength, which is high tech, Weinberger told the group. The Soviets are lagging, and some of these new systems threaten to make their current arsenal obsolete.

The buildup that Weinberger envisioned included modernizing U.S. forces across the board. He wanted to develop the Trident missile program (D-5) and build the B-1 bomber as well as proceed with developing the Stealth bomber (B-2), strengthen the U.S. land-based missile capability, and modernize the conventional forces. There would be a substantially larger navy, as well as a greater U.S. airlift capability. Reagan accepted the plan in its entirety. If it were adopted by Congress, the Pentagon budget would rise by 50 percent in only a few years.

That fall the administration received good news when the Senate approved the sale of AWACS to Saudi Arabia. Prince Bandar was enormously pleased. He even sent notes of appreciation to the president, Weinberger, and Casey. Soon after, the CIA director was off on another secret trip—to Pakistan and the People's Republic of China. Pakistan was the conduit for aid to the Afghan mujahedin and another key component of the emerging rollback strategy. China was a partner in the Afghanistan program and a thorn in the side of Moscow. In April, Al Haig had publicly suggested that if the Kremlin invaded Poland, Washington would consider selling advanced arms to China. The Kremlin had winced at the thought. Casey thought Peking could be useful, and he was eager to seal some agreements on intelligence sharing.

Pakistan was a poor country surrounded by enemies, and therefore eager to cooperate with the United States. India, with which Pakistan had already gone to war, was to the south. Radical Iran and war-torn Afghanistan were to the west. And due north, separated by only a sliver of Afghan territory, stood the Soviet Union.

In Pakistan, Casey's host would be Gen. Akhtar Abdul Rehman Khan, head of the Inter-Services Intelligence (ISI). A secretive, serious man, cold and reserved with a granitelike face, Akhtar was in effect running the resistance in Afghanistan. He was determining which weapons to buy and which Afghan leaders would get them. He was trying to lay out the general strategy for the conduct of the war. His main objective was simply to keep the resistance alive and the Soviets off balance.

Second only to President Zia in power, General Akhtar was a brusque disciplinarian. He had fought against India three times. Still it was questionable who his number-one enemy was—India or the Soviet Union. "He was totally determined, with every ounce of his body, to defeating the Soviets," recalls Brig. Mohammad Yousaf, who worked for General Akhtar and headed the ISI's Afghan Bureau from 1983 to 1987.[9]

The CIA plane carrying Casey flew into Chaklala air base outside Islamabad in the darkness of a cold night. By prearrangement, the U.S. embassy was the site of a formal dinner, a distraction to allow Casey to slip into the country without notice. General Akhtar greeted him at a secluded hangar, and soon the motorcade was headed for a secure house near the American compound. For the next forty-eight hours, Casey studied everything about the program to ship arms to the Afghan resistance. After some rest from the flight, he met with General Akhtar at the main ISI headquarters in Islamabad. Akhtar gave Casey the latest information from the front: Soviet casualties, the status of the Afghan resistance, arms shipments, and the requirements for weapons. Casey absorbed it all and began analyzing ways to make the war more costly for Moscow. "He had a quick brain, with a bold and ruthless approach to the war against the Soviets," recalls Yousaf. The DCI became famous for his verbal outbursts against the Soviets, and his "they must pay" attitude. Regulars in ISI soon gave Casey the nickname Cyclone.[10]

The director was very pleased with the way things were going under the circumstances. But he had a few questions. What would it take to increase Soviet casualties? What kinds of weapons would help? Akhtar suggested surface to air missiles to counter the Soviet air advantage. He also thought some artillery pieces would be useful. Casey agreed to all the requests, no questions asked. When some American agents on the ground objected, the DCI cut them off: No, the general knows what he wants. Get it for him.

Casey and Akhtar got along famously, united in a common mission. Yet there was tension below the surface. The operation was basically cash and carry for the CIA—the Americans provided the tens of millions, the Pakistanis ran the war. Bill Casey was an activist; he wanted strategic input. But it would not come easy. Islamabad was taking heat from Moscow for serving as a safe haven for the mujahedin. President Zia was unlikely to let distant America play too large a role in plotting the war strategy.

After two days in Pakistan, Casey's black plane took off and headed for Beijing over the disputed territory of Kashmir. Early on in the administration, senior officials had agreed that China was an ideological enemy but also a geopolitical sword pointed at the Kremlin's chest. Beijing could prove very useful.

The Chinese, with their long common border with the Soviet Union, were tying down almost half a million Soviet troops. By virtue of geography, China was also proving increasingly important as an American intelligence partner. When the shah fell in 1979, the United States had lost access to some of its most important and secret eavesdropping facilities. Located along Iran's northern frontier, they were a perfect window onto ballistic missile testing being done in the desolate plains of Soviet Central Asia. Months after the shah's fall, Stansfield Turner had begun negotiations with Chinese officials about establishing joint facilities in Western China. It was more or less a done deal; there were only a few hang-ups and technical issues. Who would man the facilities? Would China be given access to the technologies at the facilities? The issues were quickly settled. The next order of business was the Afghan project. China had been selling Soviet equipment to the mujahedin. Casey told his hosts about the problems with the Egyptian equipment; he wanted to purchase more from Beijing. Would they agree? Yes, they said, again with few questions asked.

The director then turned to a more sensitive subject related to the Afghan war—Soviet Central Asia. For years Moscow and Beijing had been bantering back and forth, trying to exploit ethnic tensions on each other's side of the border. On December 4, 1980, the prime minister of Kirghizia, Sultan Ibraimov, had been murdered in his sleep in a resort town east of Frunze, only 100 miles from the Afghan border. Officials of the KGB believed that he was assassinated by Muslim extremists and had implied Chinese participation. Beijing had denied any involvement. But the problems were not only on the Soviet side. On the Chinese side of the Kirghiz border, in the province of Xinjiang, there was also tension. In October 1980, after reports of discord and unrest, a member of China's Politburo was sent on a two-week tour of the remote province. On October 16, Wang Zhen called for increased security because of the "new czars" across the border who were "stretching their tentacles" into China. Zhen had been able while in Xinjiang to listen to propaganda radio broadcasts from Frunze criticizing Beijing and encouraging resistance to Chinese rule.

No doubt the Chinese were doing the same thing. In fact, they had only recently dramatically expanded the reach of Radio Urumqi, which was being beamed into Soviet Central Asia.[11] So Casey shared with his hosts leaflets that the Afghan mujahedin were smuggling into Soviet Tajhikistan and Uzbekistan. It was an Afghan project at this point, but Casey was thinking about backing it and turning up the propaganda a notch or two. It was sensitive because the Chinese might not like the thought of stirring the ethnic pot. After all, they might get involved in the imbroglio. Islam, like communism, had no borders. There was no guarantee that the message would not boomerang and cause problems in China. To Casey's delight, Chinese intelligence liked the idea and offered to contribute to the cause. They are soft in the South, said the director of Chinese intelligence. Casey himself couldn't have said it better. The New York Catholic Irishman and the peasant communist from Hunan Province were reading from the same script.

On the flight home, reams of financial information were coming across Casey's transom. Herb Meyer, his special assistant tasked with drawing up a vulnerability assessment of the Soviet economy, had stumbled across some interesting information. The Soviets had been selling gold heavily throughout 1981—in a very soft market. In 1980 they had sold 90 tons, their usual amount. But by early November of 1981, they had cashed in 240 tons, and the volume was increasing. "It was a telltale sign to both of us," recalls Meyer, "that they were in big trouble."[12]

1. *The Wall Street Journal*, October 22, 1981, p. 1.
2. Weinberger memo (classified) to President Reagan, March 1981.
3. Interview with the author.
4. "Polish Party Assails Appeal by Union," *The New York Times*, September 10, 1981.
5. Caspar Weinberger, interview with the author.
6. "Soviet Politburo Warns Poland on Debt to West," *The New York Times*, August 23, 1981.
7. Robert McFarlane, interview with the author.
8. John Poindexter, interview with the author.
9. Mohammad Yousaf, interview with the author. For those interested in reading more about the war in Afghanistan the author highly recommends Mohammad Yousaf and Mark Adkin, *The Bear Trap* (London: Leo Cooper, 1992).
10. Mohammad Yousaf, interview with the author.
11. S. Enders Wimbush, "Nationality Research in the PRC: A Trip Report," Rand Corporation, N-1713-NA, August 1981.
12. Herb Meyer, interview with the author.

6

A heavily fortified Soviet military transport plane escorted by fighter aircraft descended onto a secret military air base near Warsaw on the night of December 9, 1981. Onboard was Marshal Victor Georgmevich Kulikov, commander of the Warsaw Pact forces. He was met by heavily armed Soviet security service agents, who bundled him into the back of a black sedan and drove at high speed to a Soviet military installation outside Warsaw. Kulikov had throughout 1981 railed against "Western subversion" in Poland and denounced Solidarity as a "threat" to the Warsaw Pact.

Poland had been, since 1945, the most important non-Soviet member of the Warsaw Pact. Whether measured by its military or its economic strength, it was the largest non-Soviet contributor to the pact. It was the geopolitical linchpin of Moscow's hegemonic system in Eastern Europe. But control of Poland appeared to be slipping away. There was open defiance in the streets, calls for free elections and independent unions in other Soviet bloc countries. Kulikov was there to keep the lid on the boiling pot. He was in country to oversee the declaration of martial law.

Security forces had been practicing for months under the Orwellian name Operation Springtime. Kulikov had been immersed in the planning. Three days after he arrived, the operation began. In the middle of the night, Polish security forces, supported by military units acting as Soviet proxies, in effect invaded their own country. Tanks rolled into the streets of Warsaw; roadblocks were set up throughout the country. Simultaneously, 3.4 million private telephones went dead. Five thousand activists were rounded up in one night; borders were sealed with all of Poland's neighbors. The Polish internal security apparatus mobilized its force of 250,000, including motorized police units (ZOMO) and paramilitary forces under the command of the Interior Ministry's head of counterintelligence (WSW).[1] The resistance, or so officials thought, had collapsed without a fight. At 6:00 A.M., General Jaruzelski went on radio and television to announce that a "state of war" had been declared, and that authority now rested with the newly formed Military Council of National Salvation.

Halfway around the world, the Reagan administration was, despite the information provided by Colonel Kuklinski, taken by almost complete surprise. American spy satellites, hanging above Poland, did not detect the troop movements in the days and hours before the fateful night of December 12. There had been heavy cloud cover—they didn't see a thing. What was surprising was not that martial law came but that it came so quickly and powerfully.

At the White House, the staff was numb when the reports first arrived. However, the disorientation quickly gave way to anger. The president was in California, but his reaction was apparent over the phone lines. Richard Pipes, director of Soviet and East European Affairs at the National Security Council, recalls, "The president was absolutely livid. He said, 'Something must be done. We need to hit them hard, and save Solidarity.' The president was gung ho, ready to go."[2]

The declaration of martial law in Poland was a turning point for the administration. It solidified support behind an offensive strategy to roll back Soviet power. Within months, secret directives would be signed, making it explicit U.S. policy to undermine Soviet power and calling for a comprehensive economic war to be launched. And opportunities would be sought for sowing dissent in Eastern Europe.

Shortly after the declaration of martial law, the president spoke with his closest advisers about the situation in Poland and U.S. options. Much of the NSC was not included. "National Security Council meetings were not considered leak proof, he [the president] didn't want to risk anything," recalls Pipes. At the meeting were Vice President Bush, William Clark, Secretaries Haig and Weinberger, Ed Meese, Richard Pipes, and William Casey.[3]

There was a general consensus that the United States had to send a strong message to Warsaw and Moscow. Economic sanctions were universally supported as a way of demonstrating American anger. But then Pipes raised the stakes: what about doing something proactive? What about covertly funding Solidarity to ensure that the first anticommunist organization aboveground in the Soviet bloc survived this harsh political winter? The specter of such a risky operation haunted the room. After a few moments, Al Haig cut through the silence with his explosive voice. "That's crazy, it just won't work," he said. "The Soviets would never tolerate it. Solidarity is lost." Bush agreed, expressed concerns about inflaming Moscow, and counseled against any operation.

Pipes, the only NSC staffer at the meeting (and a Pole himself), tried to contain his anger. "What worries the Soviets is the survival of Solidarity," he retorted. "They are afraid of an infection, that it will spread to the rest of the Soviet bloc—even Lithuania and Russia itself. You don't know the Poles, Mr. Secretary. Solidarity will survive."[4] Weinberger, Casey, and Bill Clark voiced enthusiastic support for the operation. But the president "didn't need any encouragement," according to Pipes.[5] He immediately asked Casey to draw up a covert operation plan. "He not only wanted to free Poland but shatter the myth of Soviet invincibility," recalls Clark.[6]

A premium was placed on secrecy. In the end, the operation was funded and executed outside traditional government requirements. "No formal intelligence action was taken," recalls Pipes. "It was feared it would leak. This was a highly secret operation, handled 'off the books.'"[7]

After the meeting, Casey raced back to Langley. As his Olds sped down the George Washington Parkway, he started calling a few trusted aides. There was no time to waste. Casey worked with half a dozen aides, developing a plan to get funds to Solidarity and establish communications. They were beginning from scratch. What would Solidarity need? How could external support be funneled in? Recalls one Operations official who worked on the project, "Solidarity was a populist organization with millions of members and sympathizers. But they had not made any preparations for martial law. They had no command, control, or communications capability. They were littered with enemy agents. They had very few resources to draw upon, except the popular support of the Polish people."[8] To Casey the whole thing must have seemed like a replay of his experience during the Second World War. The problem—getting people behind enemy lines—was the same. Only the players and names were different.

At one point Casey got on the secure phone and called General Hoffi, director of Israeli intelligence. "Casey read him the riot act," recalls one official. The Mossad had promised access to the ratline into Poland more than six months ago, and the agency had received nothing.[9] After a stream of expletives, the director demanded immediate access. I don't care if martial law complicates things! he screamed. He reminded Hoffi of the satellite photos and other intelligence he had openly shared.

Slamming down the phone, he then put in a call to the Rome station. The station chief had to be awakened. Casey wanted someone to get him in contact with Cardinal Casaroli. Perhaps, given martial law, there would be an attitude change at the Vatican. Casaroli took the call at home. Casey received an encouraging response: there was a willingness to cooperate. The assassination attempt on the pope and the declaration of martial law had affected him deeply. The foreign minister agreed to a meeting.

By late January 1982, things were falling into place. General Hoffi had called; the CIA would be plugged into the ratline at once. Cardinal Casaroli of the Vatican was scheduled to meet with CIA representatives in an effort to "cooperate." The Church insisted from the outset that it would never play a covert role with the agency, nor would it serve as a cover for CIA operations. But it was critical in providing information and contacts inside Poland. John Poindexter, a chief military adviser to the national security adviser and one of the few NSC staffers with knowledge of the operation, recalls, "Clearly in terms of gathering intelligence as to what was happening and from the standpoint of talking to Solidarity and other supporters of Western objectives in Poland, the Vatican was very helpful." The Church was not a "partner" in the CIA operation, says Poindexter. "It was simply the fact that we had some mutual objectives in Poland. And we took advantage of that when we could, both to collect information and spread information."[10]

While Casey had been putting together his covert action plan, Caspar Weinberger had assembled a team of economic experts in the Pentagon. Held under the auspices of the Rand Corporation, it was sort of a classified gabfest to formulate a strategy for virtually killing off a Polish economy already in poor health. Fred Ikle, undersecretary of defense, called in economists Henry Rowen and Charles Wolf, old hands at Rand, and a few trusted outsiders, including Roger Robinson, then vice president at Chase Manhattan. Poland was already faltering on meeting loan payments to Western banks. The all-day conference, therefore, focused on the benefits and costs of throwing the country into default. A strong case was made for doing just that, potentially pushing the entire Soviet bloc into a financial crisis. According to Robinson, "The Pentagon was of a mind to do this."

But the banker from New York argued strongly against such a move. "There was a better than even chance that throwing Poland into default in this manner would actually relieve pressure on Warsaw to expend critical hard currency." A default initiative might also benefit the Soviet Union, Robinson argued, particularly if it was perceived in financial markets as a political move by Washington. There was also the possibility that a sudden Polish default could set off a worldwide chain reaction. Ironically, writing down, if not off, the $28 billion Polish debt might encourage the myriad of other troubled debtor nations to seek the same solution. Robinson added, "Playing out a politically driven default scenario involved the prospect of 'instant replays' of sovereign default throughout the world, beginning in Latin America. For those of us crafting the Polish debt rescheduling in 1981, it was quite clear that it was a harbinger of the international debt crisis to come."

Robinson also argued that a default would worsen the plight of the beleaguered and oppressed people in Poland with very little pain for the Kremlin. Now in his closing days with Chase and relieved of any possible conflict with his banking responsibilities, Robinson revealed his game plan: "If you really want to hurt Moscow," he told Pentagon officials, "let's move the targeting designator several degrees and put direct financial pressure on the Soviet Union. After all, the Soviets were the catalysts and sponsors of martial law in Poland. Let's delay the first strand of the pipeline and stop the second strand, halt subsidies on official credits and militarily relevant high-technology transfers to Moscow instead. This is our opening." Robinson's view prevailed. Weinberger took it to the president.[11]

Weinberger, who had been arguing for months for a tough U.S. position on the Urengoi pipeline, made his case before an angry chief executive bent on action. With encouragement from the NSC, the president embraced his plan almost immediately. Three weeks before martial law, the Office of Technology Assessment had sharply criticized Weinberger's repeated calls for a Western embargo of Soviet gas and oil equipment, declaring that it was "tantamount to economic warfare." But with the declaration of martial law in Poland, the administration's mood swung sharply in favor of such a war. On December 29, President Reagan took to the airwaves to announce the embargo. American involvement in the pipeline project would be prohibited. The plan affected some sixty U.S. companies but also halted Japanese and Soviet plans to develop oil and gas fields off Sakhalin Island. That arrangement was very similar to the pipeline deal: Japan was financing the project in exchange for guaranteed supplies of gas and oil. But the deal required sophisticated offshore oil-drilling technologies from General Electric, Dresser Industries, Schlumberger, and Velco to make it work.

The seven-year-old Sakhalin Island deal was at a critical stage. The area had proven reserves of 1.1 billion barrels of oil and 2.5 billion cubic feet of gas. The Tokyo-based Sakhalin Oil Development Corporation, owned jointly by Japan National Oil Company and several private companies, wanted to begin drilling in the spring, when the icy waters melted. Any delays would force the company to wait until 1983 and possibly end the project entirely. The embargo upset Japanese plans to develop an alternative to Middle Eastern oil on an accelerated basis. For its part, the Kremlin had been counting on several billion dollars a year in income from the project.

While critical technologies were being cut off to Moscow, the NSC was doing what it could to discourage bank loans to the USSR. Robinson, well known in international banking circles, offered guidance in the effort. Ikle and Weinberger wanted to take an aggressive approach, publicly prodding the financial community to stop making loans. Robinson pointed out that political intervention or diktats would not go over well in banking circles. He advocated "a lighter touch," including selective private meetings with bankers to discourage new, undisciplined lending. His approach got results.

The goal was to shake bankers' confidence in Soviet financial prowess. Western bank loans and credits to the Soviet bloc had grown rapidly based on the so-called umbrella theory. Throughout the 1970s, bankers had eagerly made loans to Eastern Europe, under the impression that if any of the Soviet satellite states could not make their payments, Moscow would intervene as a payer of last resort. The theory hinged on the assumption that the Kremlin placed a high premium on its fine credit rating, and that it had the financial reserves to meet such a crisis. The umbrella theory had, however, never been tested. Recalls Robinson, "Bankers had great faith in Moscow's creditworthiness and financial solvency. It was supposed to have some $25 to $30 billion in gold reserves that could be called upon to ensure repayment. Trouble was, no one ever inspected these reserves or held gold as collateral—it was a mystery."[12]

Under the guidance of the new national security adviser, Bill Clark, it had been decided that the administration would discourage new Western lending to the Soviet Union. Political or humanitarian appeals would not be enough: bankers had fiduciary responsibilities to shareholders. Their job was making money. And some bankers saw martial law as a way of actually making their job easier. "Most bankers think authoritarian governments are good because they impose discipline," one banker told The New York Times shortly after martial law was declared. "Every time there's a coup d'etat in Latin America, there's much rejoicing and knocking at the door offering credit. Who knows what political system works? The only test we care about is: Can they pay their bills?"[13]

Taking Robinson's advice, the administration would try to put the umbrella theory to the test. Casey wanted to discourage Western bankers from giving short-term credits that would allow Warsaw to meet its payments. He felt that if these loans were suspended, Moscow might be forced to step in. If it failed to do so, bankers would be discouraged from making further loans to questionable East European debtor nations and possibly the Soviet Union itself. It was a deft manipulation of the credit market for national security ends. And the thing was, it wouldn't have U.S. government fingerprints all over it.

In early February, Bill Casey and Treasury Secretary Don Regan were working the phones, calling friends in banking circles. Roger Robinson, still vice president at Chase, recalls, "There was subtle guidance in meetings on the Polish rescheduling to discourage new, unsecured rollovers. Moving to secured short-term transactions through means of collateralized accounts would enable bankers to better manage repayment. This revised approach reduced the flexibility of both Warsaw and Moscow."[14]

The effort to make financial markets jittery about the Soviet bloc continued throughout the year. On April 26, Lionel Olmer, the undersecretary of commerce for international trade, told a group of international bankers that loans to the Soviet bloc were "fraught with risks." At the sixty-first annual meeting of the Bankers Association for Foreign Trade, Olmer declared that "the growing crisis in the Soviet Union could bring as many risks for creditors in a few years as Poland presents now."[15]

These actions and the financial crisis throughout Eastern Europe had a chilling effect on loans going to the rest of the Soviet bloc. During the spring of 1982, Hungary saw the termination of short-term credits amounting to $1.1 billion. Romania was hit even harder, experiencing the withdrawal of $1.5 billion. Even East Germany felt the tightening credit, losing $200 million in liquid assets. Several of the countries for the first time had trouble making loan payments.

Casey and Weinberger wanted to force Moscow to step in and fill the gap or risk seeing the creditworthiness of its allies plummet. Moscow elected to go the latter route. "They had forced our hand in Poland," recalls Vladimir Kutinov, then an officer at the Central Bank in Moscow. "There was no proof that the emperor had no clothes."[16] By now, Robinson had made a big impression in Washington. In early March, he was asked by the new national security adviser to join his senior staff. He soon became senior director of international economic affairs at the NSC and executive secretary of the cabinet-level interagency body mandated to manage international economic policy. Bill Martin, an energy expert, was also brought on the staff at this time and later played a key role in gaining European agreement to limit Soviet gas deliveries to the continent. This NSC economic team proved very formidable. At the outset, staff planning director Norm Bailey instructed Martin to wear the "white hat" and Robinson the "black hat" during interagency deliberations and meetings with U.S. allies.

By mid-February, Bill Casey had put the final touches on his proposal for covertly funding Solidarity. The plan had four central elements:

- Provide critical funds to Solidarity to sustain the movement. These could take the form of cash, both U.S. dollars and Polish zlotys.
- Supply advanced communications equipment to organize an effective C3I network for the Solidarity underground. This would enable the movement to communicate even under martial law.
- Offer training to a few select individuals in the movement to use the advanced communications equipment that would be provided.
- Use CIA assets to serve as the eyes and ears of Solidarity, sharing critical intelligence when appropriate.

Casey next identified three institutions that he planned to use as tools in the venture. The AFL-CIO had been funneling aid to Solidarity since 1980. He thought learning from the union might prove "very fruitful." Solidarity activists trapped in the West might also provide a lift. The French SDECE (Service de Documentation Extérieure et de Contre-Espionnage) was smuggling some activists out of Poland who wanted to leave. Casey hoped to use some of them for information and operations. Finally, once contact with Solidarity had been made, Casey wanted to relay information through code words used on Voice of America radio broadcasts.

Casey met privately with the president and Bill Clark in late February to discuss his plan. Reagan saw it as risky but well worth it. He seemed intrigued by the idea of supporting workers to undermine the workers' state. He signed off on the plan but did not issue a covert action finding. That was deemed too risky. The president asked that

Casey notify the chairman of his Foreign Intelligence Advisory Board, Dr. Glenn Campbell. Casey did, but Campbell didn't get too many specifics. "He mentioned it to me in general terms," recalls Campbell, "and then went into his mumbling act. He never mumbled about generalities, but usually about specifics. I thought it was a great idea and said, 'OK, Bill, do it.' " At its peak, $8 million per year were being transferred into Solidarity coffers.[17]

To carry out the operation and maintain supreme secrecy, Casey constructed a complex web of international financial institutions. The money trail was constantly shifting to avoid detection. Polish officials' uncovering the channel and following it to the source could spell the end of Solidarity and might also precipitate an international crisis.

The difficulty was getting currency into the country. The zloty was not convertible. The Church could get enormous sums of money into Poland but appeared unwilling to become so deeply involved in the covert action. Casey ended up relying on a chain of sources throughout Europe. Several European companies unwittingly had funds transferred into Poland through accounts established for legitimate projects. Electronic transfer was preferable, because by this means the funds would be automatically converted into zlotys. Thankful for the business it was getting, one company agreed to set up a separate account for the agency. By late March to early April, the financial channel to Solidarity was in place.

In conjunction with the decision to support Solidarity covertly, the president ordered the NSC to draw up a document outlining American objectives and goals in Eastern Europe. Bill Clark felt it was important for U.S. objectives to be spelled out explicitly, in accordance with the president's wishes. A document written by Richard Pipes and touched up by Clark emerged several weeks later. It was radical: the explicit purpose of U.S. policy was to "neutralize efforts of the U.S.S.R." to maintain its hold on Eastern Europe. "In effect, we believed that the Yalta Agreement was irrelevant," recalls Edwin Meese, then on the NSC.[18] The document was signed by the president and became a national security decision directive (NSDD), a formal written order directing senior advisers and departments on policy. "NSDD-32 was proactive and broke with the past," recalls Clark. "In NSDD-32, Ronald Reagan made clear that the United States was not resigned to the status quo of Soviet domination of Eastern Europe. We attempted to forge a multipronged strategy to weaken Soviet influence and strengthen indigenous forces for freedom in the region. Poland offered a unique opportunity relative to other states like Bulgaria, Romania, and Czechoslovakia. This is not to say that we did not pursue activities—both overt and covert—in these other countries to loosen Moscow's grip."[19]

National Security Decision Directive-32 outlined a number of principal objectives:

- Covertly support underground movements in the region attempting to throw off communist rule
- Intensify psychological operations directed at the region, particularly radio broadcasts such as Voice of America and Radio Free Europe
- Seek through diplomacy and trade to wean away the regimes' heavy reliance on Moscow

The U.S. embargo on technologies for the natural gas pipeline was seen in Europe for what it was: a declaration of economic war on the Soviet Union. Washington made the statement with more than a hint of moral outrage over what had happened in Poland. But Europe was mute. West German Chancellor Helmut Schmidt even went so far as to declare that, given the turmoil in Poland, martial law was "necessary." There existed in Western Europe an overwhelming desire to continue to trade with the Kremlin, regardless of events in Poland.

Economic realities made European leaders hungry for exports. Unemployment was running at 14 percent in Britain, 9 percent in France, and almost 8 percent in West Germany—the highest levels since 1954. The pipeline would create tens of thousands of jobs all over Europe. In mid-January, there were two meetings between the Western allies to discuss sanctions: one with the Coordinating Committee on Export Controls (COCOM), the other at the North Atlantic Congress. At the insistence of the president, the U.S. position was to push hard for the Europeans to follow the American lead in cutting off oil and gas technology to Moscow. A few days before the COCOM meeting in Paris, Chancellor Schmidt was in Washington for consultations with the president and the secretary of state. At the stately Blair House, where the

German chancellor was staying, Secretary Haig joined Schmidt for a breakfast of fruit, toast, and eggs. The meeting did not go well. Haig chastised Schmidt for not condemning the crackdown in Poland hard enough. At one point, shouting between the two could be heard from the dining room. There was no progress.

In Paris on January 19, COCOM was meeting in secret to discuss several American proposals. Created in 1949, COCOM was an attempt to forge a unified Western response on technology and strategic trade with the Soviet bloc. It is a secretive body, its internal actions unknown except to a precious few. The American delegation to the Paris meeting, headed by Undersecretary of State James Buckley and Undersecretary of Defense Fred Ikle, proposed three specific changes to the COCOM process in light of current realities. First, the United States wanted stricter enforcement of the ban on the sale of critical technologies to the Soviet Union, including advanced computers and electronics, fiber optics, semiconductors, and various metallurgical processes. The United States also wanted to restrict the building of Western industrial sites within the Soviet bloc which might aid the Soviet military or train personnel in advanced skills that would help their economy. The second U.S. proposal was that all contracts with the Soviet bloc worth $100 million or more automatically be submitted to the committee for approval to ensure that they did not result in the transfer of sensitive technologies. This would in effect offer Washington veto power over European trade agreements with Moscow. The third proposal constituted the first major attempt to tighten the embargo list since the committee was set up. The American delegation wanted the highly classified list expanded to reflect new technologies and products. France and Great Britain were willing to accede to some U.S. demands, but the Germans were unbending in their opposition. The economic war would have to wait, or proceed at least initially without European cooperation.

At a meeting of the North Atlantic Congress, NATO foreign ministers struck a middle position on the issue of pipeline sanctions. They agreed that Europe could continue to develop the pipeline but that they would not undermine U.S. sanctions. In other words, European companies would not step in and fill contracts the Americans had abandoned. European foreign ministers did not realize what a critical victory this was for Washington. They assumed that the Reagan administration would never actually enforce the agreement, that it was only a triumph on paper to offer the American public. How wrong they would be.

On March 15, Buckley and a team of financial experts began a swing through five European capitals to tighten the noose on credits going to the Soviet Union. Not only were the West Europeans loaning Moscow vast amounts of money but they were doing so at well below market rates. The interest on the subsidized loans going to the Kremlin was incredible. Not even Western Europe's best domestic clients would receive these rates. The French government was financing part of the pipeline deal at 7.8 percent, less than half of what the Soviets would have had to pay at current market rates.

The Buckley team wanted to curb such subsidies by reclassifying the Soviet Union as a "relatively rich" country instead of an "intermediate borrower" under the existing agreement on government-backed export credits established by the Organization for Economic Cooperation and Development. That would require the Soviets to pay a minimum 11.25 percent interest on official export credits. But beyond that, Washington had proposed on March 10 that all subsidized credit to countries in the "relatively rich" category be halted. Moscow would thus face interest at real rates, then approximately 17 percent.

1. "Security Forces of Polish Rulers put at 250,000," *The New York Times*, January 5, 1982.
2. Richard Pipes, interview with the author.
3. Richard Pipes, interview with the author.
4. Richard Pipes, interview with the author.
5. Richard Pipes, interview with the author.
6. William Clark, interview with the author.
7. Richard Pipes, interview with the author.
8. U.S. intelligence official, interview with the author.
9. U.S. official, interview with the author.
10. John Poindexter, interview with the author.
11. Roger Robinson, interview with the author.
12. Roger Robinson, interview with the author.
13. "Banking on Repression," *The New York Times*, January 5, 1982, p. A14.
14. Roger Robinson, interview with the author.

15. "U.S. Stresses Risks of Credit to Soviets," *The New York Times*, April 27, 1982.
16. Vladimir Kutinov, interview with the author.
17. Glenn Campbell, interview with the author.
18. Edwin Meese, interview with the author.
19. William Clark, interview with the author.

7

In early 1982, Caspar Weinberger and his aides were putting the final touches on a top-secret, five-year planning directive for the Department of Defense. The document laid down several important elements in the emerging campaign to undermine Soviet power and made them guiding principles of the largest peacetime military buildup in U.S. history. It emphasized the important role "economic and technical war" would play in administration policy. *The New York Times* described the document "as a peacetime complement to military strategy, the guidance document asserts that the United States and its allies should, in effect, declare economic and technological war on the Soviet Union."[1]

The guidance document placed a premium on reducing Soviet access to technology from the United States and other noncommunist countries by a variety of means, in keeping with efforts in 1981 to cut back high-tech exports to the Soviet bloc. But the document also outlined the Pentagon's intention to execute a complex strategy designed to erode Soviet economic strength by forcing Moscow into a technological competition. That strategy included

- Identification of technologies critical to Soviet economic strength and establishment of policies to limit access. This could include preemptive buying and pressure on suppliers.

• "Investment in weapon systems that render the accumulative Soviet equipment obsolescent."

The document reflected Weinberger's plans for forcing the Soviets to make more and more difficult decisions on how increasingly limited resources would be allocated.

These elements of the Department of Defense planning directive became a central tenet of the president's top-secret strategy for dealing with the Soviet Union. In May 1982, President Reagan signed a secret eight-page national security decision memorandum (NSDM), laying out U.S. military strategy vis-à-vis the Soviet Union. It gave the bureaucracies their first set of coordinated marching orders for conducting Reagan's Soviet policy. Drawn up by the NSC under the direction of William Clark, the NSDM reflected a strong emphasis on exploiting Soviet economic weaknesses. "We must force our principal adversary, the Soviet Union, to bear the brunt of its economic shortcomings," Clark proclaimed in the only public mention of the secret strategy.[2] "The NSDM purposefully reflected the president's strategic view that trade and finance should emerge as new priorities in our broader effort to contain and roll back Soviet operations worldwide," recalls Clark.[3]

Increasingly, administration officials were pointing to the reality of profound Soviet economic weakness as a strategic vulnerability to be exploited. On June 16, Thomas Reed, a consultant to the NSC and special assistant to the president, made a controversial speech before the Armed Forces Communications and Electronics Association. He declared the Soviet Union "an economic basket case," and said the United States "should not provide the trade and credits necessary to prop up the Soviet economy."[4]

The intelligence analysis being done at the NSC indicated that cutoff of U.S. technology in the short term was critical to the pipeline project. Moscow had purposely developed a purchasing strategy for the pipeline technologies it would need from the West with the hope that the deal would therefore be embargo proof.

The Kremlin was signing agreements down to the subcontractor level to ensure that the Urengoi pipeline construction would go ahead despite objections from Washington. However, it inadvertently overlooked a critical link—the rotor shafts and blades driving the gas turbines for the forty-one compressor stations along the 3,300-mile line. These parts were made by General Electric, which was now prohibited from providing them.

The Soviets could find an alternative to the GE rotors, but the search would delay construction and increase costs considerably. A thirty-member Soviet delegation based in Cologne was tasked by Moscow to find an alternative. It quickly identified Alsthom-Atlantique, the giant French machinery maker. It was the only other company producing the rotor blades and shafts, and they were under license to GE. Getting approval for purchase of the French blades and shafts might prove pretty easy. In most European capitals, the agreements were fudged. The Europeans interpreted the NAC agreement, concluded in January 1982, that Europe would not undermine U.S. sanctions as covering only deals in which American companies were the main contractors, not where they served as subcontractors. So the French government gave the go-ahead to Alsthom-Atlantique to supply the technology to Moscow. "It was evident between January and June of 1982 that they [the Europeans] had dismissed the NAC agreement and had begun replacing U.S. suppliers at flank speed," recalls Roger Robinson. "This despite a solemn pledge not to undercut American sanctions during the period of Soviet-sponsored repression in Poland."[5]

Additional intelligence reports confirmed that pipeline sanctions were coming at a time when they could have the maximum effect as an economic weapon. On January 25, intelligence at the NSC indicated how serious the Soviet cash crunch really was. It included figures on Soviet bank deposits in the West compiled by the Bank for International Settlements in Basel. Soviet deposits in Western banks had fallen from $8.5 billion at the start of 1981 to about $3.0 billion at the end of the year. Soviet trade figures were equally dismal. In 1980, Moscow had experienced a $217 million trade surplus with the industrialized non-communist countries. But in 1981 that had turned to a $3.0 billion deficit. The gambit over Poland, pushing Moscow into the role of financial guarantor, had been timed perfectly. The financial markets would become much more cautious in their dealings with the Soviet bloc.

At the Kremlin, the leadership was sweating rubles. And the pipeline—at a minimum delayed—would pinch them even more. The

Siberian gas pipeline and the oil and gas exploration project off Sakhalin Island were deemed critical if the Kremlin was to generate the hard currency income needed to purchase Western technology, fill the large gaps in the Soviet economy, and fund its global empire. "Hard currency earnings were a central part of the Soviet economy," recalls Yevgenny Novikov of the Central Committee staff. "And completing the pipeline without delay was most important. There was no breathing room."[6]

Encouraged by Bill Casey and Caspar Weinberger, Bill Clark had the NSC undertake a series of studies exploring other ways to damage the Soviet economy. It would assess the viability of a broadscale economic war against Moscow. Directed by staff planning director Norm Bailey, the study explored the possible mechanisms for undermining the Soviet economy, including forging a grain cartel—to include the United States, Canada, Australia, and Argentina—to limit exports to the USSR.[7]

As the volleys flew back and forth between Washington and Europe over the pipeline, the first contact was made with remnants of Solidarity, now underground. The situation in Poland was grave. Solidarity activists were being systematically hunted down by security forces. There were food shortages and security personnel on the streets of every major city and town. On February 2, the coal mines in Poland slowed down in symbolic protest. So did mines at Donbas in the Soviet Union, a dangerous precedent for the Kremlin. It was the first visible and tangible sign of worker support for Solidarity aims in the Soviet Union itself. In the Soviet Central Committee, there was continuing concern. If Solidarity was not stamped out, it might very well spread to the Soviet Union. But the days of the labor union did appear to be numbered.

In February, two Polish-Americans boarded the Chopin Express train in Vienna destined for Poland. They had been involved in Solidarity activities in the West. Carrying false identity papers and information, they were planning to meet with remnants of the underground. A meeting was to take place outside Zyrardow, just west of Warsaw. The town had just over 40,000 people, and it was relatively quiet. On February 17, there had been another massive sweep by security forces. In what was officially called Operation Calm, tens of thousands of militia had arrested 4,000 people over a two-day period. The two Americans were to rendezvous with a Solidarity activist on the run.

The Solidarity representative was a colleague of Lech Badkowski, the Solidarity spokesman in Gdansk. Badkowski had lived in London during the Second World War and fought in Polish naval units organized in England. He had maintained some contact with British intelligence after his return to Poland and was now advocating communication with the West as the only hope for saving the movement. The Americans had left Warsaw four days before the meeting in Zyrardow and had slept in a church on the outskirts of the city. The parish priest asked no questions. He was part of the vaunted Israeli ratline. It was finally paying dividends.

The meeting was the first inside Poland. In late January, the CIA had been in touch with émigrés in West Germany who had contact with activists across the Iron Curtain. They had made the initial arrangements. The hope had been to identify a senior Solidarity official caught outside Poland who would be returning shortly and make arrangements through him. But that proved impossible, as did getting anybody out of the country on short notice. The two Polish-Americans would relay information to the CIA.

The activist told the Americans that Solidarity had been hit hard. In the first night, December 12, security forces had rounded up 5,000 leaders, many of them core activists in the opposition. The movement had been taken by complete surprise, unwilling to believe that martial law was possible. By mid-February, estimates of arrests ran as high as 40,000. Not much of the Solidarity leadership was left, and the embers of the movement were scattered. Those leaders who had gone into hiding included Zbigniew Bujak in Warsaw, Wladyslaw Hardek in Krakow, Bogdan Lis in Gdansk, and Wladyslaw Frasyniuk in Wroclaw. The financial assets of the movement had been seized, as had all their property. The leadership could not communicate effectively with the rank and file except through passed notes and crudely duplicated letters. Solidarity may not have been dead, but it had been effectively lobotomized.

The initial meeting outside Zyrardow was tense. The Solidarity representative, in hiding and on the run, was very nervous. Despite their fluent Polish, he wondered if these Americans could be trusted. The Americans, for their part, were equally nervous, afraid of being picked up for "spying."

The meeting lasted for six hours and covered an array of topics—what type of support from the West would be most helpful, the amount, how it might be distributed and accounted for. The Solidarity representative made it clear that it was assumed that "no strings" were attached to the aid. Technical matters were also discussed—how the funds might be transferred and possible means of communication. The Americans passed the Solidarity man the name of a European businessman in Warsaw who could hand over funds. He had access to a special account.

Shortly after their return to the West, the Americans wrote reports that were forwarded to Bill Casey. In keeping with the president's orders, he began constructing a financial pipeline. "Bill was a master at moving money around in secret," recalls Glenn Campbell. "He was getting millions in every year. He had it so they could have never figured out how he got the funds into Poland."[8]

It was also assumed that the underground would need technical help in reorganizing itself. Specifically, it would require advanced communications equipment. The agency was exploring several suggestions. One was to bring the equipment in as diplomatic material and then try to smuggle it out of the embassy compound. But that would not do. The embassy was being watched closely and surrounded by armed militiamen. The second proposal was to ask the Catholic Church to smuggle the contraband in as part of its regular shipment of relief supplies. But Casey didn't want to risk it. The Church seemed uncomfortable enough just sharing intelligence. There was no way it would do this.

Then the agency got a break. A contact in the Israeli ratline proved to be not only a resident of Gdansk but a manager at the shipyard. The Israelis asked the contact to make arrangements for two shipments. The communications equipment would be arriving from Sweden as part of a shipment of machine tools for tractors and then four days later as engineering equipment. He was provided with the invoice numbers and dates of shipment. His job would be spiriting the equipment to a Solidarity safe house before customs and/or security officials inspected it. On the nights of the drops, the manager had the crates immediately put in a storage facility. They were perhaps the most important cargo shipments he had ever handled. The equipment, according to Robert McFarlane, "gave them the means of communicating with their own membership and the country at large and the means of staying in touch with each other and avoiding compromise. It was a C3I program, to give them an infrastructure of command and control."⁹

Distributing the equipment throughout the underground took months. At one point, equipment destined for Krakow didn't arrive when members of the underground had been expecting it. It was feared that it had been intercepted by Polish intelligence. If so, the whole operation would be at jeopardy before it even got started. And the reputation of Solidarity would be sullied. Fortunately, the missing crates turned up days later. The truck carrying the precious cargo had blown out a tire. In martial law Poland, finding a spare tire had proven difficult.

Casey watched the operation from afar, biting his nails and hoping that his gambit would succeed. The president was anxious— aware that assets were in place and sensitive operations under way. That spring Casey met with the president in private in the White House Situation Room. They discussed a variety of issues—chief among them the circumstances in Poland. Reagan enthusiastically received the news that the operation was off the ground. Casey even passed him some documents that had been received from the underground. Included was a letter written by Solidarity activist Jacek Kuron in prison. It was a defiant and open statement of protest. It declared that "a mass insurrection" was around the corner in Poland: oppression would not stand. The president kept the letter in the drawer of his desk in the Oval Office. He and Casey agreed that they would only discuss the Poland operation in private in the Oval Office. When they discussed particulars over the phone, the DCI would call from a secure phone at home or from his office in the West Wing.

There was never any doubt that the Soviets figured something was going on. "I think it would be foolish to believe that they didn't have a reasonable idea of the things we were doing," recalls John Poindexter. "They had informants that were telling them what was going on. And so I think our assumption when we planned operations was that they knew in general terms what we were doing. They fussed about it and raised threats, but it never got to a threshold where we even considered changing our policy. We tempered what we would do for Solidarity by not doing those things that would provide the trigger that would provoke the Soviets into military intervention."¹⁰

In late March, Bill Casey was bringing together his Directorate of Operations to put the third strand of his Solidarity support strategy in place. Because the weak often rely on cunning instincts and intelligence to survive against a more powerful foe, Casey wanted the agency to serve as the eyes and ears of Solidarity. The underground needed intelligence from the highest levels of the Polish government so it could counter the regime's next move. While the movement had many sympathizers in place who relayed information, it lacked the capacity and resources to maintain a flow of intelligence on what the government planned to do next. Casey had dispatched a joint CIA-NSA team to the embassy in Warsaw in late 1981 to rapidly expand electronic intelligence operations in the city.

The team included four people, highly skilled in the use of advanced electronic intercept technologies. Called a Special Collection Element, the employees were brought in as part of the ordinary rotation of embassy employees. The element was in operation by late January 1982. The team was running a sophisticated electronics intercept system and succeeding in eavesdropping on Polish communications. Later they would increase dramatically the use of bugs and other electronic intelligence devices.

Casey had also been pushing for more aggressive recruitment of human assets. He wanted operatives to penetrate their host countries more effectively, particularly in the Soviet bloc. Operatives had been much too cautious when it came to recruiting agents. In the early months of his tenure, Casey had replaced the CIA's lengthy handbook on agent recruitment with new guidelines. The old handbook was too laborious; it "got in the way" he told aides; it set up a rigid code of conduct that stifled creativity and encouraged agents to be skeptical of walk-ins. Operations, according to Casey, were about results, not rigid rules. The 130-page book was reduced to a few paragraphs. In particular, Casey encouraged aggressiveness on the part of agents working behind the Iron Curtain.[11]

American intelligence hoped to serve as an early warning system for Solidarity. If there was going to be renewed repression or there were leads on Solidarity leaders in hiding, the president and Bill Casey wanted them warned. As time went on, the system worked very well. "We had good intelligence about what the Polish government was doing and what it was about to do," recalls Poindexter. "And as it was appropriate, that information was passed on to Solidarity."[12]

One of the most effective means of getting the message to the underground was the Voice of America (VOA). The United States Information Agency was being run by longtime Reagan friend Charles Wick. Casey had hit it off well with Wick since the campaign days and made arrangements to use the VOA as an intelligence signaling device. "They would come in with a request for a message to be sent," recalls Wick. "Because it was in the national interest, so long as it didn't hurt the integrity of the Voice, we would broadcast it."[13] Information was relayed through a series of complex codes. Voice of America broadcasts, at certain times, would use specific code words or phrases. A special song might be played; a carefully crafted broadcast could pass along information about an impending crackdown, a special shipment, or a meeting time and place. Sending intelligence signals was prohibited by the VOA charter. But these were desperate times, and for Casey it was all right to bend some rules.

The money channel to Solidarity started in March 1982. It went primarily to support the publication and distribution of underground literature. Martial law had created a greater demand for reliable news. The regime controlled the media even more tightly and gave out even less information. In many instances, the underground publishing houses would be starting from scratch. Clandestine publishers had been caught off guard by the declaration of martial law. Police had confiscated equipment and materials. Many activists working in the underground publishing houses were arrested.

Early funds were also used to buy radio transmitters. Solidarity had placed some in hidden locations just before martial law, but they were largely antiquated and of limited range. Agency funds were used for the purchase of fifteen portable radio transmitters. On April 12, four months after the crackdown, citizens in Warsaw heard the inaugural broadcast of Solidarity radio. Zbizhek Romaszewski, a member of Solidarity's Warsaw leadership, was responsible for the program. On May 9, he managed to broadcast a brief appeal for a general strike.

The transmitters were being moved constantly to prevent detection. On April 30, police conducted a massive citywide search. Special equipment had been brought in from the Soviet Union and East Germany to trace the radio signals. A high-stakes game of cat and mouse was being played out daily on the streets of Warsaw. House-to-house searches and the cordoning off of large parts of Warsaw turned up nothing.[14]

On the advice of Solidarity activists in the West, funds were directed primarily to NOW-a, a publishing house that printed dozens of works dealing with politics, economics, and literature. (The other main publishing house, Krag, concerned itself with history.) NOW-a had managed to survive relatively intact even after the anvil of martial law had fallen. Its main problem was financial. Solidarity union dues, which had helped finance the house, were drying up. Production costs were skyrocketing. The cost of printing alone went from one zloty per page to about four. In January 1982, the house started slowly producing new materials. It began printing the newspaper *Tygodnik Mazowsze* and the intellectual periodical *Krytyka*. *Tygodnik Mazowsze*, with a circulation of 50,000, was the voice of Solidarity in Warsaw. An ingenious and clandestine distribution network was put together. The production of *Tygodnik Mazowsze* required workers at thirty-seven secret locations throughout the country.

The communications equipment and financial support to the underground had almost an immediate impact. In late April 1982, the first statement emerged from an independent group of prominent Solidarity activists who had escaped internment. Called the Provisional Coordinating Committee (TKK), it was an underground organization that hoped to coordinate activities of resistance to martial law. The original TKK members included Zbigniew Bujak in Warsaw, Wladyslaw Hardek in Krakow, Bogdan Lis in Gdansk, and Wladyslaw Frasyniuk in Wroclaw. At the first meeting, the TKK was a provisional directorate, loosely linking conspiratorial networks in all regions. The committee was defiant in its initial statement. Conditions for holding negotiations were the release of all internees and an amnesty for everybody convicted of crimes under martial law.

Western funds and technical support were going to the TKK. The committee members maintained contact with one another, sometimes arguing over strategy. The joint declarations of the TKK were widely circulated, inspiring many and embarrassing the Jaruzelski regime. The underground was somehow going to survive the long winter of martial law.

The only region not represented on the new body was Katowice, the center of Poland's mining industry. Phone lines were still down in the area, and no communications equipment had been smuggled in. A union stronghold, Katowice was under tight police surveillance.

On May 17, Konstantin Rusakov, a secretary of the Soviet Communist Party, paid a surprise visit to Jaruzelski in Warsaw. He was dispatched to gather firsthand information about the political situation. A flurry of symbolic strikes and protests continued to plague Poland. Somehow Solidarity was breathing, and the Kremlin was not pleased.

The Jaruzelski government appeared to be following an ambiguous strategy. It was unclear whether they would try to co-opt Solidarity or crack down even harder. Rusakov ordered Jaruzelski to beef up internal security. As he put it, "Facts show that the aggressive circles of the imperialist states, above all the United States, are conducting a subversive policy against the socialist countries. The subversive actions conducted in the framework of this policy are assuming ever more acute forms."[15]

In Moscow there was concern about the Americans "meddling in internal affairs." Ever since trouble had begun in Poland, the Kremlin and the Polish government had been blaming Washington for their difficulties. When Reagan had announced sanctions would be imposed, he had very clearly linked renewed economic ties to the Polish government with the fate of Solidarity. Now Soviet and Polish security officials were seeing hints that Washington was helping to bankroll Solidarity. But those in the know realized that Washington really was beginning to support Solidarity. "We in the security services had never believed much of the propaganda about U.S. support for Solidarity," recalls one former Soviet intelligence official. "Ideologically to us it made sense; but we had no evidence. Beginning in the spring of 1982, the telltale evidence began to appear. They were well funded. They had sophisticated means for carrying out their activities. We knew then they were getting something from someone."[16]

As Solidarity not only continued to survive but seemed to be garnering further resources, security officials in Warsaw decided to lash out at Washington. At the beginning of May 1982, Polish officials staged a KGB-like setup.

John Jerolis, a scientific and technical affairs officer, and James Howard, the first secretary for cultural affairs at the U.S. embassy, had met with Ryszard Herczynski, a scientist with the Polish Academy of Sciences and a former internee, at his apartment. Police officials accused the diplomats of receiving information from Herczynski.[17] Suddenly, plainclothes police and security officials seized them and roughed them up. They were thrown into a van and driven to headquarters. There officials accused them of supporting Solidarity and "engaging in activities prejudicial to the process of stabilization in Poland." They were declared persona non grata and expelled. Other embassy employees were harassed, followed, and threatened by plainclothes security officers.

Warsaw was playing a war of nerves with the Reagan administration. The security services were desperate to find the channel and expose the operation. They concentrated on the U.S. embassy, which played only a minor role in the plan. Little did they know that the operation was being run independently, but the embassy was an important diversion.

As the clandestine effort in Poland was getting under way and the Pentagon's secret directive was being implemented, Caspar Weinberger was strengthening his ties with a potentially helpful ally in the economic war against Moscow. On February 19, he was in Riyadh for secret talks with the Saudi leadership. Weinberger was close to Prince Bandar and got along well with Prince Fahd, the apparent heir to the throne. Fahd was fluent in English and sent his sons to the West for schooling—three to the University of California and one to the Royal Military Academy at Sandhurst. He had a reputation for pro-Western attitudes and preferences. He reportedly had opposed the Arab oil embargo of 1973 and wanted close military cooperation with the United States. His personal life was flamboyant. He had been quite a gambler in his youth. He lost $6 million one evening in Monte Carlo.

The defense secretary was there both as a symbol and to work out a complex defense cooperation agreement. The Iran-Iraq War was dragging on, and that was not a good sign for the pro-Western royal family. The longer it continued, the more Iran's natural advantage in manpower and religious fervor would tip the scales against Baghdad.

Fahd saw Saddam Hussein as a bulwark against Khomeinism, the most substantial threat to his kingdom. When Weinberger saw Fahd, the prince was clearly nervous.

Only two months earlier, Saudi and Bahraini security officials had arrested sixty-five people in a plot to bring down the governments of both oil-rich, conservative states. The men had been trained in Iran and had in their possession a large quantity of weapons. The group went by the name al Dawa, or The Call. The underground Shiite organization had been developed to recruit Muslim Shiites from all over the Arab world to export the Iranian revolution to the Persian Gulf. American intelligence had managed to get a whiff of the plan through some electronic intelligence, and the CIA tipped off Prince Nayef, the Saudi minister of interior.

But Weinberger was in Saudi Arabia to hammer out details on the U.S. military presence in the Persian Gulf. His basic aim was pure and simple: provide the military muscle necessary to keep the oil spigot open. That meant military protection for the generally pro-Western states of the Persian Gulf, most important, Saudi Arabia. On April 21, 1981, Weinberger had announced that the Rapid Deployment Task Force (RDF), proposed by President Carter to develop a capability to deploy forces in the Middle East if necessary, would be dramatically upgraded and expanded. It would become a unified command, with its own forces, intelligence, communications, and its own unified commander, responsible for all aspects of U.S. military planning and operations in the central region. The new U.S. Central Command (USCENTCOM) would be much larger than the RDF, boasting nearly 300,000 U.S. troops. It was a nice security blanket for the royal family and a unique venture that symbolized just how closely Riyadh was wedded to Washington for its security needs and how important Saudi oil was for America. The new command was not part of any formal alliance such as NATO, and it had no treaties governing its role. To soothe Saudi sensibilities about the political hazards of U.S. forces based on Saudi soil, the headquarters and forces for USCENTCOM would be located outside the theater.

Fahd reiterated to Weinberger his gratefulness for USCENT-COM. It was the only military deterrence that the royal family could count on in a sea of hostility. By supporting al Dawa, Tehran had made its intentions to seek the violent overthrow of the Saudi royal family very clear. It had already pushed Iraq back to its border, despite Iraq's estimated $20 billion financial backing by Saudi Arabia and other oil-rich Arab states. On top of it all, the number of Soviet advisers in Syria had jumped from 2,500 to nearly 6,000 in one year, and there were now nearly 100,000 Soviet troops in Afghanistan.

The Reagan administration's commitment to Saudi security had already been demonstrated several times in the last twelve months. The White House had gone to the mat for the Saudis in the fight for the AWACS. The president had expended serious political capital to get the deal through Congress. He had even made a verbal commitment that he would ensure the integrity of the Saudi government and prevent another Iran from occurring. While these words were welcomed in the halls of the Royal Palace, there was still distrust of Washington. Fahd did not want a public treaty guarantee from Weinberger—that would be too politically explosive in the Middle East. But could Washington express its commitment to Saudi security in a more tangible and direct way? Could they have reassurance from Reagan that if they were attacked the United States would spring to their defense?

Weinberger said he would have to take the matter up with the president. He also had to massage the sensitive issue of U.S. military policy toward the Persian Gulf. The new Pentagon strategy, "Fiscal Year 1984–88 Defense Guidance," directed U.S. forces to be ready to force their way into Saudi Arabia if necessary, and not wait for an invitation from a friendly government.

1. Richard Halloran, "Pentagon Draws Up First Strategy for Fighting a Long Nuclear War," *The New York Times*, May 30, 1982.
2. "Reagan Aide Tells of New Strategy on Soviet Threat," *The New York Times*, May 22, 1982.
3. William Clark, interview with the author.
4. "Soviet Economy Called 'Basket Case,'" *The Washington Post*, June 17, 1982.
5. Roger Robinson, interview with the author.
6. Yevgenny Novikov, interview with the author.
7. "Economic Leverage of Moscow Sought," *The Washington Post*, June 15, 1982; interview with NSC staff member.
8. Glenn Campbell, interview with the author.

9. Robert McFarlane, interview with the author.
10. John Poindexter, interview with the author.
11. U.S. official, interview with the author.
12. John Poindexter, interview with the author.
13. Charles Wick, interview with the author.
14. "Solidarity Broadcasts Calls for General Strike," *The Washington Post*, May 10, 1982.
15. "Ranking Soviet Makes Surprise Polish Visit," *The Washington Post*, May 18, 1982.
16. Interview with the author.
17. "Poland to Expell Two U.S. Diplomats, Who Met with Activist," *The Washington Post*, May 11, 1982.

8

In May 1982, it was Bill Casey who was on the Saudi peninsula. Casey was a guest of King Khalid, the aged patriarch of
the royal family. He was a simple man in delicate health, the product
of a previous era who could recall the days before vast wealth had risen
from the desert floor. He was in many ways a mystic. The fact that he
got along well with the earthy CIA director mystified others. They
discussed chivalry and honor in a modern era that seemed to have little
of either. Khalid was proud of his Bedouin past and gave Casey the long
version of the royal dynasty's family history.

After a brief discussion about politics and world affairs, the king
insisted on showing Casey some of his treasures. They went first to his
dairy herd. Fed by imported foodstuffs, the herd was tended by an Irish
family. The DCI was delighted, breaking into an Irish brogue as he
chatted briefly with them about the "old country." But there was not
much time; the king was waiting impatiently. He wanted his guest to see
his pride and joy—the royal camels. They were enormous creatures,
hundreds of them. The king offered Casey a ride on one, but he
declined. He then offered the director "a real treat," a glass of warm,
thick camel's milk. Casey refused this too, citing something about his
health.

The time spent with King Khalid was a nice diversion, but Casey was really in Saudi Arabia to see Crown Prince Fahd. The warm relationship that had developed in 1981 between the crown prince and the DCI continued where they had left off. Fahd thanked Casey for what he and the administration had done for the AWACS deal. They covered much of the same ground Fahd had with Caspar Weinberger only weeks earlier. As Bandar had requested in Washington, the Reagan administration was also doing everything it could to keep a lid on information pertaining to Saudi financial holdings in the United States. On May 6, 1982, the House Subcommittee on Commerce, Consumer and Monetary Affairs was holding a private hearing on the matter. Chairman Benjamin Rosenthal had written to President Reagan on February 9 threatening to release the details of Saudi financial holdings in the United States. On February 17, heavily pressed by Casey, Don Regan, Bill Clark, and Weinberger, the president responded: "Disclosure of this information would be likely to cause grave injury to our foreign relations. . . . the public interest in avoiding such injury outweighs any public interest served by disclosure."

One hour before the May 6 subcommittee hearing, ten CIA officials descended on the second-floor room in the Rayburn House Office Building. Half of the contingent swept the room for electronic bugs; the other half stood guard. This was unusual, even by CIA standards, in that it overstepped the boundaries of the agency's authority. Only the Capitol Police Force had jurisdiction over Capitol buildings. Once the hearings began, the CIA was uncompromising. It did not want any of the data made public. After the last word was spoken, CIA security officials took possession of the stenographic tapes of the hearing and escorted the House reporter to subcommittee staff offices three floors below to pick up additional copies of the transcript. Agency officials informed the committee that the transcription would be done at Langley, not by committee staff.

A shouting match ensued. Peter Barash, the subcommittee staff director, glanced out of his office and saw the House reporter surrounded by CIA types. He quickly headed over to find out what was going on. The tapes were the property of Congress, not the CIA, he told agency officials. "This was not a meeting of the Central Intelligence Agency," he said. "This was a meeting of a subcommittee of the

Congress!" A CIA official returned verbal fire, saying that he had specific instructions not to part with the tapes. A standoff followed until Rosenthal was reached on the House floor. He declared forcefully that the CIA could not take possession of the tapes. The agency reluctantly had to capitulate.[1]

After this scene, the subcommittee members met in private. A compromise was reached with the CIA: only summaries of the documents would be released. It had not been a complete victory, but once again the administration had pushed hard to protect Saudi interests and had prevailed. President Reagan had become personally involved in an effort to stop the congressional subcommittee from attempting to declassify materials. Keeping the financial information secret was an important test of the Saudi relationship, and the administration had passed.

The National Security Council and the CIA had also been of assistance on other fronts. Several intelligence tips had helped the royal family avert serious internal threats. And the administration was going ahead with plans to erect a military shield around Saudi Arabia.

As Casey and Fahd dined in the Royal Palace one evening, they took a geopolitical tour around the world. They discussed Afghanistan, Central America, Western Europe, and the Palestinian question. But again and again the travelers found their way back to the Soviet Union. It was, in their eyes, the source of many of the world's problems. Fahd was as obsessed with the USSR as Casey was.

Fahd asked Casey about the sanctions on oil and gas technology against the Soviets. After all, Soviet oil was a leading competitor of Saudi crude. "It was directly in their interests for the United States to restrict Soviet access to oil and gas technology," says William Schneider, undersecretary of state for military assistance and technology. "They encouraged us."[2] Casey told Fahd that the sanctions on technology to build the Soviet natural gas pipeline along with restrictions on oil-drilling technologies would remain in place. Your Highness, if we had our way, they wouldn't be pumping one quart of oil, Casey said. Fahd laughed.

The American sanctions were at a minimum going to delay construction on the massive gas pipeline. Fahd took particular pleasure in that fact, given that the project had been touted in European capitals as a reliable alternative to Middle Eastern oil. Sanctions were serving not only American strategic interests but Saudi petroleum interests as well.

Your Highness, we want to do everything we can to stop countries from buying Soviet crude, Casey told the crown prince. He reiterated how the administration was pressuring the French government and the national oil company not to purchase Soviet crude but to buy from others. The importance Moscow placed on the hard currency earnings generated by energy exports was demonstrated by its decision to reduce oil exports to Eastern Europe by 10 percent. That cutback would allow Moscow to sell more oil to the hard currency–paying West. The Soviet drive for Western exports was threatening to squeeze the Saudis out of certain markets. Both Belgium and France were attempting to renegotiate expensive state-to-state contracts signed with the Saudis. State-run companies in France such as Elf-Quitaine were being given a freer hand to seek out new sources of crude, and the prospect of sales from the Soviets was being raised at the negotiating table. Over the course of the year Moscow was successful in its venture: by the end of 1982, Soviet oil exports to the capitalist West would increase by 32 percent.[3]

The reduction in exports to Eastern Europe was expected to have serious consequences for the region. The cutbacks would cause "significant" reductions in the already low rates of economic growth. *The Wall Street Journal* even predicted that the cutbacks "could push a number of countries in Soviet Europe to the brink of economic insolvency and political collapse."[4]

Casey told Fahd that the administration would continue to take steps to limit Soviet energy programs as best it could. But he suggested that the administration wanted lower oil prices in return. Lower energy prices would boost the U.S. economy, Reagan's primary domestic goal. It was in the Saudi interest to see a strong United States, particularly since the United States was quickly becoming the key factor in Saudi survival. At the same time, lower oil prices would end the rush to alternative energy sources, such as Soviet natural gas. And they would hamstring the sworn enemies of the Saudi regime—Iran and the Soviet Union—both of whom had cashed in on the price surge in the 1970s.

The crown prince, with incredible business acumen, no doubt knew these points as well as the administration. But to hear them from a chief ally and guarantor was something different.

Their relationship was based on mutual respect, but Casey clearly took the role of nurturing and tutoring the crown prince. Fahd liked to listen to Casey's stories about the OSS and the threat posed by expansive totalitarianism, first in Germany and now in the Soviet Union. To Fahd, the nominal Muslim and friend of the West, the Soviets were true "infidels."

Casey counseled the crown prince about other possible internal threats to the Saudi regime. Some Saudis had been educated at Soviet bloc universities, and they were now working in the government. I would fire them, Casey told Fahd. They might be enemy agents, spies or saboteurs. It would be best not to hire anyone educated in the Soviet bloc. The crown prince eventually took this advice, proclaiming such a policy in 1983.

Palestinians were another potential problem. According to CIA reports, factions of the PLO were working with organizations in Saudi Arabia trying to undermine the king. Replace them with more reliable groups—Pakistanis or Egyptians, Casey said. Fahd eventually took this advice too, expelling thousands of Palestinians and bringing in Pakistanis.

One of the projects closest to Fahd's heart was the effort to support Islamic movements in Soviet Central Asia. This was done through the Wahhabi clan and was top secret. "The Wahhabis—it was very important for them to fund Muslim projects in Soviet Central Asia," recalls Vincent Cannistraro, a former senior CIA operations official.[5]

Casey was naturally interested in this subject too, but for geostrategic not spiritual reasons. Central Asia was the Russian Achilles heel, Casey told Fahd. Until we take the war there, the Soviets will not leave Afghanistan. Fahd, eating dates, agreed. They talked a bit about Russian domination of the area, and then about the mujahedin. The jihad in Afghanistan was a revolution without borders, just like communism, Fahd told Casey. The DCI was intrigued.

The Afghans were making regular contacts with Muslims across the Amu River in the Soviet Union. These mostly involved distribution of Afghanistan resistance membership cards, dissemination of revolutionary Islamic literature, holding of meetings or discussions, and mine-laying operations on a small scale. Casey wanted something more—a systematic campaign to subvert Soviet power in Central Asia.

Later that evening, Fahd and Casey sat with Musa Turkistani, a historian of Central Asian origin living in Saudi Arabia. He had written on atrocities committed by the Russians against local ethnic groups and still had contact with individuals in the region. Turkistani told Casey that there had been rioting in Alma-Ata in March 1980 over the Afghan war, and that the underground movement was flourishing. The Saudis were, no doubt, financing some of these organizations.[6]

The Soviet press was abuzz with Saudi meddling in Soviet Central Asia. Professor A. Doyev singled out the Saudis for spreading "lies" to the people of Central Asia.[7] Major General N. Ovezov, deputy chairman of the Turkmen SSR KGB, claimed the Saudis were using Islam as an offensive instrument to incite Muslims in the USSR against the Soviet system.[8] The Saudis had contacts in the region, money, and the will to subvert the atheistic Soviets. Perhaps all they now needed was encouragement.

It was the first Thursday in April 1982. The Solidarity operation was off to a good start. Casey just hoped that nothing would go wrong. He was with David Wigg, one of his White House liaisons. The DCI often stopped by the Old Executive Office Building to pick a former business partner's brain. "We would just sit in the foyer," recalls Wigg. "He would start bouncing things off me—how the Soviets might be vulnerable, what we could do to cause them problems." But this time the meeting was less speculative and more definite, at least in Casey's mind. Says Wigg, "Bill had spent the first year trying to reconstruct what the Soviet economy actually was, how it worked. In the spring of 1982 he felt he was finally putting his finger on the pulse."

"This is a mafia-style economy," Casey told Wigg, still staring at the ceiling. "They're bleeding off technologies that are necessary to the survival of the Soviet Union. The only way they can generate hard currency is by exporting oil and gas at higher prices. This thing is so haywire, if we play our cards right, it's going to implode."[9]

For Wigg, who was used to Casey's bluntness, such a statement came as a surprise. He had spent years at the agency tracking Soviet resource flows and balance of payments. But he had never heard someone so senior say such a thing. Bill Casey had been doing his homework.

That spring several new reports started crossing Bill Casey's desk, which were immediately forwarded to the NSC and the president. These weren't the regular agency reports, which he tended to discount. These were the first of his prized "vulnerability assessments" of the Soviet Union that he had asked Herb Meyer and Harry Rowen to put the staff to work on. The vulnerability assessments had a profound effect on Casey, reinforcing in him what he had felt all along. They also convinced Ronald Reagan that the United States could seriously damage the Soviet economy. "Bill used to go into the Oval Office and sit down with the president," recalls Wigg. "They would go over a lot of subjects, including the Soviet economy. It was pretty informal really, but it certainly helped shape Reagan's views." The vulnerability assessments were, in retrospect, a work of near prophetic insight. They began with a general statement on the nature of the Soviet economic system. It was, the authors pointed out, "rigid and inflexible." There was no flexibility of the marketplace for the reallocation of resources. What was more, the infusion of technology and equipment from the West was "a rigid requirement" to alleviate bottlenecks and maintain production levels. Cutoffs of critical technologies would severely damage the Soviet economy.

> The Soviets must now rely on Western imports of capital and technology to increase and maintain production of some of the raw materials with which they are abundantly endowed and self-sufficient. Imports from the West can play a critical role in relieving critical shortages, spurring technological progress. The Soviet Union is blessed with enormous quantities of energy sources for export. These materials are increasingly inaccessible, and thus the cost of exploiting them has been rising sharply. The Soviet economic system is peculiarly ill-suited to promote efficiency and technological progress. Oil production continues to

increase, though slowly. Even the very small growth of the last few years has required an enormous effort. Inputs of Western technology will be immensely important in sustaining this critical hard-currency earning sector of the economy.

The USSR will have to import a broad range of Western oil and gas equipment if it is to minimize the fall in production in fields where depletion is at an advanced stage, increase output elsewhere, and help locate and develop reserves. Pipe-laying equipment capable of handling large-diameter pipe is produced only in the West, and we estimate that the Soviets will need to import at least 15–20 million tons of steel pipe during the remainder of the 1980s to build pipelines they have scheduled. They will also continue to need sophisticated exploration equipment, high capacity submersible pumps for the oil fields, and probably high-powered turbines for gas compressors.

The USSR's ability to earn the hard currency it needs to pay for its Western imports is, however, already under pressure and may well diminish in the future. The main reason is the leveling off and possible decline in Soviet oil production. According to our projections the rise in hard currency earnings from stepped up exports of natural gas will only partially offset the anticipated decrease in receipts from oil. Primarily because of the softening of energy prices, Soviet terms of trade vis-à-vis the West will be less favorable in the 1980s than they were in the 1970s, when upward spiralling oil and gold prices brought the USSR windfall gains. OPEC countries would be less able to pay cash for Soviet arms.

The vulnerability assessments zeroed in on the Soviet energy sector as an area to exploit. They emphasized that it was critical in sustaining the Soviet economic machine. Oil and natural gas exports made up between 60 and 80 percent of Soviet hard currency earnings during most years. And those earnings were "a pillar" of the economic system. Hard currency from the West was required to purchase food-stuffs from the West and technologies that sustained the economic monolith. Some hard currency was thrown back into the energy sector to squeeze out even more production. It was Western technology that allowed the energy sector to grow and thrive. In a special annex on the energy sector, several important conclusions were reached:

> Moscow's desire to maintain steady economic growth re-quires an expanding energy resource development program as reflected in the eleventh five-year plan (1981–85). En-ergy exports are the principal source of Soviet hard cur-rency earnings. Revenues from exports to Western countries permit the acquisition of equipment and tech-nology for a variety of Soviet activities; particularly impor-tant are energy efforts to increase oil recovery, transport natural gas, and exploit offshore energy resources.
>
> The recent expansion of Soviet exports to the West has been responsible for important increases in hard currency earnings necessary for the development of new energy resources. The Soviets have used much of the new revenue to purchase Western equipment and technology for oil and gas exploitation and production.

Moscow was adopting an enhanced oil recovery (EOR) program to tap oil from deposits that were impossible to retrieve using conventional methods. Old fields in Volga were declining in production. It was hoped that EOR would use new technologies to increase production. The vulnerability assessment notes:

> The Soviets have expressed high hopes for EOR tech-niques to increase oil recovery from older fields and to produce undeveloped fields that contain heavy oil. Soviet EOR efforts have been hampered by severe shortages of equipment and chemicals. . . . The Soviets have not as yet been able to build the steam generators needed for thermal

recovery or to produce sufficient amounts of surfactants or polymers for chemical and polymer flood programs. Continued efforts are being made to acquire Western technical assistance and equipment to promote EOR.

The report then pointed to the critical factor regarding Soviet hard currency earnings—world oil prices. In the 1970s, when the price of oil went through the ceiling, Moscow's hard currency earnings from oil went up 272 percent, while the volume of exports increased only 22 percent. Meyer concluded that for every $1 increase in the price of a barrel of oil, Moscow would gain nearly $1 billion per year in hard currency. But the converse was also true. A drop in the price of oil by perhaps $10 a barrel would cost Moscow dearly—$10 billion. "The price of oil on world markets will be a critical determinant of Soviet economic viability."

"Bill latched almost immediately on to that report," recalls Meyer. "For him it became the gospel. He said, 'We can do them in.' "[10]

A few days after one of his regular strategic seminars with Wigg, Casey was in the Indian Treaty Room with the president going over a variety of issues. Caspar Weinberger and the new national security adviser, Bill Clark, were there too.

Reports were coming back almost daily that the Europeans were undercutting American sanctions. Two European manufacturers in particular, John Brown in Britain and Atlantique in France, were gearing up to sell to Moscow the very technologies that Washington was cutting off for the pipeline. The Versailles Summit was coming up in June, and sanctions were likely to be issue number one. Casey had brought with him the vulnerability assessments, which he had shared with Clark and Weinberger before the meeting.

Casey passed out sheets of paper with a summary. Mr. President, he began in his typical chaotic jargon, the stakes in the pipeline are huge. We're not just talking about a project that will help them, we're talking about a project that they need to go on. They desperately need the hard currency that this massive project is going to generate. With two strands, they are looking to take in between $15 billion and $20 billion a year.

If we can stop it or delay it, they'll really be in a bind. Clark had discussed the issue in private with the president, and they agreed to take a strong position.

"This thing was a big cash cow," recalls Weinberger. "I kept telling the president, we need to keep the sanctions on. This was economic warfare, and it would cripple them."[11]

Reagan left the meeting convinced that crippling Moscow economically was a good strategy and the pipeline was a great place to start.

The machinery of U.S. diplomacy was working slowly in the spring of 1982. Europe was not budging on its commitment to construct the full two-strand natural gas pipeline. Moreover, European companies were being given the green light by their governments to undercut U.S. sanctions, despite the agreement made months earlier at the North Atlantic Council. President Reagan was leaving open the possibility of rescinding the sanctions, but only if Europe were willing to commit to a cutback on subsidized credit and technology flows to Moscow. Haig was shuttling back and forth to Europe trying to work out some sort of compromise. In May 1982, George Shultz (still then in the private sector) was dispatched by Reagan to meet with the major Western allies to discuss the pipeline and other contentious issues. He reported back to the president, "Your views about credit to the Russians and their satellites have made a real impact, and I sense that sentiment on this issue is coming your way. No one will defend subsidizing the Soviet economy."[12] But would Europe agree to cutting off or reducing the flow of critical Western life support?

From June 4 to June 6, the spotlight turned to Versailles, where the G-7 countries were meeting. Reagan had alternatives to the Siberian pipeline and ending subsidized credits to Moscow at the top of the agenda. The summit did not go well. The president had offered a compromise: the pipeline could be built if it was limited to one strand, not the originally planned two; if official subsidized credits to Moscow were stopped; and if the G-7 could agree to tighten severely the export of technologies to the Soviet Union. The Europeans agreed to a line in the final summit communiqué about "fighting preferential agreements" when trading with Moscow, but that was it. France had only recently signed another subsidized credit deal with Moscow. "Mitterrand and Schmidt left the final ceremony and told their media and publics that there would be no change in their pattern of financial or energy relations with the USSR," recalls Roger Robinson, who was closely monitoring the summit from the White House.[13]

On June 7, President Reagan flew to Rome for a six-hour meeting with the pope. They met in private for forty-five minutes in the ornate sanctum of the Vatican. The pope, dressed in white cassock and coif with a silver cross around his neck, welcomed his first opportunity to meet with Reagan.

Behind the men was Perugino's famed painting *Resurrection*. Reagan began the meeting by noting how appropriate it was. Both had faced a brush with death, shot by assassins only weeks apart. "He told him that they had been spared by God, for a purpose," recalls Bill Clark. And that purpose was freeing Poland.[14]

Before he had left on his European trip, Bill Casey had briefed Reagan and Clark on the Polish operation. The president raised the subject with John Paul only briefly by saying, "Hope remains in Poland. We, working together, can keep it alive." The pontiff had subtly nodded in agreement.

After the private meeting, the two men stood before the press and read official statements. Reagan made specific and prolonged mention of Poland. He declared, "A special area of mutual concern is the martyred nation of Poland—your own homeland. Through centuries of adversity, Poland has been a brave bastion of faith and freedom in the hearts of her courageous people, yet not in those who rule her. We seek a process of reconciliation and reform that will lead to a new dawn of hope for the people of Poland."[15]

While the pope and the president met, Bill Clark was meeting with Vatican officials about the situation in Poland. He did not go into too much detail about the CIA program in Poland, but he did say that the Church could be useful if it would share intelligence on a regular basis with Washington. He also sought to make clear that Washington wanted to work jointly with the Church in staking out a proper diplomatic tone in relations with Warsaw. It would be a deft hand. On the one hand, there should be firmness, making it clear that repression was unacceptable. On the other hand, to appear too unyielding might push Poland under even more direct Soviet control. Clark also let Vatican officials know that the United States had an efficient means for relaying information into Poland, and that if the Church needed to get information there fast, it could be arranged.

After the six-hour excursion to Italy, Reagan and his aides boarded Air Force One and returned to Great Britain.

After Versailles, there was a meeting in Bonn of Western leaders. The president at one point stood up and made an impassioned plea for curtailing the Siberian pipeline, restricting subsidized credits, and resisting "business as usual" with Moscow. The appeal fell on deaf ears. But, perhaps more important, Reagan felt slighted. "While [Reagan] was making this impassioned plea, Schmidt was looking out the window at the garden—purposely ignoring him," says Robinson. "He was deliberately snubbing the president. Upon his return to Washington, the president was keenly aware that he had been treated dismissively, even contemptuously, as a neophyte who doesn't really understand the fine point of East-West economic relations. That was a mistake."[16]

Fuming, the president called for an NSC meeting on June 18—later referred to in Europe as "Black Friday." He wanted to know his options and choose a course of action. Bill Clark chaired the meeting. The assembled were tense. By now, the administration was deeply divided over the sanctions issue. Weinberger, Clark, Meese, and Casey were in favor of keeping the sanctions in place. Everyone else at the table was in favor of lifting the sanctions immediately. Al Haig, the most persuasive opponent of sanctions, was in New York. Lawrence Eagleburger, number two at State, sat in for him. After some discussion, Clark noted that the president had essentially three options:

- Lift the sanctions completely, despite no letup in Soviet-sponsored repression in Poland
- Keep the unilateral U.S. sanctions in place, even though they were being systematically undercut by European suppliers and governments
- Expand the sanctions to include American licensees and subsidiaries abroad as authorized by the Export Administration Act

The first option meant a blatant reversal in policy, and the United States pocketing a nothing agreement on subsidized credits that West Europeans had reluctantly signed off on at the Versailles summit to mollify Washington. The second option meant imposing unilateral penalties on U.S. companies and accepting the fact that the original two-strand pipeline would eventually be built with American technologies licensed to European companies. Caterpillar Tractor lost a $90 million order, General Electric an order worth $175 million. They were quickly filled by European competitors. The third option meant hardball—and a real economic war against Moscow.

Casey, Weinberger, and Clark had prepared themselves to make the case for option three, although Clark, as usual, would stick to his role as "honest broker" during the NSC meeting itself. They expected a long, drawn-out argument among NSC members about the relative merits of the sanctions. But the president didn't seem in the mood to have the issue debated at great length. He told a few anecdotes about how Schmidt had treated him with contempt and his past experience with the French. He indicated his fatigue with empty allied agreements. Then he summed up: "They can have their first pipeline [the Soviets and Europeans]. But not with our equipment and not with our technology."[17]

Clark immediately jumped in. "We have a presidential decision on this." The third option, initiating a real economic war with Moscow, became U.S. policy.

In Europe there was a thermonuclear reaction to the news. The American president was extending sanctions to include European companies operating under American licenses. Even the predictably pro-Reagan Margaret Thatcher was outraged. All the major West European leaders let it be known that they would defy the new order. Unbeknownst to the president, Al Haig began giving the West Europeans assurances that everything on the policy front would be fine. He quietly counseled European officials that they should just sit tight and wait the crisis out. William Brock was dispatched to West European capitals to deal with the fallout. Several days later, he delivered the bad news that Europe would not budge. Haig, Clark, Meese, and other cabinet and subcabinet officials sat in the White House Situation Room with Brock going over the sensitive issue. After a few heated words, Haig went ballistic. He pointed toward Clark and bellowed, "You people [at the White House] planned this [the NSC meeting of June 18] when I was in New York. You knew this was going to happen. It wouldn't have happened if I had been here!"

Haig's explosion proved his final mistake. Soon after the meeting, Clark consulted with the president. "Haig was screaming at a very close personal friend and adviser to the president over the course of more than twenty years," recalls a senior NSC staff member. "There was an extraordinary chemistry and implicit trust between Reagan and Clark. Haig, in short, was dismissed shortly thereafter."[18]

The expanding U.S. sanctions led the Kremlin in coordination with the Soviet Gas Ministry to begin a strenuous internal effort to complete the pipeline without U.S. technology. There was soon a massive—and debilitating—diversion of supplies from other priority projects. It became a matter of national pride to complete the project somehow. Roger Robinson, who was tracking the issue from his office at the NSC, recalls, "These major diversions of equipment and personnel were having a harmful ripple effect on the Soviet economy by, in effect, delaying or bringing to a halt other national projects. The completion of the pipeline became a kind of Manhattan Project equivalent. The money they were spending overseas in a largely failed effort to substitute for American equipment was enormous. They were dipping quite heavily into their limited pool of hard currency in an attempt to jerry-rig the pipeline. Their brightest technical people were pulled off their existing jobs, and they still could not get it done."[19] According to estimates by the Soviet Gas Ministry in 1986, these internal efforts had a high price—almost $1 billion in hard currency. Yet in the end, the Soviets couldn't make it work. They needed the U.S. technology. "We tried to build a twenty-five-megawatt turbine, threw resources into a crash program," recalls one engineer who worked on the pipeline project for Moscow. "We failed. It was a huge drain on our resources. It cost us dearly."[20]

When the Reagan administration got wind of the Soviet effort to complete the pipeline using internal resources, Casey and senior NSC officials went into mental overdrive trying to come up with ways to complicate matters further. The Soviet oil and gas industry always relied heavily on Western designs of components to build their own, and the new internal push would be no different. In Washington, several officials concluded that a disinformation program, including the sending of purposely false and distorted technical data, might do the trick. And some work was done.

The firing of Al Haig over the pipeline issue led the new secretary of state, George Shultz, to come in cautiously. He treaded lightly on the pipeline issue. "He knew that Haig had been fired over this," says one former NSC staffer. "He told the Europeans, 'This is serious. This is no joke. We just lost the previous secretary of state over this.' "[21]

Somehow Shultz had to settle the issue with entrenched European leaders. Thatcher and Mitterrand were telling their companies to ship the equipment in violation of the American order. The sanctions were an extraterritorial application of American law rejected by Europe. Thatcher told Reagan personally, "Your law doesn't apply here." In Paris, the minister of industry, Jean-Pierre Chevenement, was threatening to "requisition" any French companies that did not ship their goods to Moscow. Crevoit-Loire, a French licensee of Dresser Industries, went ahead and started shipping in the summer.

1. U.S. official, interview with the author.
2. William Schneider, interview with the author.
3. *Oil and Gas Journal*, May 13, 1985, p. 74.
4. *The Wall Street Journal*, February 11, 1982.
5. Vincent Cannistraro, interview with the author.
6. U.S. official, interview with the author.
7. A. Doyev, "Islam and Atheistic Work," *Kommunist*, no. 2, 1984, pp. 68–74.
8. N. Ovezov, "On the Occasion of the 60th Anniversary of the Cheka," *Soviet Turkmenistany*, December 19, 1982.
9. David Wigg, interview with the author.
10. Herb Meyer, interview with the author.
11. Caspar Weinberger, interview with the author.
12. George Shultz, interview with the author.
13. Roger Robinson, interview with the author.
14. William Clark, interview with the author.
15. *The New York Times*, June 8, 1982.

16. Roger Robinson, interview with the author.
17. William Clark, interview with the author; Roger Robinson, interview with the author.
18. Senior NSC official, interview with the author.
19. Roger Robinson, interview with the author.
20. Interview with the author.
21. Interview with the author.

9

In August 1982, Bill Casey was aboard his black mechanical bird again, headed for Africa. He was interested in talking over several issues with his South African counterparts. He admired the tenacity of the South African intelligence service, its reach and capability. On the inbound flight, he instructed his pilot to fly low over the Zambezi River so he could get a good look. The plane banked up just above the spectacular Victoria Falls.

When his plane touched down in Pretoria, Casey was met by the CIA station chief and escorted to the embassy. After freshening up, he received a briefing on the internal situation in South Africa and the civil war raging just north in Angola. Next he was off to his meetings with South African intelligence officials.

The meetings were cordial. The South Africans were backing Jonas Savimbi in his war with the Marxist government of Angola. They wanted Casey's help in supporting Savimbi, who was doing real damage to Angolan and Cuban forces in the country. Savimbi was a perfect test case for supporting anticommunist insurgents, a policy Casey had first proposed in early 1981.

He also raised the prospect of sharing intelligence. American satellite photos of Angola could benefit Savimbi greatly, just as they had the Israelis a few months earlier. The South Africans relished the thought, and said they would be very pleased to have access to such information.

The DCI then turned to the business that related to the secret war against Moscow. The Kremlin had been selling gold heavily. In 1981 they had dumped almost four times their usual amount on the international market. Obviously they were strapped for cash. Casey wanted to project how much hard currency Moscow could expect to generate from sales. Where were world gold prices going? What would the South African response be in terms of production? He also wanted to head off any collaboration in the international market between Moscow and Pretoria.

South African officials, the dominant force in gold production and sales, had immense insight into the world gold market, so they seemed the logical people to ask. The South Africans had long been rumored to maintain top-secret contact with Moscow in the hopes of regulating the market in gold, diamonds, platinum, and precious minerals, in which they together had something approaching a world monopoly.

The KGB took a prominent part in arranging sessions between South African and Soviet officials. The meetings usually took place in Switzerland, where the first had been held in 1978. These dealings were closely guarded secrets; after all, Moscow's closest allies in black Africa were the sworn enemies of Pretoria. The Kremlin was backing the African National Congress and the South African Communist Party in their efforts to overthrow the South African government.

When gold had climbed high in the 1970s, both Pretoria and Moscow had made a fortune. Moscow had sought a dialogue to see if the two could not develop some mutually beneficial arrangement for regulating the international markets in the precious commodities. The initial meetings had yielded few results. But by 1982, with prices precipitously dropping and Moscow unloading, there was a renewed interest by both parties in trying to stabilize the world market.[1]

South African intelligence was less than forthcoming in response to Casey's questions. After all, when it came to world gold pricing and regulating the market, Pretoria and Moscow had common cause. They wanted to maintain high prices and their ability to control world prices. Why share the information with the Americans?

Look, Casey told them, You might find common cause with them on this, but everywhere else they are going to screw you. I can help you in Washington and with intelligence. But I need some things from you.

The South Africans wanted to think it over. Intelligence was sympathetic; it was the most consistently anti-Soviet department in the government. But the departments responsible for gold production and sales would not view things quite the same way. Their job was high production and high prices. If Moscow made that possible, so be it. In stern language Casey made it clear that the Reagan administration did not want any manipulation of the international precious metal markets, particularly if it benefited a cash-strapped Kremlin.

After Pretoria, Casey's next port of call was Cairo. The Egyptian end of the Afghan project had improved greatly since his first trip. Casey was meeting for the first time with the new Egyptian president, Hosni Mubarak. The two discussed the Middle East, the loss of Anwar Sadat to an assassin's bullet, and the Afghan project. Casey then turned to more intriguing subjects.

What do you think is the mood of the Muslims north of the Amu River, in Soviet Central Asia? They could be a powerful ally.

Mubarak paused. It was a supersensitive question. Exactly what was Casey driving at?

Mr. Casey, the situation is tense. I have seen reports that there are groups underground in the region. There is literature crossing the border.

Casey knew all about that—he was bankrolling some of it. But he wanted to know everything Egypt knew about underground organizations in Soviet Central Asia. The Egyptian intelligence officials he had met with said they didn't know anything about it. The serene Egyptian president suggested that Casey get in touch with the mujahedin leaders themselves.

Casey nodded and thanked his hosts. When he returned to the embassy, he assembled his team. He would be in Pakistan in four days.

When Casey's plane touched down in Islamabad, the course of

events was fairly routine. An official function at the embassy served as a decoy against any possible terrorist attack. The director was bundled into a secure car and whisked away to a secure house. Casey had thought long and hard about Afghanistan since his last visit. The president, Bill Clark, and Weinberger were asking for regular updates. The resistance was in better shape now than it had ever been. There was deeper cooperation between the factions, and they were better equipped. But serious problems remained. Vincent Cannistraro was a career CIA operative assigned to the NSC to oversee the Afghan project. He recalls, "You basically had a modern army facing a band of ragtag guerrillas fighting in the hills in the early years. Effective because they knew the terrain, but they still lacked arms and a coherent strategy." There was a stalemate, but that was it. "You didn't have tremendous Soviet losses," says Cannistraro. "There was a stalemate but Soviet troops were not hemorrhaging in terms of losses." The resistance was only a low-grade infection. The president and others in the administration wanted to increase the costs of the occupation exponentially.[2]

The conduit of arms was running smoothly. In one of the most extensive and sophisticated covert operations in history, supplies were being delivered by the CIA through three routes. Arms were being purchased on the international market with Saudi money, and the CIA was flying them from Dhahran to Islamabad. The CIA was also flying in weapons and ammunition from China, over sensitive Kashmir. The third conduit was by ship. A variety of states—China, Egypt, Israel, and Great Britain—were chipping in, and the contributions were being brought to the port of Karachi. The Pakistani ISI then loaded the cargo on heavily guarded trains, which carried it to Islamabad or the border town of Quetta. Ten thousand tons of arms and ammunition were going through the channel every year. By 1985, this would rise to 65,000 tons.[3]

General Akhtar greeted Casey warmly at the ISI compound. The material coming from Egypt and elsewhere had improved significantly, and Akhtar knew that he largely had Bill Casey to thank. The DCI had been working the phones from Langley, calling everyone involved in the operation to ensure that the quality of weapons was high. The two now wanted to see how, working together, they could more effectively "bleed" Moscow.

Half the Soviet troops were tied up in or around Kabul. Yet most of the fighting was actually being done by the demoralized Afghan army. Akhtar proposed that they zero in on the northern provinces. He was planning to increase operations there for two reasons. First, it was an important Soviet base of operations for the war effort. Just north of the Amu River were several basing facilities for troops and material coming into Afghanistan. The lifeline for the Soviet contingent in Afghanistan was the Salang Highway, a winding road through mountainous passes. Increasing activity in the north would threaten those Soviet supply lines—which were narrow and concentrated. But it would also preclude Moscow from bringing more troops into the country. "We determined that the inability to maintain secure supply routes was a critical factor in limiting the size of Soviet forces in Afghanistan," recalls Mohammad Yousaf.[4]

Akhtar proposed activity in the north also because the region had great economic value to the Soviet Union. There was a natural gas field near Shibarghan in the northern province of Jowzjan that was estimated to have reserves in excess of 500 billion cubic meters. Eighty percent of the production was going to the Soviet Union—free of charge.[5] There was oil approximately 150 miles west at Sar-i-Pul and Ali gul. There were also valuable deposits of copper, iron, gold, and precious stones near Kunduz and Mazar-i-Sharif. The Soviets were having these resources extracted and brought to the Soviet Union, and they were paying ridiculously low prices for them. It all meant $100 million or so in basically free commodities for the Kremlin.

Casey agreed with Akhtar's reasoning. But he also felt that the north was important because the northern provinces bordered Soviet Central Asia. The maps, as in Africa, had been poorly drawn. The people on both sides of the border were Uzbeks, Tajiks, and Turkomans. They shared an ethnic identity and a faith. Northern Afghans had more in common with the peoples of Soviet Central Asia than they did with the peoples of Southern Afghanistan.

The Soviet strategy in Afghanistan was to grind down the enemy through a combination of airpower and patience. "The Soviets were by and large content to hold a series of major military bases or strategic towns and the routes between them, which indicated a mainly static, defensive posture," recalls Mohammad Yousaf.[6] They were relying on massive bombing campaigns—largely indiscriminate—to weaken and wear down the enemy. It was a "low-calorie" war for Moscow, Casey said. Only if resistance activity increased would the burdens of war begin to wear on the Soviet army. Casey and Akhtar came up with two assets that might help do just that.

The mujahedin were getting good quality arms, but their capability to inflict damage was limited. They were getting small arms, rocket-propelled grenades, and some small artillery pieces. Akhtar and Casey decided to give them heavier weapons, including 122-mm rocket launchers and artillery batteries. We'll get them the stuff to do the job right, Casey said. Akhtar in particular wanted better quality surface to air missiles (SAMs) to counter the Soviet airpower advantage. The current system being supplied, the SAM-7, was showing a poor success rate. "The quality of these systems is no good," Akhtar told Casey. By contrast, CIA officers on the ground in Pakistan tended to discount complaints about the quality of the SAM-7. According to Vince Cannistraro, "The Americans on the ground said, 'They're just stupid mujahedin and store these things in caves. No wonder they don't work.' "[7]

Casey promised to look into the matter personally. A sensitive intelligence operation was launched. Several weeks later agents working behind the Iron Curtain identified the problem. The defective SAMs came from an international arms dealer who had bought them from Poland. The Soviets, having discovered that the SAMs were destined for the mujahedin, decided to do something about it. "It turns out that the SAMs weren't very effective for a reason," recalls Cannistraro. "The Soviets had interrupted the supply channel and had deliberately sabotaged SAM-7s. The muj had been right all along."[8]

Casey and Akhtar concluded that it would be a good idea to use the CIA's spy capability to make the resistance more effective. Longer-range weapons meant the mujahedin would need satellite intelligence. Up until then, CIA spy satellites had been used exclusively for damage assessments. Now they would be used for targeting. The arrangement was direct and efficient. Agency experts in Langley would pull photos off the satellites and send them by courier to the CIA office in Pakistan. They would then be brought every few months to the Pakistani ISI, which was coordinating the resistance strategy.

The satellite photos proved a boon to the mujahedin. "This was a tremendous help," says Yousaf. "The CIA would show us the maps and help target vital areas. CIA satellite information would include exact targets, location of posts; it would also indicate the strength of the enemy and show possible routes to get in and out of the area. This satellite information played a major role in the victory."[9]

The photos would give the resistance the opportunity to distinguish Afghan from Soviet facilities. Casey and Akhtar decided to use the information to shift targeting from Afghan military targets to Soviet installations. It was hoped that some attacks on economic targets would hamstring efforts to extract commodities and export them to the USSR. Soviet technicians were procuring Afghan natural gas, oil, and precious metals, and they were paying very little (if anything at all) to the Afghan government. According to intelligence reports reaching the ISI, the Soviets had conducted a detailed survey of the mineral resources of Northern Afghanistan. It determined that the area was very rich, and the Soviets began to invest heavily in development of the region. Akhtar and Casey decided to concentrate on these economic targets.

The attacks would become fierce and sophisticated. The mujahedin quickly began targeting pipelines carrying natural gas from Afghanistan to the Soviet Union. "The value of the pipelines was demonstrated by the fact that when the mujahedin would attack these pipelines, the Soviets would strongly retaliate with indiscriminate killings of civilians," says Yousaf. Parts of the Soviet Union were already reliant on Afghan energy supplies. "On two occasions, Soviet industry in Central Asia came to a halt for at least ten to fifteen days when the mujahedin damaged the pipeline," according to Yousaf.[10]

As the bloody war raged in the hills and valleys of Afghanistan, a shadow war of nerves and wills was being fought halfway around the world in Poland. In October, General Jaruzelski raised the political stakes in an attempt to further weaken the underground, the embers of which were still visible. The Polish Parliament passed a law on trade unionism that outlawed Solidarity. Article 52 of the so-called trade union bill read: "All previous registrations of unions made before this law are canceled and no longer valid." With a stroke of a pen, Solidarity was officially no longer legal. Activists had been expecting it; the law was only the next logical step for a military government that was already rounding up activists and treating them as criminals. The bill was introduced and passed without any fanfare in Warsaw. Jaruzelski hoped that might be the end of it.

But the response in Washington was almost immediate. Bill Clark conferred with Reagan about the next step. Senior officials were unanimous that sanctions should be expanded. "It was very important that we do something," remembers George Shultz. "The funds [to the underground] were one thing, but we had to let them know psychologically that we stood with them."[11] On October 9, President Reagan suspended Poland's most-favored-nation (MFN) trading status, the last major economic bridge the Jaruzelski government had to the United States. Suspending MFN increased tariffs on Polish products exported to the United States by 300 to 400 percent and effectively priced them out of the American market.

The administration had spent months deciding what U.S. economic policy toward beleaguered Poland should be. It had wanted to send a clear message that martial law was unacceptable and raise the costs for Moscow of sustaining the military government. But it did not want to make the populace suffer. Outlawing Solidarity effectively ended the debate. In a radio address to the nation on Solidarity and U.S. relations with Poland, President Reagan said, "By outlawing Solidarity, a free trade organization to which an overwhelming majority of Polish workers and farmers belong, they have made it clear that they never had any intention of fostering one of the most elementary human rights—the right to belong to a free trade union."

The Jaruzelski government's action had come on the heels of renewed Solidarity activity, possible in part because of the funds flowing from the West. The "infection" was not going away; it was undergoing a metamorphosis. On August 31, there had been mass demonstrations to commemorate the second anniversary of Solidarity's founding. The movement was somehow surviving, and the authorities didn't quite know why.

"U.S. financial support was critical to sustaining Solidarity," says Robert McFarlane. A sophisticated C3I communications system was in place by the fall of 1982. It was being used to help organize protests and other mass actions. Radio transmitters were spreading the word while playing their cat and mouse game with authorities. Funds from the CIA were being used to purchase everything from printer's ink to gasoline.[12]

In addition to covertly funding the opposition, the Reagan administration was trying to pull the right levers of the diplomatic machinery to link the survival of Solidarity with economic benefits for the Polish government. "It was a very specific goal of sanctions to sustain Solidarity," says McFarlane.

At the NSC, staffers were tasked with setting up criteria for progress that would link specific political concessions by the Polish government with U.S. economic concessions and benefits. Roger Robinson was part of that process. "We had an incremental, step-by-step strategy," he recalls, "in effect, a left-hand column and a right-hand column. On the left were those trade benefits and concessions, including MFN and debt rescheduling, which corresponded to specific, concrete progress on Warsaw fulfilling the political preconditions of the legalization of Solidarity and restored national dialogue."[13]

In keeping with NSDD-32, the United States had as its formal goal the reversal of Soviet power in the region. President Reagan was talking to his advisers not only about keeping Solidarity intact but about overturning Yalta, which had divided Europe since the end of the Second World War. "Reagan had no time for the Yalta agreements, which divided Europe into spheres," says Richard Pipes. "To him it was unjust and unfair. Covertly supporting Solidarity was one of the ways to try to change that."[14]

The CIA was in contact with Solidarity activists on a regular basis. By meeting with them in Frankfurt, and later by using burst communicators, the CIA was relaying to the underground the specifics of U.S. policy. "We briefed Solidarity on our policies," recalls John Poindexter. "We wanted to eliminate surprise, which could in turn be demoralizing. They knew rather specifically what they would get before U.S. policies were announced."[15] Every week, at a different time, an updated message was relayed over Voice of America broadcasts.

In November, Bill Casey was in West Germany for a whirlwind tour and would get his first chance to touch the edge of what he liked to call "the Network." Ted Atkeson, his national intelligence officer for foreign military assessments, was on the trip. The director wanted to talk out the NATO–Warsaw Pact numerical balance with American analysts and European intelligence officials. But he was also in Germany to talk about Poland. The Frankfurt office of the agency was serving as a temporary forwarding base for operations in Poland. Casey met with operatives running the program. "He wanted to know everything," recalls one official, "down to the minutest detail. 'Do they need more newsprint paper? Do they have enough and the right kind of transmitters?' He wanted to be hands on."[16]

Field agents and analysts were pessimistic about the future. The Solidarity underground was recovering from the crackdown and was even growing in confidence. But the Polish people appeared to be exhausted, their passion for mass action against the Jaruzelski government waning. On October 11 and 12, the underground had called for nationwide protests and strikes in response to the banning of Solidarity. Public participation in the rallies was substantial but not overwhelming. Strike organizers and activists were languishing in jail, serving out long sentences. The food situation was deteriorating. Hope, like everything else, was being rationed. The insurrection that some in the administration (including Bill Casey) thought might be just around the corner had failed to materialize. It would be a long, hard struggle for the underground.

For their part, Polish leaders were holding intense discussions on how to smother the enemies of the regime. Through the spirit of the people and external financial support, the opposition had managed to get by.

On November 16, 1982, a meeting of senior party activists and military commanders took place in Warsaw. It included Politburo member and Central Committee Secretary Kazimierz Barcikowski; Gen. Florian Siwicki, the deputy defense minister and chief of the General Staff; and General R. Baryla, another deputy defense minister and head of the main political directorate of the army. They hashed out a report, assessing the political situation in the country. The officials were quietly optimistic about their new assertiveness:

> The opposition has lost its ability to mobilize strike actions and demonstrations in major enterprises. The authorities gained control over the traditional region opposition centers by isolating the leaders and individual

activists, by surveillance and stiff sentences. The official propaganda campaign and disinformation circulated in flysheets prevents mass demonstrations and stoppages at work. . . . Official propaganda must point to the danger of underground extremists determined to lead the country into bloody confrontation. Under martial law 1,100 sub-machine guns have been confiscated—these weapons could have been used against Party, militia and security functionaries.[17]

The turmoil that was turning Pole against Pole was making for some interesting intelligence-gathering opportunities. Casey had bolstered the Warsaw station in the last months of 1981, making it one of the most resourceful CIA facilities in the world. As a result, the penetration of the Polish government was increasingly successful. The agency had managed to recruit a deputy minister of defense who was soured by the whole martial law process. He was privy to defense plans and some of the internal security discussions being held in secret by the government. He was passing information slowly, every month or so, through a series of drops and signals. Most of the information concerned force structure and procurement plans. Political intelligence came later. At first agency operatives had been reluctant to deal with the officer. After all, they were under martial law, and there had already been provocations against American embassy officials. But they had taken the risk, and it had panned out. More sources in Poland would soon follow.

As operations in Poland and Afghanistan were gaining momentum, the U.S. effort to delay the first strand of the Siberian gas pipeline and terminate the second strand was running into trouble. The administration was facing vigorous, widespread discord within the Atlantic alliance. The president wanted the pipeline impeded but not at the risk of destroying the NATO alliance. "The embargo was not sustainable," recalls George Shultz. "The alliance was severely strained. Some sort of compromise had to be struck."[18]

On the advice of the new secretary of state, a novel strategy was hammered out at the National Security Planning Group in early July. Bill Clark, Caspar Weinberger, and Bill Casey wanted to take a hard-line approach. "This might be our best chance to gain leverage over the Allies and cut off Western resources going to the Kremlin," Weinberger counseled. But the president opted for a two-track strategy that included both a public and a private approach to reaching an agreement with the Europeans. Publicly, the administration would take a hard line with Europe. Privately, however, Reagan would be willing to compromise— but only to help Europe save face.

The president signed a national security decision memorandum drafted by Robinson and others on his NSC staff outlining the strategy for dealing with the fracturing pipeline issue. The United States would continue to play hardball with anyone violating U.S. sanctions. European countries that were using U.S.-licensed technologies or U.S. subsidiaries would have access to U.S. markets denied and face import controls if they continued to circumvent pipeline sanctions. That meant violators would be punished severely; most of the European companies involved could not survive a sustained closure of the American market. At the same time, Reagan wanted to negotiate some sort of agreement with the allies to hold their feet to the fire over time. He told Shultz he did not want to appear "overly anxious" to negotiate with Europe. "The president didn't want a nothing agreement," recalls Robert McFarlane. "He wanted something real and with teeth. Hence, he didn't want to appear to be weakening."[19]

Fortunately it was Europe that took the first tentative step toward a compromise. British Foreign Minister Francis Pym called George Shultz in early July and suggested that a special meeting be organized to discuss the issues surrounding the pipeline. Shultz took the offer to the president, who gave his secretary of state the go-ahead, but under the strictest NSC guidance; it was Europe that was backing down, not Washington. Shultz called Pym, and a meeting was set.

On September 16, the cabinet-level Senior Interdepartmental Group on International Economic Policy (SIG-IEP) met to outline the U.S. strategy for the talks. There was genuine concern that the Europeans might gang up on Shultz and equal concern that he would cave in. The talks were slated for early October at La Sapinière in Canada. The agenda would be wide open. There would be no staff present, and no communiqué would be issued. Out of the SIG came a tough line. "We were dead serious about this one," recalls one NSC aide. "We were determined to get the result that would cost Moscow dearly."[20]

At La Sapinière, Shultz argued forcefully for a trade-off: the sanctions would be lifted only if Europe agreed to a security-minded trade and credit regime. But the allies were not easily persuaded. French Foreign Minister Claude Cheysson argued that there should be no linkage. The meeting ended with an impasse. Out of the discussions emerged a nonpaper, a diplomatic term for a document that only outlines areas of potential agreement.

Shultz returned to Washington "feeling good" about the progress he had made. On October 15, he presented the results of the talks to the National Security Council. Weinberger and Casey were not impressed. "I don't know that this is enough to give up the pipeline sanctions," Weinberger said. Casey echoed the defense secretary's sentiment with NSC staff concurrence.[21]

Shultz challenged them to offer an alternate approach. "These sanctions are not viable, not sustainable," he retorted. "What's the alternative?" Clark, Casey, and Weinberger continued to insist on a fundamental change in Western economic and financial policy toward Moscow. So the negotiation process continued. Working through ambassadors in Washington and under tight parameters laid down by the NSC, Shultz hammered out an agreement. On November 12, an end to the impasse was in sight. On November 13, the president went on the air to announce that the sanctions were being lifted and consultations on conducting a unified "security-first" allied economic strategy vis-à-vis the Soviet bloc would begin. Reagan said, "First, each partner has affirmed that no new contracts for the purchase of Soviet natural gas will be signed or approved during the course of our study of alternative Western sources of energy. Second, we and our partners will strengthen existing controls on the transfer of strategic items to the Soviet Union. Third, we will establish, without delay, procedures for monitoring financial relations with the Soviet Union and will work to harmonize our export credit policies."[22]

The day before Reagan made his announcement, he signed the most important secret document concerning the Soviet economy in U.S. history in the form of a national security decision directive (NSDD). The directive—NSDD-66, drafted by Roger Robinson—reflected a seismic shift in the U.S. economic warfare strategy from sanctions to other critical issues. Unable to secure allied cooperation over the pipeline earlier in the dispute, National Security Adviser Bill Clark had asked the international economics directorate of the NSC to draw up a coherent U.S. approach that would exploit Soviet economic vulnerabilities. This directive was the result, and it guided the Shultz negotiations in La Sapinière even before the president signed it.

"NSDD-66 was tantamount to a secret declaration of economic war on the Soviet Union," says Roger Robinson, its principal author. "It is the document that, along with the U.S. military buildup and SDI, charted the ultimate demise of the Soviet Union." Only a few pages in length, NSDD-66 made it U.S. policy to seek to rapidly construct a "strategic trade triad" to curtail "western life-support" to Moscow.[23]

According to Robert McFarlane, NSDD-66 had three central elements:

- It was U.S. policy to gain the concurrence of European allies that credits would not be extended to Moscow at better than market rates.
- The United States would not allow access to Western high technology critical to sustaining the Soviet military and economy. The policing of COCOM would be enhanced.
- The United States would try to work with its allies in a proactive way to develop alternative sources to reduce the dependence on Soviet gas in Europe. There would also be a threshold. The goal would be preventing Europe from dependence on the Soviet Union for more than 30 percent of their natural gas needs (i.e., no second 3,600-mile strand of the Siberian pipeline and no new contracts).[24]

The compromise over sanctions had not been favored by Clark, Weinberger, or Casey. They wanted to tough it out and delay the first strand of the pipeline even further. But even after the pipeline sanctions were dropped with European adoption of the "strategic trade triad" approach, Casey, Clark, and Reagan remained of the opinion that the Soviet economy could be severely damaged. And certain voices within the administration were giving officials the same message. In late November 1982, the National Security Planning Group was in special session. One important area of discussion was the Soviet economy.

Usually NSPG meetings included only the president, vice president, secretaries of state and defense, and the CIA director. But that day Henry Rowen was in the White House Situation Room presenting his views of Soviet economic vulnerability. Rowen began describing methodically the declining health of the Soviet economy. "We have simply got to sustain our military challenge to Moscow and cut off their Western life support, because in this decade we are going to see the combined weight of that burden cause such stress on the system that it will implode," he said.[25]

1. Former Soviet official, interview with the author. See also Christopher Andrew and Oleg Gordievsky, *KGB: The Inside Story* (New York: HarperCollins, 1990), p. 560.

2. Vincent Cannistraro, interview with the author.

3. Mohammad Yousaf, interview with the author.

4. Mohammad Yousaf, interview with the author.

5. Mohammad Yousaf, interview with the author.

6. Mohammad Yousaf, interview with the author.

7. Vincent Cannistraro, interview with the author.

8. Vincent Cannistraro, interview with the author.

9. Mohammad Yousaf, interview with the author.

10. Mohammad Yousaf, interview with the author.

11. George Shultz, interview with the author.

12. Robert McFarlane, interview with the author.

13. Roger Robinson, interview with the author.

14. Richard Pipes, interview with the author.

15. John Poindexter, interview with the author.

16. U.S. intelligence official, interview with the author.

17. *Serwis Informacyjny Malopolska*, no. 42 (1982).

18. George Shultz, interview with the author.

19. Robert McFarlane, interview with the author.

20. Interview with the author.

21. George Shultz, interview with the author.

22. George Shultz, interview with the author; see also his *Turmoil and Triumph* (New York: Scribner's, 1993).

23. Roger Robinson, interview with the author.

24. Robert McFarlane, interview with the author.

25. Robert McFarlane, interview with the author.

10

November 10, 1982, was bitterly cold in Moscow. The snow was falling heavily. At 7:30 A.M., Leonid Brezhnev was reading *Pravda* and having breakfast at his dining room table. The Soviet premier was in ill health and pretty shaky, but he was still strong enough to get around on his own. In a room nearby sat the aging man's ever-present bodyguards. Personally assigned by KGB Director Yuri Andropov to protect the general secretary from harm, they were a constant fixture almost everywhere he went. Twenty minutes after breakfast, Brezhnev headed up the stairs to his bedroom. His protectors followed him and closed the door behind them.

A few minutes later, a bodyguard descended the stairs and politely informed Victoria Petrovna that her husband had just died. She broke into tears. Collecting herself, she headed quickly for the bedroom, but she was stopped by the bodyguards. No doctor was called. The body was embalmed, and no autopsy was apparently ever performed. Victoria Petrovna didn't see her husband's body until two days later at a ceremony in the Hall of Columns of the House of Unions. Until her dying day, she remained convinced that her husband had met a violent end.[1]

Perhaps her suspicions were justified by her husband's successor.

Just five days after the death of the Soviet Union's second longest ruling leader, the new captain of the Soviet ship of state was firmly in command. Yuri Vladimirovich Andropov, head of the KGB and the official who had handpicked the Brezhnev bodyguards, was now the protector of the Soviet empire. He was a complex man, full of apparent contradictions, at least in tone and taste. His complexities were symbolized by the objects he prized. Although his office at KGB headquarters had been spartan, two adornments had dominated the room: a large picture of Felix Dzerzhinski, the founder of the Soviet secret police, and a statue of Don Quixote.

Days after assuming his new post, Andropov and Foreign Minister Andrei Gromyko were meeting with General Zia of Pakistan and his foreign minister, Yaqub Khan. The site was St. Catherine's Hall of the Great Kremlin Palace, a grand room full of czarist treasures. Andropov was seething about Afghanistan, his dark, steely eyes piercing his guests. He had opposed the 1979 invasion, but that didn't matter now. It was a matter of Soviet pride and honor, not to mention geostrategic interest. "Pakistan is a partner in the war against Afghanistan," said Gromyko to the visiting Pakistanis in a script prepared by Andropov. "You must understand that the Soviet Union will stand by Afghanistan." The Soviets were doing just that, and more. Separatists in the province of Baluchistan were being backed in their efforts to break away from Pakistan. The KGB and the Afghan KHAD were running destabilization operations against Islamabad, trying to sow dissent against Zia's rule. And Afghan fighter aircraft were flying into Pakistani airspace to attack mujahedin targets.

Andropov and Gromyko knew that Pakistan was the cornerstone of the Afghan resistance. Without an external base of support, the resistance would be sunk. The Reagan administration had recognized the very same thing and was providing billions in aid on the condition that Zia continue to give shelter to the mujahedin.

The Pakistani president did not take kindly to the threats Moscow was making and responded coolly to this verbal assault. "Pakistan genuinely wishes to have friendly relations with Afghanistan and the Soviet Union and seeks a peaceful political solution of the Afghan problem," he said mechanically.[2] The Pakistani general was defiant. Both

Caspar Weinberger and William Casey called Zia after he returned from Moscow. Casey offered to do whatever he could to help Pakistan. The general continued to play his role as a conduit.

In late 1982, National Security Adviser Bill Clark directed the NSC to outline the Reagan strategy for dealing with Moscow in a secret directive for the president to sign. This was no easy undertaking. Administrations since 1945 had attempted to enunciate policies that had their own imprints. Nonetheless, since 1950 American foreign policy had been essentially driven by the assumptions and policies expressed in a document signed by Harry Truman in 1950 called NSC-68. The main drafting of that report had been undertaken by Paul Nitze, who had recently replaced George Kennan as head of the State Department's Policy Planning Staff.

The document called NSC-68 rested on a number of assumptions that were to leave a long-lasting impression on American foreign policy. It described a persistent East-West struggle and a sustained Soviet military challenge. To respond to this reality, American foreign policy would be essentially reactive and defensive. It assumed, as did Kennan in his famous article "The Sources of Soviet Conduct," that "a long-term, patient but firm and vigilant containment of Russian expansive tendencies" would eventually produce fundamental changes in the Soviet system, making it far less menacing to the West. In the 1970s, successive administrations expanded on this stripped-down version of containment, adding a litany of inducements in the hope of inviting a change in Soviet conduct. Little, however, seemed to divert the Kremlin's actions on the international stage.

Reagan and his senior advisers did not share many of the assumptions of "containment." The problems posed by the Soviet Union were not to be resolved through "behavior modification" (to use the clinical term); they were inherent in the Soviet system. Instinctively, Reagan wanted to take the strategic initiative and not be forced into a reactive position. It was necessary to change the nature and scope of the superpower competition. The singular focus on a quantitative arms competition was to the Soviets' advantage. Administration officials wanted to amplify the competition to include economics and technology. What emerged from Richard Pipes's pen was an attempt to incorporate these instinctive concepts into policy. Touched up by others on the NSC staff and only several pages long, the result was a farsighted document that codified the Reagan approach for dealing with the Soviet Union.

The Harvard historian had spent late nights in his small, nondescript office in the Old Executive Office Building writing and rewriting the pivotal document. His work became the basis of NSDD-75, the first and only formal presidential directive during the Reagan administration on U.S. strategy, goals, and objectives vis-à-vis the Soviet Union. It remains one of the administration's most highly guarded secrets.

"NSDD-75 was a clear break from the past," says Pipes. "It was the first document which said that what mattered was not only Soviet behavior but the nature of the Soviet system. NSDD-75 said our goal was no longer to coexist with the Soviet Union but to change the Soviet system. At its root was the belief that we had it in our power to alter the Soviet system through the use of external pressure."[3] The U.S. strategic goal became undermining the Soviet system, by exploiting its internal weaknesses. The political ligaments of the Soviet empire were seemingly weak and should be probed in the hope of "rolling back" Soviet power around the globe. The earlier NSDD-32 had stressed U.S. interest in rolling back Soviet power in Eastern Europe, but NSDD-75 took things a step further.

The new document was comprehensive and offered policy prescriptions and explicit aims for American policy on a number of fronts. "What we tried very hard to do in NSDD-75 was to have an integrated policy that incorporated actions in all areas," says John Poindexter, who was in concurrence in the document. "In my view that was one of the most effective things about the policy."[4]

The document was fairly pointed and started with "working principles":

- "The United States does not accept the current Soviet sphere of influence beyond its borders, and the U.S. will seek to roll it back."
- "The United States will not contribute to enhancing the welfare of the Soviet economy and will do what it can to restrict any

means that could serve that end"; in particular the document
mentioned technology, credits, and hard currency earned
through energy exports.
- "The United States will seek opportunities to roll back the level
of Soviet influence overseas."[5]

This pivotal document reiterated the U.S. strategy of seeking to exploit
Soviet vulnerabilities. "NSDD-75 did not say we should confront the
Soviets at every point. It said we would look for vulnerabilities and try
to beat them," says Robert McFarlane.[6]

Chief among those vulnerabilities was the Soviet economy.
Echoing the Defense Department directive and the national security
decision memorandum of 1982, NSDD-75 declared that it would
henceforth be administration policy to exacerbate the Soviet economic
problems in the hope of plunging the system into a crisis. "The economic area we frankly felt had been ignored—certainly not used the way
it could be in terms of an economic weapon to hurt the Soviets,"
according to Poindexter. "In the economic area there were a lot of
nonbelievers in the executive branch of government. I can recall senior
officials taking the position that there was no way that actions taken by
the United States could cause the collapse of the Soviet economy. On
the face of it, that didn't ring true to me. It was much too dogmatic and
unscientific. In general I think we were faithful to the NSDD. It was
signed by the president for a specific purpose."[7] That purpose was to
squeeze the Soviet economy, by both reducing income and forcing an
increase in expenditures.

"Ronald Reagan wanted a complementary relationship between
the U.S. military buildup (to redress years of neglect), futuristic defense-
related technologies like SDI, and economic security policies directed at
Moscow," recalls Bill Clark. "Frankly, our intention was to divert
priority Soviet resources to meeting future U.S. capabilities beyond their
grasp and to persuade Moscow that they would not prevail in a toe-to-
toe technological competition."[8] In the past, technological superiority
had been viewed as an advantage that could be used to counter Soviet
numerical superiority on the battlefield. The Reagan administration
wanted to take things a step further. By forcing the tempo of the

technological race, this American advantage could become a powerful weapon.

In late 1982, the president lost a critical vote in Congress for funding the MX missile. It was nothing new; the Pentagon had proposed three basing modes for the new intercontinental ballistic missile over the course of 1981–82. All three plans had been rejected by Congress. "The bottom line was we weren't putting any missiles in the ground," says McFarlane.[9]

Shortly after the failed MX vote, Adm. John Poindexter approached McFarlane. Poindexter, who had graduated at the top of his class at the Naval Academy and possesses a keen scientific mind, suggested that the administration explore the possibility of researching and even deploying a strategic defense system. The idea had been percolating in the White House since early 1981, when Gen. Daniel Graham, head of a group called High Frontier, met with the president and members of the NSC. There had been a quite detailed discussion, but no action had followed.

Several Reagan aides had long counseled for a stronger American commitment to strategic defense. Richard Allen, a longtime foreign policy adviser to the president, had for years educated Reagan on the antiballistic missile debate. Martin Anderson, a domestic affairs specialist, had vividly demonstrated America's vulnerability to Soviet nuclear missiles when he visited NORAD with candidate Reagan. Caspar Weinberger had repeatedly emphasized the promise of a high-tech strategic defense system since the earliest days of his tenure as secretary of defense. On October 2, 1981, at a White House press briefing on strategic weapons, Weinberger emphasized that "there are some broad new things that look quite promising that we are going to be exploring because obviously, if we are able to destroy incoming missiles, I don't think it would be destabilizing; I think it would be extremely comforting."

McFarlane told Poindexter that he liked the idea and had in fact been thinking along similar lines. "It had seemed to me for about ten years, since the Nixon and Ford years, that we were competing with the Russians militarily on the wrong terms," recalls McFarlane. "Our comparative advantage was in quality and technology. It really caused me to pause and look back. I asked myself, How could we reorient our investment strategy? How do you spend your resources? It seemed to me that spending on offensive systems and numbers was less effective than investing in our comparative advantage—technology. And I began to look at what were the areas in which we could invest and that we needed an investment strategy for high technology that could be played out."[10]

Poindexter pulled together some of the brightest strategic minds in the U.S. military-science community to talk about a resource shift from the traditional emphasis on nuclear weapons to high-tech systems in strategic weapons. The group included Bob Lenhart of the NSC, Gen. Richard Bovery, and Al Keel of the Office of Management and Budget; John Foster of TRW; Richard DeLauer, a scientist and engineer; and Dr. George Keyworth, President Reagan's science adviser. "We met in the Situation Room and brainstormed for a while," Poindexter remembers. "The conclusion of the meeting was that the technology had progressed so much since the days of the ABM that the idea of strategic defense deserved a lot of research."[11] Poindexter reported back to McFarlane the group's general conclusions and assigned several research and policy papers.

In the interim, McFarlane broached strategic defense with Paul Gorman of the Joint Chiefs of Staff (JCS). Gorman told him that the joint chiefs had an interest in the strategic defense concept, driven mainly by Adm. James Watkins. Watkins was a serious student of science who believed that the state of the art had so improved as to enable a shift in U.S. strategic policy from mutual assured destruction (MAD) to strategic defense.

After the consultation with the JCS, Poindexter and McFarlane went to Bill Clark, who wanted to act immediately. In December 1982, he arranged for members of the Joint Chiefs to meet privately with President Reagan. It was part of a series of regular monthly meetings between the president and the JCS.

There was a tremendous snowstorm that day. Clark was out of town, so McFarlane ran the meeting. The roads were so bad that the joint chiefs had to come to the White House in a tracked vehicle. McFarlane broached the subject first. The joint chiefs recommended that the United States consider abandoning its complete dependence on MAD and move toward the research and development of a strategic defense initiative (SDI) system. The president took to the idea immediately. He did so, according to most of his advisers, out of strong moral conviction. "He thought MAD was quite simply immoral," recalls George Shultz.[12] "What if," Reagan asked the brass, "we began to move away from our total reliance on offense to deter a nuclear attack and moved toward a relatively greater reliance on defense?"

Shortly after the meeting with the JCS, Clark sat down with McFarlane and Poindexter to determine how to proceed. It was McFarlane who suggested that the president mention the idea in a speech—a sort of public affirmation of the shift in the American strategic vision.

The plan to explore a strategic defense system was kept very secret. Shultz, Weinberger, and members of the JCS were not consulted about the speech until two days beforehand. McFarlane was working feverishly to hammer out a strategic missile defense statement. He was using his own typewriter—no secretaries—to maintain strict secrecy. George Keyworth made some final edits.[13]

On March 23, 1983, the president addressed the nation. With intensity, he outlined his commitment to a new direction in the strategic field. The United States would begin research on the Strategic Defense Initiative (a term coined by Poindexter). Reagan concluded by saying, "Let me just say I am totally committed to this course." Two days later, the president issued an executive order in which he instructed William Clark to supervise an "intense effort" to define a long-term research and development program for the system.[14] While the president's interest in SDI was largely based on his vision of a world no longer facing nuclear peril, the system was also pursued because of the strain it would place on the Soviet economy. In one national security decision directive, for example, the value of the system was to be measured in part by a "cost-effective criterion." It was "couched in economic terms; it is more than just an economic concept." That meant that the system's value would be measured not only in strategic terms but by how severe the economic penalties would be of Soviet attempts to counter it.[15]

Reagan's announcement sent a shock wave through Moscow. "I remember these days pretty well," says Aleksandr Bessmertnykh. "The atmosphere in Moscow was very tense for the first few years of the Reagan administration, especially because of the SDI system: it frightened us very much."[16] "SDI frightened them to death," says Allan

Whittaker, formerly with the Political Psychology Division at the CIA. "They were extremely insecure—in the clinical sense—about their research and development capability. They took our technological sprint capability very seriously."[17]

For McFarlane, the issue was not strategic defense but a battle of resources. "It was really about how we could reorient our investment strategy," he recalls. "I called it that—an economic term more than a military strategy—because it is really a resource concept. I put myself in the position of the Russians in the Politburo. How would I react if the Americans began investing in what they really did well? You knew that when you turned the labs and companies loose with $26 billion [for SDI], you knew they would come up with something."[18]

Why Reagan so strongly backed SDI has been a source of speculation. Was it to redirect American nuclear strategy? Or did he see the system the way McFarlane did, as a resource question? According to longtime Reagan associate and former National Security Adviser Richard Allen, "I don't believe Reagan saw SDI as a shield you could put over the United States, and it would be invulnerable. I believe that he thought that this was far out enough that if we put some big bucks behind it, the Soviets would have to fall for it."[19] Most senior Reagan officials believe Reagan's unshakable embrace of SDI was motivated by both the hope of changing American nuclear doctrine and an attempt to change the terms of the military technical competition.

The Soviet leaders took Reagan's SDI speech for what it was—a technological challenge. As *Izvestiya* put it: "They want to impose on us an even more ruinous arms race. They calculate that the Soviet Union will not last the race. It lacks the resources, it lacks the technical potential. They hope that our country's economy will be exhausted."[20]

The fierce defense buildup was heading in the direction Moscow feared most. The Soviet General Staff took the Department of Defense five-year plan, with its commitment to developing weapons that might render Soviet systems "obsolete," with a seriousness bordering on hysteria. The early 1980s were a "revolutionary period" in military affairs for Moscow. Marshal Nikolai Ogarkov, the Soviet chief of the General Staff, had written in 1982 that "the rapid development of science and technology in recent years creates real preconditions for the emergence in the very near future of even more destructive and previously unknown types of weapons based on new physical principles."[21]

The Soviet brass believed that radical technological developments had twice in the past created military "revolutions." The first had occurred in the 1920s, when the tank and airplane replaced the cavalry and horse. The second occurred in the 1950s, when atomic weapons were attached to ballistic missiles to replace the bomber and conventional bombs. In both instances, military weapons reached a new level of development. And in both Moscow had managed to keep up fairly closely with the West.

But now the third revolution was coming—and Moscow was nervous. The application of emerging technologies such as microelectronics and computers to military systems would be even more challenging since it placed a premium on high quality in production, not a Soviet strong point. Because of its complexity, a precision-guided munition, for example, with only the slightest manufacturing flaw could be useless. The MIG-25 aircraft contained only vacuum tubes and no solid-state circuitry in its avionics.[22] According to a Department of Defense assessment, Moscow was ten years behind the United States in computer electronics and trailed in many of the most important third revolution technologies—electro-optic sensors, robotics and machine intelligence, signal processing, stealth, and telecommunications.[23]

The prospect for developing these new systems did not look good anytime soon. Moscow had been working for years on a strategic defense system of its own, spending billions and committing thousands of scientists to the effort. But they were confronting unique technical and logistical problems. The Soviet system did not emphasize initiative and creativity, critical ingredients in a high-tech economy. The troubles had mounted so high that the military was virtually abandoning any hope of developing new systems. Rather, they were trying to apply off-the-shelf technologies to their system.

On the American side, things were shaping up to be quite different. Suddenly a whole array of U.S. high-tech systems were being developed and deployed, threatening to make expensive Soviet systems obsolete. The Kremlin had expended great resources to achieve military parity with the West. "The attainment of military strategic parity between socialism and capitalism was one of the most important results of the last several decades," said Yuri Andropov. "It took great resources and effort on the part of our people to achieve this parity."[24] But now that was increasingly at risk.

In his 1982 book *Always on Guard in Defense of the Fatherland*, Marshal Ogarkov expressed a concern about the "fast pace" of the development of American military technology. He warned, "In these conditions, the failure to change views in time, and stagnation in the development and deployment of new kinds of military construction are fraught with serious consequences." Those repercussions were being worked over in secret tests under the direction of Gen. K. U. Kardashevskiy. Military officials wanted to assess the magnitude of the American technological challenge. In laboratories Soviet military scientists were testing everything in their arsenal against the new generation of American high-tech weapons that were being deployed or would be coming shortly. Their results shocked the Soviet establishment.

Kardashevskiy concluded that new technologies posed a dangerous threat to the conventional backbone of the Soviet armed forces, the tank. If deployed in large enough quantities, antitank systems being developed by the United States could form a virtually impenetrable wall.[25] The Soviets could respond with upgrades of their own, but the race would get costly. As one analyst lamented, "The West prefers to invest funds in improvements of antitank weapons, thus creating a need for us to constantly modernize our tank fleet and as a result pushing us toward ever greater expenditure of economic resources."[26] In short, the tank might go the way of the dinosaur.

With technology changing at a revolutionary pace, the high-tech industrial bases of both superpowers became a large determinant of military power. "What was worrisome to the leadership was the American emphasis on high tech," recalls Yevgenny Novikov. "They knew they could not keep up. Our technology base was not sufficient. They knew that in multiple areas new technologies would make old systems obsolete."[27]

The challenge the Reagan administration's high-tech arms development program posed to the Kremlin was reflected in new Soviet intelligence goals. Overseas officers of the KGB were to give "priority" to collecting intelligence on "third-generation" military technologies.

According to KGB documents, the "list of priority questions of military strategy on which the intelligence service abroad is required to throw light" included "active utilization of important inventions and discoveries, and designs and ideas for military technology, which would ensure that a really new qualitative level was reached in the upgrading of individual types of strategic and tactical nuclear and conventional weapons."[28]

- While the administration was intensifying the high-tech arms race, it was also trying to limit Western exports that were helping Moscow stay competitive. Technology transfer from West to East was an acute Soviet vulnerability, one the Reagan National Security Council wanted to exploit. Technology exports had been part of the "strategic triad" outlined in the secret NSDD-66. Bill Casey had been pushing for the CIA to have more authority in constricting the flow of technologies since the earliest days of the administration. He got his wish in 1983, when the secret Technology Transfer Intelligence Committee was established and based at Langley. Its sole responsibility would be to track Soviet bloc technology acquisitions. It was a clearinghouse to which twenty-two departments in the federal government would contribute manpower and other resources. For the first time, there was a systematic process for collecting and disseminating information on this area. The data gathered by the committee was a gold mine for Casey. He could track which technologies the Soviets were trying to acquire. That would let him know their economic needs. "Now I have my finger on their pulse," he told Herb Meyer.[29]

The flow of high technology from the United States was dramatically declining, thanks in large part to new restrictions on exports that the Department of Defense and State Department (in part) had been pushing for. In 1975, of all the manufactured goods sold to the Soviet Union by the United States, 32.7 percent were high-tech products. That amounted to $219 million in sales. By 1983, the sales that were high tech dropped to 5.4 percent, amounting to a paltry $39 million.[30]

While administration officials were pleased with these results, they understood that unilateral restraint would accomplish little. Only with the cooperation of key allies would technology restrictions yield results. Assistant Secretary of Defense Richard Perle had been making secret trips to allied capitals since the earliest days of the administration, hoping to gain cooperation. The bilateral talks were slow going, but there were some marked results.

After two years of secret shuttle diplomacy, a unified strategy was beginning to emerge in COCOM. The allies had reached a tentative consensus on technology transfer at La Sapinière in 1982. Members of COCOM had acted on over one hundred U.S. recommendations regarding exports to the Soviet bloc over the past year. But the United States was now looking to broaden dramatically the number of technologies included on the export control lists. No longer inclined to base Western export control policy solely on goods with obvious military relevance, it wanted to include any products and technologies that were somehow "strategically important," even civilian technologies if their range of application could not be precisely determined. The United States also wanted COCOM's policing powers to cover exports to third countries, because transactions with them were a favorite Soviet technique of obtaining sensitive technologies.

Better policing began to have a significant effect. By the fall of 1983, U.S. customs investigators, in collaboration with their European counterparts, had been able to seize approximately 1,400 illegal shipments valued at almost $200 million. Many of these were critical technologies that helped sustain sectors of Soviet industry.[31]

The administration was also making progress on limiting Soviet energy exports to the West. American officials had forced an agreement at the International Energy Agency (IEA) in the spring of 1983, in effect capping European imports of Soviet natural gas. It committed Western Europe to seek out alternative sources of energy, and it precluded Europe from relying on the Soviets for more than 30 percent of their energy needs. The agreement was codified at the G-7 Williamsburg Summit in May 1983. It was a potentially enormous financial blow to the Kremlin, a blocking maneuver denying it large sums of hard currency.

As the United States closed the deal at the IEA, interest in Soviet oil exports continued. Oil was the Kremlin's most significant export earner, in some instances accounting for more than half of Soviet hard currency. In early 1983, the Treasury Department concluded a massive secret study on international oil pricing. Treasury often did reports on such subjects, but this one received considerable interest at the NSC. Bill Casey and Caspar Weinberger also reviewed it. The study took six months to write and was hundreds of pages long; it was an impressive compilation of data. World oil prices were an important determinant of both U.S. and Soviet economic health. But exactly how significant were they to each superpower?

The report argued that the optimum oil price for the U.S. economy was approximately $20 a barrel, well below the 1983 price of $34. At the time the United States was spending $183 billion on 5.5 billion barrels of oil a year. Of that, imports amounted to 1.6 billion barrels. A drop in international markets to $20 a barrel would lower U.S. energy costs by $71.5 billion per year. That was a transfer of income to American consumers amounting to 1 percent of existing gross national product. "Lower oil prices were basically like a tax cut," recalls Weinberger.[32] The report concluded that with a drop to $20 a barrel, "the nation as a whole would be unambiguously better off. . . . The initial effect of reducing oil prices would be a substantial transfer of income from foreign producers to U.S. users of oil. This would represent an unambiguous increase in U.S. income and purchasing power. . . . The lower oil price means a transfer of income to this country—a larger share of the command of the world's resources."[33] Few segments of the U.S. economy would be losers in such a scenario, and the effect on them would be minimal. "What stands out is that the only loser among U.S. industries is mining, as oil and gas drilling activity falls off. All other industries benefit from the price reduction."[34]

A lower price for oil would occur with either a drop in demand (not very likely) or a dramatic increase in production. Concerning the latter, the report noted that if Saudi Arabia and other countries "with available oil reserves should step up their production and increase world output by . . . about 2.7 to 5.4 million barrels a day and cause the world price to fall by about 40%, the overall effect on the United States would be very beneficial."

While the effects for the United States were "unambiguously good," dropping oil prices would have a "devastating effect on the Soviet economy." The report noted Moscow's heavy reliance on energy exports for hard currency. By Treasury Department calculations, every one-dollar rise in the price of oil meant approximately $500 million to $1 billion extra in hard currency for the Kremlin. But the reverse was also true: dropping prices meant plunging incomes. And Moscow, unlike other producers, could not raise production to increase earnings. It was already producing at maximum capacity.

The massive report was arcane like most of the reports coming out of Treasury. But Bill Clark, Casey, and Weinberger made sure the president received a summary of it. Pushing for lower prices was very inviting. "It was a no-lose situation," recalls John Poindexter. "We came out ahead on both counts."[35] The message was not lost on the president. "Ronald Reagan was fully aware that energy exports represented the centerpiece of Moscow's annual hard currency earnings structure," recalls Bill Clark. "He likewise understood the benefits to the U.S. economy of lower, stable oil prices."[36]

World markets seemed to be moving downward. Only a few months before the report was released, four U.S. oil executives had sat down with the Saudi oil minister, Sheik Ahmed Zaki al-Yamani, in Geneva. Yamani had summoned the executives—George Keller, chairman of Standard Oil of California; Clifton Garvin, Jr., chairman of Exxon; William Tavoulareas, president of Mobil; and John McKinley, chairman of Texaco—for a private chat about the world oil market. They had lunch in the oil minister's elegant suite in the InterContinental Hotel, with its spectacular view of the lake and skyline. There were phones scattered all over, and several screens in his office constantly alerted him to changes in contract and spot prices for crude being sold around the world.

Yamani was an imposing figure in the international oil market and the enforcer for OPEC. It was his job to ensure that production was strictly controlled, keeping prices stable and relatively high to enhance earnings. To that end, Saudi Arabia served as the swing producer, adjusting its production levels to maintain price stability—lowering production to bring the price up or increasing production to lower the cost of crude. Yamani did not have the protection of being a member of the royal family to keep his job. He was a businessman who, by sheer wit and brilliance, had risen to the top in a society that placed a premium on familial history. If he failed at his job, he could be gone instantly. It was that simple.

In the past it had been Yamani who established the tone and

terms of any decision with American oil executives. But this time it was the Americans who did the blunt talking. The oil shortages of the 1970s had given way to the oil glut of the 1980s. The price of Saudi light crude was quite simply too high, and the American firms were losing big money. "We can live with $30-a-barrel oil," Keller told Yamani. "We can live with $34 oil. But we can't live paying $34 for $30 oil." The meeting ended at an impasse. The Americans left frustrated.

Administration officials had been tipped off about the gathering by friends in the oil business. Specialists from the NSC and CIA met with one of the executives who had attended.[37]

Despite the lower prices that had come to mark the international market, a variety of political and economic factors could easily push prices higher, something Moscow would no doubt relish. The Iran-Iraq War made the markets nervous with every changing tide. Radical states such as Iran and Libya were trying to force OPEC prices up. Concerned about this prospect, U.S. officials were dispatched to try to keep markets calm. In early February 1983, two Department of Energy officials were sent to London to meet with British Energy Secretary Nigel Lawson. The purpose was to urge him to reduce the official price of crude and raise production in the North Sea. "We were working hard to persuade the British to increase production and bring down prices," recalls Weinberger. "The Soviets were going to bring natural gas on line to Western Europe very soon. If the price of oil stayed high, Europe would convert to gas. It would be a boon to the Soviets."[38] Bill Schneider remembers the same thing. "We saw Britain as a catalyst for bringing down oil prices. The North Sea had the capacity to drive the market down dramatically."[39]

Anything that could be done to suppress prices was being pursued. One easy way was cutting purchases of crude for the Strategic Petroleum Reserve (SPR). Established as a result of the Arab oil embargo of 1973–74, the SPR was a stockpile designed to offer a reserve in case an oil crisis developed again. Millions of barrels were being stored in underground salt caverns along the coasts of Louisiana and Texas. Congress had stipulated that the reserve be stocked with 750 million barrels by 1990. But in early 1983, the administration announced that it would begin dramatically cutting the amount of oil it would purchase. Instead of 220,000 barrels per day, mandated by Congress, the administration was budgeting for purchases of only 145,000 barrels. Bill Schneider, who handled budgeting for the reserve at the Office of Management and Budget before becoming undersecretary of state, said the purpose of the reduction was to help the budget but also to reduce demand and hope to achieve some drop in prices.[40]

In late February, Prince Bandar of Saudi Arabia met with several senior officials in the administration, including Bill Casey and Caspar Weinberger. Bandar wanted an independent channel to the Oval Office. The State Department and Secretary Shultz were seen as too pro-Israel, he told several officials. The emerging special relationship between Saudi Arabia and the Reagan administration warranted easy consultations with the right people. "The Saudis always viewed the Pentagon and the CIA as the best channels of communication," recalls a senior official from the region. "The State Department was viewed as ineffectual."[41]

The Saudis were particularly concerned that their interests be heard given the current state of the Middle East. Lebanon was in pieces; the Iran-Iraq War was proceeding with a bloody vengeance and hanging over the region like the sword of Damocles. Syria and Israel were standing eyeball to eyeball. And the threat of Khomeinism hung over the entire region.

In Poland, the underground war was continuing. Although the government had formally ended the internment of political prisoners on December 30, 1982, authorities were still incarcerating activists. The newest wave of arrests was directed at underground printing presses and aimed at breaking up the remnants of Solidarity and preventing any released internees from reviving the organization. On New Year's Day, the police seized an underground printing plant near the city of Poznan; fifteen activists were arrested. Officials uncovered a foreign money trail in the operation. The activists had scarce food supplies, which had been imported from the West, and some hard currency.

Distribution of literature was getting more difficult. Two underground organizations that produced and distributed leaflets in Gdansk were smashed; two centers in Warsaw and another in Leszno were also exposed in early 1983. But perhaps the biggest coup came with the arrest of Stanislaw Zablocki, who headed the strike committee in the Szczecin shipyards. The underground had lost another leader. Every arrest of a senior Solidarity official brought more anxiety to those in Washington in the know about the covert supply line. Exactly who in the underground knew about the support coming from the United States? Would anyone be willing to talk? Was there incriminating evidence of any sort? Seven leaders of Solidarity and five of the intellectual dissident movement Committee for the Defense of Workers (KOR) had been captured in recent months, and Polish authorities were determined to make examples of them. The activists were being charged with seeking to overthrow the State, and that meant the death penalty.

But despite the setbacks, the underground was more organized than ever. Zbigniew Bujak, the twenty-seven-year-old president of Solidarity in the Warsaw region, was now handling the funds for the underground and distributing foreign support to various groups. He concentrated resources on the large Warsaw region but also maintained contact with the leaders from other regions to coordinate a general strategy of resistance. Wictor Kulerski was in charge of liaison with groups of teachers, doctors, lawyers, and intellectuals who all published regular underground journals and papers. He was a troubleshooter, helping editors come up with paper to print their publications and money to pay for printer's ink. He was meticulous, working eighteen-hour days.

A bureau had been established to deal with administrative tasks. These included lining up apartments, cars, and false credentials for members of the underground. It was headed by Ewa Kulik and Konrad Bielinski. Kulik was trying to complete doctorate work on William Faulkner; Bielinski was a mathematician. Perhaps most important, the resistance had established a security and intelligence bureau, which was euphemistically referred to as the Bureau of Hygiene and Safety. It was made up of security and intelligence experts (some trained by the CIA in the West) to check out reports of infiltrators and penetrations by the Polish secret police. It was this unit that maintained the secret communications equipment smuggled in by the agency and inspected apartments to make sure they were suitable hideouts. This was the command, control, and communications unit of the underground.

The covert operation program in Poland had been growing rapidly, so Bill Casey sought to overhaul its structure in 1983. From its infancy, the operation had been run through the Frankfurt office of the CIA, working in lockstep with agents in the Warsaw station. But this process was cumbersome, and so far it amounted to a large "black bag operation"—bankrolling the resistance. Several million dollars a year was being smuggled to the underground. But funds alone were not going to be enough, particularly if NSDD-32 was to be carried out in full. The president wanted the level of support to grow, and it was up to Casey to construct a covert supply line for critical materials. It would be similar to the Afghan supply operation, the only difference being that the cargo for Poland would not be lethal. In addition to the high-tech communications equipment that had been supplied the previous spring, the administration wanted the underground fully equipped with fax machines, computers, advanced printing equipment, and more. The AFL-CIO had been providing some materials and doing a pretty good job of keeping it covert. John Poindexter, who had been meeting regularly with AFL-CIO officials, asked Irving Brown a little bit about the union's setup in Poland.

Sweden had already proved quite effective as a transit point for smuggling out activists and sending in the communications gear. It was nearby and had plenty of commerce with Poland. Perhaps more important, it was officially neutral, and therefore was more trusted by Polish authorities.

Casey instructed the Stockholm station to make preliminary arrangements for meetings with Swedish officials during his visit in October. "He planned to persuade the Swedes to go along and help out in the effort to support Solidarity," recalls one aide. "No one thought he could pull it off."[42]

The material conveyor belt for Poland was simple in design. Equipment and supplies would be purchased with CIA funds and managed in Brussels, where one of the largest and most effective Solidarity offices was located. Strategic goods would be brought to Brussels and stored in several warehouses. There they would be repackaged by Solidarity activists and shipped to Stockholm. Once on Swedish soil, the containers would be re-marked and put on a ship in crates marked "tractor parts," "machine tools," and "fish products," bound for a Polish port. The only ingredient missing in this recipe of conspiracy was Swedish cooperation.

1. This series of events is described in Vladimir Solovyov and Elena Klepikova, *Behind the High Kremlin Walls* (New York: Berkley, 1987); one former KGB official interviewed by the author tells the same.
2. Andrei Gromyko, *Gromyko* (New York: Doubleday, 1989), p. 247.
3. Richard Pipes, interview with the author.
4. John Poindexter, interview with the author.
5. Robert McFarlane, interview with the author.
6. Robert McFarlane, interview with the author.
7. John Poindexter, interview with the author.
8. William Clark, interview with the author.
9. Robert McFarlane, interview with the author.
10. Robert McFarlane, interview with the author.
11. John Poindexter, interview with the author.
12. George Shultz, interview with the author.
13. John Poindexter, interview with the author; Robert McFarlane, interview with the author.
14. William Clark, interview with the author.
15. Caspar Weinberger, interview with the author.
16. Aleksandr Bessmertnykh, comments at Princeton University conference "A Retrospective on the End of the Cold War," February 26, 1993.
17. Allan Whittaker, interview with the author.
18. Robert McFarlane, interview with the author.
19. Richard Allen, interview with the author.
20. "Chance Missed, Search Continues," *Izvestiya*, October 17, 1986.
21. *Krasnaya Zvezda*, May 9, 1984.
22. "MIG-25 Based on Technology Spinoffs," *Aviation Week and Space Technology*, October 11, 1976, pp. 18–19.
23. Department of Defense, "The FY 1986 Department of Defense Program for Research, Development and Acquisition" (Washington, DC: U.S. Government Printing Office, 1986), pp. II–15.
24. "Materialy Plenuma Tsentralnoga Comiteta KPSS," Moscow, June 14–15, 1983, p. 25.
25. See Peter Schweizer, "The Soviet Military Today: Going High-Tech," *Orbis: A Journal of World Affairs*, vol. 35 no. 2, pp. 195–206.
26. Vitaly Shlykov, "The Armor Is Strong," *Mezhdunarodnaya Zhizn*, November 1988.
27. Yevgenny Novikov, interview with the author.

28. "Measures Designed to Step Up Work on Problems of Military Strategy," KGB memo no. 2106, December 17, 1984.

29. Herb Meyer, interview with the author.

30. U.S. Department of Commerce, International Trade Administration, "Quantification of Western Exports of High-Technology Products to Communist Countries Through 1983" (Washington, DC, 1985), pp. 12, 28, 29.

31. "Geheimclub COCOM," *Die Zeit*, October 10, 1983, p. 34.

32. Caspar Weinberger, interview with the author.

33. U.S. Treasury Department, "International Oil Pricing, 1983," Executive Summary, pp. 1, 3.

34. Ibid., p. 21.

35. John Poindexter, interview with the author.

36. William Clark, interview with the author.

37. U.S. official, interview with the author.

38. Caspar Weinberger, interview with the author.

39. William Schneider, interview with the author.

40. William Schneider, interview with the author.

41. Interview with the author.

42. Interview with the author.

II

In the earliest days of the Reagan administration, great empha-sis had been placed on changing the psychological dynamics of the Cold War. Putting Moscow on the defensive would provide opportunities to redirect the currents of the competition. The massive defensive buildup being orchestrated by Caspar Weinberger was a tech-nological challenge that went to the heart of Moscow's vulnerabilities. And Moscow was beginning to notice. "Overall, viewed from Moscow, the U.S.-Soviet military balance seemed to be tilting in favor of the United States—and along with it, the perceived aggregate 'correlation of forces,' " recalls Sergei Fedorenko, a division chief with the USA and Canada Institute of the Academy of Sciences.[1]

But the administration did not want simply to check the Soviet military advantage. The president wanted to strike Moscow a geopoliti-cal blow, one that would potentially echo throughout the empire. A possible spot was Afghanistan.

In late March 1983, Bill Casey was back in Pakistan. Estimates put the number of Soviet casualties in the conflict at between 12,000 and 15,000. Spring was just around the corner, and that meant two things in Afghanistan: planting season and major antiguerrilla sweeps by Soviet-backed forces. When the snow lifted and the climate improved, Afghan government and Soviet forces would be on the move again.

But to see in 1983 the covert operation to support the mujahedin was to observe a surprisingly effective machine, in spite of its far-flung components. Beginning in early 1981, Casey had ordered the Directorate of Operations to seek out and recruit Afghans living overseas to help run the international conduit of arms to the rebels. By the spring of 1982, more than one hundred Afghans were trained by the CIA in the art of international arms shipping. Soon they were coordinating the purchase of arms and arranging shipment to the mujahedin under the guidance of CIA officials.

The CIA had gone to great lengths to keep the Afghan project as quiet as possible, particularly for the sake of Pakistan's President Zia, who was walking a geopolitical tightrope. Zia was courageously allowing Washington to use his country as the logistical supply line to the Afghan resistance. Moscow of course knew how the mujahedin were being supplied and pointed an accusatory finger in Zia's direction. "Keep his hands clean," Casey kept telling his people. To that end, there were only six agency officials on the ground handling the entire operation. Rifles, ammunition, and rockets were coming in crates marked "television sets" and "appliances." A whole army of Pakistani ISI officials was put to work carrying the equipment by unmarked trucks to mujahedin staging areas. It was hoped that this might give Zia a fig leaf of deniability.[2]

In 1983 Moscow began turning its gaze toward Pakistan. "The Kremlin and the Soviet General Staff knew that without Pakistan, the resistance was doomed," recalls Mohammad Yousaf.[3] The Soviets were purposely trying to drive millions of Afghan refugees into Pakistan to destabilize the country; there was a massive subversion effort, including thousands of agents from the Afghan KHAD. Bombs were going off in street bazaars across the country; aircraft were increasingly crossing the border to hit mujahedin bases and facilities; and thousands of Soviet weapons were being passed out to every group or tribe with a grudge against Zia. Yuri Andropov and Andrei Gromyko had been unsuccessful in proving their point to Zia in Moscow the previous year. Perhaps a more aggressive course would send the appropriate signal.

Casey's most important meeting was with Zia, who greeted him warmly as he entered the presidential office. Zia offered Casey a seat in a heavily gilt chair with historical symbols from Pakistani provinces etched on it. An aide brought out two glass cups and filled them with a hot, sweet drink. Zia encouraged his guest to try the libation. There was little opening chatter; as always, it was all business between them. The Irish-Catholic businessman and the devout Muslim general had a relationship bordering on comradeship, hammered out in the face of a common threat. But neither had the patience or the taste for small talk.

Casey had brought with him a stack of satellite photos, in this instance of Soviet military deployments in Afghanistan and the placement of troops by Zia's archenemy, India. Zia was always eager to get the folders. The meeting lasted three hours. They talked about Afghanistan, India, and China.

The president, the NSC staff, Caspar Weinberger, and Bill Casey had grown concerned about the possibility of a Soviet thrust into Pakistan. Although there was no intelligence indicating that an attack was pending, there was a consensus that such a move would fit a Soviet pattern. Casey passed along the president's reassurances that the United States was fully behind Zia.

Next Casey raised a "theoretical" military question. In early 1983, he had met with the president and Bill Clark in the Oval Office to discuss the situation in Afghanistan. The conversation turned to raising the stakes for Moscow. The DCI suggested taking the war into the Soviet Union itself, and Reagan liked the idea. "The president and Bill Casey were determined that Moscow pay an ever greater price for its brutal campaign in Afghanistan, including the possibility of taking the war into the Soviet Union itself," recalls Clark.[4]

Pakistani cooperation in such a venture would be absolutely essential, so with the president's blessing Casey raised the subject with Zia. The Pakistani president was evasive, saying that it depended on a variety of circumstances. The issue was dropped, but it would be picked up later.

Aid from the United States was allowing the ISI to conduct extensive training of the mujahedin. They were brave, but published accounts of the mujahedin being "natural warriors" were a myth. After his session with Zia, Casey met with General Akhtar to discuss the battlefield situation. The two had decided early on that a training program was essential in making the mujahedin more effective. The resistance needed to learn tactics, how to function as a military unit, and how to get the best out of their weapons.

Because of a lack of money, only a couple of hundred mujahedin were being trained per month. Akhtar wanted to know if Casey could get more funds for the program. Casey likened the situation to his experiences with the OSS in World War II. Training had been an ingredient in his success. Poorly trained mujahedin were simply wasted. Casey promised more money and also offered CIA specialists in explosives and electronic devices to consult the ISI on special operations.

Missions were becoming increasingly specialized, and the resistance would be making greater use of high-tech explosives and sensitive electronic equipment. Despite the imagery of the mujahedin relying only on faith and an AK-47 rifle, this was going to be a high-tech war.

To make up for the lack of trained mujahedin, Akhtar and Casey developed a sensitive and secret operation to hit targets deep inside Afghanistan of particular economic or military interest to the Soviets using Pakistani specialists directly trained by the CIA. Akhtar would put together teams of ISI volunteers highly trained in special operations who could be trusted completely. The teams would carry out critical tasks—blowing up fuel depots, bridges, roads, and ammo dumps. Casey promised experts in explosives to teach operatives how to use chemical and electronic timing devices, and special control switches.

Akhtar and Casey also agreed that the various factions and tribes in the resistance had to work more closely if the effort was to succeed. Unity would bring greater professionalism. And a resistance that could be more efficient and strategic in its planning and operations would be more effective. But Akhtar pointed out that cooperation between the various groups would be difficult to achieve. Many of the leaders disliked each other; they were competing for power and had different ideologies. Some were religious moderates and pro-Western, others fundamentalist and anti-American.

Casey wanted the war escalated, the stakes raised. This was a chance to get even with the Soviets for Vietnam, he told his hosts, so he wanted the job done right. Maximum casualties and cost to the occupier. "The Soviets had kept the Vietcong supplied with hardware to fight and kill Americans," says Yousaf. "So the United States would now do the same for the mujahedin so they could kill Soviets. This view was prevalent among CIA officials, particularly William Casey."[5]

Soviet casualties were not running high enough as far as the

Reagan administration was concerned. The Kremlin could sustain these losses, Reagan told aides and colleagues, because of the closed nature of its system. He wanted the numbers up, and he wanted the Soviet high command further demoralized. Until recently the guerrillas had lacked area weapons, so killing had been done at relatively short ranges. Now that artillery and rockets were being delivered by the CIA in fairly large quantities, the dynamics of the war would change. There were some intelligence reports that the Soviets were trying to "share the human burden" of sustaining the regime in Kabul by bringing in Warsaw Pact and Cuban personnel. An Afghan officer who defected in October 1982 reported seeing both Cubans and Bulgarians in the field, wearing Afghan army uniforms. The guerrillas claimed that a Bulgarian military base had been set up in Southern Mazar-i-Sharif to provide protection for a fuel pipeline.[6] If true, the reports meant that the human costs of the war were becoming uncomfortable for the Kremlin.

In Kabul, things were also heating up. The resistance had begun a series of bomb attacks against Soviet military targets, and they were having a numbing psychological effect on Soviet commanders and officials. Previously the war had been largely confined to the countryside. Now it was being brought to the cities. Only recently guerrillas had kidnapped a senior Soviet Communist Party official on the streets of Kabul in broad daylight. E. R. Okrimyuk, a personal friend of the Soviet prime minister, Nikolai Tukhonov, was counselor at the Soviet embassy. On his way to Khwaja Ruwash to meet an incoming flight, he was an easy target for abduction. His personal driver, from Tajikistan, stopped the bullet-proof vehicle at a prearranged spot. Okrimyuk was knocked unconscious and driven in his own car past military checkpoints into the countryside.

For Casey operations against the Soviet leadership were an important step in the escalation of the war. So long as the Soviet elite were immune to attacks and threats, they would continue to back the war in Afghanistan. But when the sons of senior party officials and military officers started coming home in pine boxes, things might change. Targeting these individuals was an excellent idea, Casey told Akhtar.

☆   ☆   ☆

That spring Casey was on the picturesque Spanish coast on a stopover. He was visiting his good friend King Fahd, recently elevated from crown prince following the death of King Khalid. Fahd had just completed construction on an enormous villa on the sea. They met beside the deep blue waters of the Mediterranean, under a deep black and starry sky. It was late evening, and there was a slight breeze.

The jittery oil markets were foremost on Fahd's mind. Weeks earlier, oil ministers from around the world had convened a meeting in London to discuss the international market. A collapse in prices appeared to be at hand. The ministers had met at the InterContinental Hotel at Hyde Park Corner for twelve tense and frustrating days. The British National Oil Company had precipitated the crisis by cutting the price of North Sea oil by $3, to $30. Some figured it might trigger a price war. In the end, OPEC backed down, cutting its price by about 15 percent—from $34 to $29 a barrel. It was the first time OPEC had cut prices.

At Fahd's villa the two sat and talked while security personnel wandered around the perimeter of the grounds. The Saudis were facing an economic crunch with revenues down from oil exports. They were being squeezed from the market as they cut production in an attempt to maintain international prices. At the same time the geopolitical seas around Saudi Arabia were increasingly hostile. There had been attacks on oil suppliers in the Gulf. No Saudi boats had been hit, but Tehran was making veiled threats.

The Soviets were stepping up their diplomatic efforts in the region. In early March 1984, Geidar Aliyev was in Syria, a visit wrapped in significance simply because it was taking place. For the first time since Andrei Gromyko had visited in 1974, a senior Politburo member was in Damascus. An Azerbaijani, Aliyev was tall and athletic, favoring English suits and Italian loafers. He was the Middle East expert for the Soviet leadership and was in Syria to try to cement a relationship with that country. He was also there to put pressure on the Saudis. The Syrians were aggressively broadcasting anti–royal family propaganda throughout the Persian Gulf area and trying to inspire subversion. Fahd was also concerned because the Syrians were heavily backing Iran in its war with Iraq. In early 1982, Syrian President Hafez al-Assad had shut off the Iraq-Mediterranean oil pipeline. There were rumors that Syrian

troops were in Iran fighting against Iraq. Shiite extremists, sworn enemies of the royal family, were being fed by Iran and protected by Syria
in Baalbek and the Bekaa. Now Aliyev was indicating a heightened
Soviet interest in the region. It appeared that all of Saudi Arabia's
enemies were conspiring against it. As Caspar Weinberger recalls, "The
Soviets were trying their best to frighten the Saudis, to influence them
through intimidation. We had to make sure they remained wedded to
us."[7]

The king was convinced that the Iranians were going to attack
Saudi shipping and try to close the Strait of Hormuz, the narrow
passageway that tankers take out of the Persian Gulf into the Indian
Ocean. Tehran is getting more aggressive, Fahd told Casey. They will
resort to anything. Casey agreed. The radicalism of the Iranians could
not be contained. It was only to be expected that they would lash out
against the conservative monarchies across the Gulf that represented
everything they rejected. Fahd had a request for Casey. Could the
kingdom buy some "special missiles"? Fahd had in mind Stingers, the
advanced surface to air missiles highly touted as the best in the American
arsenal, or the world for that matter. It was a substantial request. Some
of America's closest allies had not yet received the Stinger. It had been
deployed by U.S. forces in Germany just two years earlier.

Sale of the Stinger might pose an even more difficult challenge
in Congress than the AWACS deal. The Iranian threat to Saudi shipping came not so much from aircraft as from speedboats. No doubt
congressional critics would also raise the augur of Stingers' falling into
the hands of terrorists or a radical Arab state. Casey promised to take
the request back to Washington, where Prince Bandar was already
raising it with other officials.

The two discussed Afghanistan, and Casey brought up the
prospect of escalating the war. Fahd was all for the idea. He would raise
the Saudi contribution to $120 million if necessary. The king also
agreed to cooperate with an anti-Qaddafi operation being planned with
Egyptian Defense Minister Abdel Halim Abu Ghazala. Then Casey
raised the more sensitive issue.

What do you think about taking the Afghan war into Soviet
Central Asia? he asked. He knew that Fahd and the royal family were
smuggling funds to support the burgeoning underground Muslim move-

ment in the region. Some estimates put the figure in the tens of millions. The DCI had in mind an anti-Soviet political campaign, something to stir up the locals and fan nationalist flames in the Soviet Union. He made his request on moral and religious grounds. This would be an ecumenical holy alliance of sorts, the deeply anticommunist and Christian administration in Washington would join forces with the equally anticommunist and Muslim Saudis in common effort against the atheistic Soviet Union.

Fahd was intrigued by the idea, and the two decided to discuss it in greater detail at a future meeting.[8]

The next stop on the itinerary was the People's Republic of China. It had been quite some time since his last visit to Beijing, and Casey was anxious to discuss some sensitive matters. The president, who had so strongly backed Taiwan during the 1980 campaign, was beginning to see the merits of cooperating with the Communist Chinese on several fronts. The enemy of my enemy is my friend, was Casey's view of geopolitics. That had been the case during World War II, when the Western democracies had fought off the Nazis and the Japanese with the help of the Soviets.

Both Weinberger and Casey saw the value in cultivating Beijing in their efforts to deal with the Soviet Union. Weinberger was advocating closer military cooperation. In May, the White House had announced a liberalization of restrictions on technology exports to China. Under the new policy, China was classified as a country friendly to the United States, so acquiring technology would become dramatically easier. Where they shared common interests, Casey wanted to work with Beijing in intelligence and covert action. Afghanistan was a case in point. Dealing with China on sensitive matters was particularly easy: it had no parliament or free press, so covert operations would be simpler to manage and keep secret.

There was already close cooperation between Beijing and Washington on a number of fronts. The electronic eavesdropping facilities along the Soviet border were proving invaluable. Technicians from the United States were secretly manning the facilities in the heart of Central Asia. The Chinese were very helpful in carrying out the Afghan program, providing Soviet bloc arms and other assistance. Casey briefed his hosts on the successes in Afghanistan and the plans for the future.

At the same time, there were growing tensions between Beijing and Moscow, particularly along the common border. The two communist powers were, among other things, fighting for the allegiance of the region's Muslims. The presence in Inner Asia of 45 to 50 million Muslims distributed between the Soviet Union and China had forced the two to devise "Muslim strategies" that were both defensive and offensive. The Soviets had been aggressively working to sow dissent and penetrate the Chinese Muslim populace. An agent named Nikolai Petrovich Zhang and two ethnic Chinese had recently been picked up for spying. Yue Zhongue, a Chinese citizen, was jailed for antistate activities. He had reportedly crossed the border from China into the USSR in 1980 and been recruited by the KGB. He had been sent back to China several times to collect political, military, and economic intelligence.[9] The Soviet effort was tenacious, particularly as it coincided with the thrust into Afghanistan. Soviet propagandists were targeting the Muslim population of Xinjiang Province, using radio stations in Tashkent, Alma-Ata, and Frunze to beam anti-Chinese messages in almost all the Turkish languages as well as Chinese.

Until 1980, the odds in the fight for Muslim loyalty had been stacked heavily in favor of the Soviet Union. Moscow could offer a higher standard of living, while China required greater ideological orthodoxy. But in 1980 two things changed to make the Chinese more aggressive and successful in their operations. The Soviet invasion of Afghanistan provided ample ammunition to the Chinese claim that the Soviets were anti-Muslim. Propaganda broadcasts from China into the USSR consistently played to that theme. At the same time, China made important concessions to Muslim minorities, including the suspension of antireligious crusades and the reopening of old mosques. Salim An-Shiwei, imam of the Dongsi Mosque and chairman of the Islamic Association of Beijing, was invited to Islamabad and elected a member of the Moslem League. He had even approached the Saudis about building a new mosque in China. For Beijing, Islam was emerging as an asset, or at least a tool to use against Moscow.

In addition to consultations with his counterparts in Chinese intelligence, Casey met with Zhu Qizhen, an assistant foreign minister in direct charge of relations with the United States. Any concerns that Beijing had about American intentions were more than covered by what was seen as a greater Soviet challenge. It was apparent that Moscow was trying to encircle China geopolitically. Vietnam, the Vietnam puppet government in Cambodia, and the Soviet invasion in Afghanistan were all part of this strategy, Zhu said.

When the topic turned to Afghanistan, Casey steered the conversation to what the Soviets called "the nationality question." Without being too direct, he hinted that the United States was running a propaganda campaign aimed at Soviet Central Asia, designed to sow dissent. Zhu said such an idea had merit and proposed possible cooperation.

In the spring, there was another of the regular meetings of the National Security Planning Group. Much of the agenda concerned the Middle East, particularly diplomatic efforts in the region. The peace process was stalled, and tensions were still high. The Iran-Iraq War continued to boil, while the threat of Islamic fundamentalism to the modern regimes of the area continued to grow.

Most of the talking was done by Secretary of State George Shultz, who had proposed a comprehensive plan for peace in the region. Casey and Weinberger didn't say much; the peace process was largely the State Department's domain. But they did make a hard pitch for selling Stinger missiles to the Saudis. The Saudis needed another tangible sign of America's commitment to their security, Casey argued. Robert McFarlane agreed that the sale should be considered but pointed out that Congress was unlikely to go along without substantial restrictions. There would have to be a long fight to secure the missiles.

The proposal was tabled so the NSC could examine the issue. Shortly after the NSPG meeting, Casey was on the road again, this time to Europe to look over the Poland operation. The president was always anxious to hear good news.

The Reagan administration was in effect forcing General Jaruzelski to make a Hobson's choice. The United States was demanding the release of political prisoners as a condition for easing sanctions. Complying would threaten the survival of the regime by invigorating the opposition. Failing to comply would keep U.S. sanctions in place. The economy would continue to sink, and Poland would become even more dependent on Moscow. Despite his solid communist credentials, Jaruzelski did not trust the Kremlin, and he loathed the idea of Poland's sinking ever deeper into the Soviet lap. Jaruzelski's father had spent time in a Russian prison camp, and the general harbored lifelong anti-Russian attitudes. Largely because of the American sanctions, Moscow had been compelled to subsidize the Jaruzelski government to the tune of $3 to $4 billion per year. As was always the case, such "aid" would come at a price.

Despite the pinch of sanctions, releasing prisoners was not yet an option. Solidarity was somehow managing to survive. Freeing detained Solidarity activists into such an explosive atmosphere would be a recipe for disaster. Jaruzelski and his men were going to have to wear down the opposition further before any amnesty could be declared.

The first stop on Casey's trip was Frankfurt. It was only a brief two-hour layover while the plane was refueled and serviced. It was 9:30 P.M., and officials from the Frankfurt and Bonn offices met with the DCI in a secure room at the U.S. air base. On hand were six officials intimately involved with the Poland operation. Someone served up hot coffee in Styrofoam cups. The group huddled around the table as jet engines roared in the background.

Reagan's NSDD-32 had made it U.S. policy to seek to undermine Soviet power in Eastern Europe. The president was clearly of a mind to expand the covert supply line once it was developed. Aid was running at just over $2 million per year. The president wanted four times that amount going to sustain the underground. He and key aides on the NSC also wanted to seek out new opportunities in the region, opposition movements that might benefit from financial support. The big question was, what sort of opportunities existed?

Intelligence reports coming out of Poland indicated that Solidarity activists had made contact with and were meeting activists from Czechoslovakia in remote woods along the Czech-Polish border. The meetings were small, and appeared to be exploratory, but they were a start, and they intrigued Casey.

There were also reports of a loose underground in, of all places, Bulgaria. It was separatist and pro-Western, and was supported by individuals near the top strata of Bulgarian life. One of its early organizers was none other than Ludmila Zhukova, daughter of Bulgarian leader Todor Zhivkov. An Oxford graduate, Zhukova was a member of the ruling Politburo. She had a close supporter in Premier Stanko Todorov. By early 1981, the KGB had ordered action taken to squelch the political movement. Todorov was dismissed suddenly. More aggressive action may have been taken against Zhukova. In March she died suddenly in an automobile accident. There was evidence of foul play, but it mattered little. The movement had lost its brightest lights, and the underground had yet to recover.

Intelligence reports on opposition movements in the Soviet bloc were circled to the NSC and read by Bill Casey. Occasionally they were passed along to the president. Along with embassies in the Soviet bloc, the Frankfurt station of the CIA was the best vantage point for this sort of information because it served as the clearinghouse for Soviet bloc defectors coming to the West. The CIA was also providing funds to some émigré groups in Europe in exchange for assistance in debriefing new immigrants from the East.

Casey reviewed the Poland operation with some intelligence officers and asked for more data on underground groups behind the Iron Curtain. This was the sort of thing he loved. Reagan had the vision, the NSC and the Pentagon were directing the strategy, and Casey was in the field carrying it out. "Old Bill would have traveled all the time if he could have," recalls Glenn Campbell. "He loved putting things together, making them happen in the field. All that crap in Washington—the committees, the meetings, the infighting—he could do without. He would much rather be out doing whatever he could making things tough for the Soviets."[10]

Minutes after Casey departed the meeting, his KC-11 was in the air, only the flames of the plane's engines visible in the distance.[11]

When Casey's plane touched down in Rome it was past midnight. The station chief was on hand to greet him, and there were several armed security officials. Terrorism was always a concern for U.S. officials traveling overseas, but extra caution was required when the port of call was Italy and the official was the director of the CIA. The name William J. Casey had appeared on a hit list put together by the terrorist organization the Red Brigades. Everyone was taking it seriously because the Brigades had demonstrated their boldness only two years earlier, when they kidnapped Gen. James Dozier, an American stationed in Italy.

Security officials of the CIA always preferred to protect the director overseas by relying on important preparations and secretiveness. Usually the DCI had a small motorcade, and his travel plans were not announced in advance. Fearing that news of his impending visit might leak, Italian authorities took no chances and were out with a visible show of force. The arrival was uneventful, and by 3:00 A.M. Casey was snug in his bed.

He was up the next morning before six, ready to go. It was a big day personally for Casey. The committed Catholic was going to meet with the pope in private. President Reagan had promised the pontiff during their first meeting in 1982 that he would keep the Vatican fully apprised of what the administration was doing in Poland. A series of envoys, including Gen. Vernon Walters, had been employed for that purpose. The subject of the meeting was going to be Poland.

After breakfast and a briefing by the Rome station, Casey was taken to the private quarters of Pope John Paul II. They met alone for forty minutes. There were no note takers. The meeting was informational. There was a continuous sharing of information at much lower levels. But this meeting was to clarify U.S. policy to the pontiff. John Paul knew that Washington was doing something to sustain Solidarity, but he did not know any specifics. Casey kept it that way.[12]

The stay in Rome was all too short, but the schedule had to be kept. It was late evening, and there was a long flight ahead. The pilot set a course almost due north, leaving the warm waters of the Mediterranean and the Latin architecture of Rome for the cold and bleakness of Stockholm.

The city was overcast, dark and damp. There was also a bone-chilling cold still coming off the Baltic. Casey was expecting his welcome from the Swedes to be about as pleasant. They were not keen about his arrival. The Reagan administration was pushing the Swedes to be more helpful in efforts to stem the flow of technology to Moscow. Sweden was officially neutral, and publicity about the visit of a CIA director could cause serious problems. For one thing, the Swedes were publicly supporting the Sandinista government in Nicaragua, which the Reagan administration was trying to overthrow. Reagan foreign policy was not particularly popular in this part of the world.

Two issues brought Casey to Stockholm. As the Pentagon had surmised, the city for both political and geographical reasons would be a critical choke point in the effort to cut off technology exports to the Soviets. As Casey had determined, Sweden would also be very useful in the efforts to bolster the support being funneled to Solidarity.

Despite Scandinavian coolness and an official policy of neutrality, leaning heavily on Stockholm to tighten up on the shipment of high-technology goods to the Soviet bloc was bearing some fruit. In the late 1970s, Sweden was a busy transshipment point for high-technology goods destined for Moscow. A number of Swedish companies had become quite adept at purchasing goods from the United States and selling them to Moscow for a markup. They were making a healthy profit. It was a foolproof system because U.S. companies eager for sales were technically selling to Sweden. They didn't need to ask what the Swedes would do with the goods. And Swedish companies did not have restrictions on what they exported to the Soviet bloc.

For Caspar Weinberger, shutting down the Scandinavian highway was critical if Moscow was going to be hit hard in the technology area. A quiet and secret campaign was launched in early 1981 to win the Swedes over to cooperating in the strategic embargo. Persuasion would not be enough. "The Swedes just didn't consider themselves to be part of the Western security system," recalls Stef Halper. "To them it was our problem, not theirs."[13] So Assistant Secretary of State Richard Perle made it their problem.

The U.S. Export Act of 1979 gave the president the option of restricting access to American technology to foreign countries or companies that did not cooperate on export issues. As had been demonstrated during the pipeline fight, the administration could restrict access to U.S. technology on national security grounds. And it was threatening just that to the Swedes if the policing of exports to the Soviet bloc was enhanced. According to a secret memo drawn up at the Department of Defense in early 1982, the U.S. objective vis-à-vis Sweden (and for that matter the other neutrals, Switzerland and Austria) was threefold.

First, the United States wanted to get the Swedes to protect the U.S. technology that they were importing for their own use. Second, the administration wanted Sweden to prevent sensitive U.S. products passing through their free ports, duty-free zones, and bonded warehouses from being diverted to the Soviet bloc. And third, America wanted to convince the neutrals to deny the Soviet bloc high-tech products that they manufactured themselves.[14]

To attain these goals, the administration was using both the carrot and the stick. On the one hand, Swedish companies such as L. M. Ericsson AB and ASEA AB were being threatened with reduced access to the U.S. market when they were accused of high-technology exports to the Soviet bloc. On the other hand, if Swedish companies and officials cooperated with Washington, U.S. export licenses would treat Swedish companies as generously as allied countries. That would be a very lucrative privilege.

In addition, the Reagan administration sweetened the pot by offering Stockholm access to cutting edge technologies. Sweden badly needed new technologies to develop a fighter-bomber it was building, the JAS 39 Gripen. Weinberger offered Stockholm the blueprints of a state-of-the-art General Electric jet engine and other aerospace technology from Honeywell, Lear Siegler, and Teledyne, if the Swedes would curtail high-technology exports destined for Moscow.[15]

Casey was in Stockholm to follow up on these efforts and to explore what sort of progress was being made. The political terrain was unpredictable. The Conservative government of Prime Minister Thorbjorn Falldin had been thrown out of office. Olof Palme, the socialist who was highly critical of American foreign policy, was now back in power. After a casual breakfast meeting in Stockholm's old town, Casey met with Swedish government officials. The series of secret gatherings with officials from the Ministry of Defense and the prime minister's office was unprecedented. The whole situation was delicate, and somewhat awkward.

To Casey's surprise, Sweden was willing to work more closely with Washington than had been anticipated. The Defense Ministry was concerned about repeated intrusions of Soviet submarines into Swedish waters, which were by now occurring almost daily. The Swedish navy was having trouble tracking the subs and was interested in any intelligence the Americans might be able to provide. Casey said he would look into it.

The prime minister's office also expressed an interest in cooperating on technology issues with Washington. They did not agree with the American strategy of "economic warfare" against Moscow, but economic realities were driving them to cooperate. The United States had replaced Germany as the largest importer of Swedish goods. Exports had nearly doubled over the last half dozen years. If the United States tightened up on Swedish export licenses, that trend would be put in jeopardy. Palme did not want to risk setting off a crisis that would damage the Swedish economy. The U.S. government wanted good relations with Sweden, Casey told his hosts. Sweden's economy would benefit greatly if the country would just cut high-tech exports to the Soviet bloc.

The DCI then raised the other topic that had brought him to Sweden. Stockholm was the best conduit to Poland. The CIA wanted to export "strategic goods" to Solidarity, but it needed the assistance of the Swedish government. Falldin's government had been helpful in 1981, when equipment had been smuggled in to set up a command, control, and communications system for the underground. But now Casey wanted to establish a permanent pipeline, to funnel material supplies to Solidarity on a regular basis.

It was no doubt a bold request of neutral Sweden. Palme was highly critical of U.S. policy in Central America and had been one of the first leaders in Europe to back the Vietcong in Vietnam. But Casey took the risk because of some promising signs. The Swedes were already cooperating with the agency on Afghanistan. Although they had balked at providing lethal aid to the mujahedin, they were donating millions of dollars' worth of medical supplies that the agency was shipping to Karachi.

Casey probably also recalled the days during the Second World War when the Swedes had been useful, despite their officially stated policy of neutrality. To get economic intelligence on the Nazi war effort, young Bill Casey had pushed for the recruitment of Swedish businessmen to collect information while visiting Germany. They were moving in and out of the country with relative ease, and they understood German industry. Perhaps, he had suggested, the Swedes might even help him recruit anti-Nazi German business.[16]

Casey had brought to Stockholm several favorable letters from senior labor leaders in the United States and Western Europe. Irving Brown of the AFL-CIO had made some calls and arranged for trusted leaders in Europe to write letters. They were brief but helpful, an indication to Stockholm that other European social democrats thought it was worth hearing what Casey had to say.

The officials from the Ministry of Defense and the prime minister's office exited and told Casey to wait for a phone call. Several hours later, the phone rang in his suite. It was the soft, gentle voice of Olof Palme.

Casey was direct and to the point. He had come to Sweden to explore the technology security precautions that had been put in place. But, he told Palme, I also want help. He appealed to the prime minister as a man committed to labor movements. Solidarity was struggling, and might not survive. The U.S. government wanted to ship some goods from time to time to Gdansk. But to make the operation a success, he needed access to a neutral port and the cooperation of government officials. He hinted that he could have just tried the operation without alerting Palme, but working together would be much more productive.

Palme was equally brief. Without hesitation he agreed to do what he could. They spoke for only ten minutes or so, and never again. But it was an enormously helpful conversation. Within weeks there was an infrastructure in place to process supplies going to Poland. Export and customs officials purposely mislabeled certain crates destined for Gdansk. It was a setup that would not be suspected by Polish authorities.

A mile high after having pulled off the impossible—convincing Olof Palme to cooperate with the CIA—Casey made his final stop in Stockholm, a small late afternoon lunch with Swedish military officials. The meeting was quick and uneventful.[17]

Shortly after Bill Casey returned to Washington he read an intelligence assessment by Herb Meyer that painted a stark and desperate portrait of the Soviet economy. The report began by noting the poor economic performance and shortages that were plaguing the "ailing" superpower. It then outlined the "heavy burdens" on the system. Foremost was the weight of defense spending, which consumed an ever greater share of the economy. But it was the conclusion that intrigued Casey: failure to arrest these trends meant "the Soviet system could implode." Meyer's assessment ran contrary to everything the Soviet section of CIA and other intelligence agencies were reporting. Modest growth with perhaps some structural difficulties was the conventional wisdom. Casey sent the report to the president and the NSC.[18]

The situation in Moscow was like the Russian winter—very bleak. Yuri Andropov's health had taken a turn for the worse. He was now a permanent guest in the heavily protected VIP suite of the Kuntsevo Hospital. He was running the country by phone and dictated memoranda. One kidney had been removed, but the kidney disease that plagued him persisted. On top of that he was having heart trouble and had diabetes. He was flat on his back, and his movement was restricted. When Ali Nassar Mohammad al-Hassani, the president of South Yemen, arrived for a state visit in November 1983, Andropov was in a weakened state, with a hollowed face and soft voice. Andropov received the visitor from his bed.

As the general secretary dangled between life and death, Washington was a constant preoccupation in the halls of the Kremlin. The anticommunist rhetoric, the tightening technological web, a defense buildup seemingly without end, and covert operations in places such as Afghanistan and Poland would have been of serious concern taken individually. But their combined weight created a strong sense of foreboding and alarm in Communist Party circles. In response, the Central Committee began a concerted effort to prepare the party cadre and the general populace for what they believed might become a serious crisis or confrontation with the United States. Hundreds of select meetings were held across the USSR in which 18 million members of the CPSU were briefed about the "aggressive intentions of the enemy" in October 1983. A crude documentary film produced by the Defense Ministry was broadcast on Soviet television. It portrayed an administration in Washington committed to world dominion through military power and economic subversion. There were images of U.S. nuclear explosions and American military hardware. There were also graphic pictures of severely injured or dead war victims.[19]

These efforts were more than the usual propaganda antics designed to manipulate the Soviet populace by cynically sowing fear of the West. "The Central Committee realized that they were facing a committed government in Washington," recalls Yevgenny Novikov. "They saw activity on all fronts; not just reactions and reflexes, but initiatives that were testing Soviet power. It frightened them to death."[20] Aleksandr

Bessmertnykh recalls, "All the leaks and all the reports that we were getting from our own intelligence in the United States . . . indicated that the United States was serious about overwhelming the Soviet Union in one basic strategic effort."[21]

At the same time, the KGB was finalizing a plan to counter a perceived intelligence challenge posed by the United States. Entitled "Plan of Basic Counterintelligence Measures for Intensifying to a Greater Degree the Struggle Against the Subversive Intelligence Activities of the American Special Services in the Period 1983–1987," it established priorities for KGB residences abroad. It noted that "the United States special services are continually increasing their subversive intelligence activities against the USSR and expanding the scale on which hostile methods are used to undermine the military and economic potential." As a result, a key priority for the KGB had become "obtaining intelligence" on "the adversary plans and actions to undermine the Soviet economy, or commercial and economic, scientific and technical cooperation between the U.S.S.R. and other countries."[22]

For the KGB, the American offensive and the strategy of exploiting Soviet weaknesses created new demands. "Now is the time for us to anticipate literally every large scale operation of the United States," the report said. "To seek to achieve that is our primary task."

At the end of 1983, the heads of the intelligence service convened a special meeting at KGB headquarters to review the work of the past two years. It was organized and directed by Vladimir Kryuchkov, the head of the KGB's First Service. Kryuchkov (code-named Alyoshan) was an aggressive, almost mechanical personality, with real-world working-class credentials. He was an Andropov protégé and was rumored to work sixteen- to eighteen-hour days, six days a week. He was fascinated by the career of the British agent Sidney Reilly, the spy active in revolutionary Russia, and sometimes unnerved his colleagues by squeezing tennis balls to strengthen his grip, an image comparable to Captain Queeg and his steel balls in *The Caine Mutiny.*

At the session, Kryuchkov stressed that Moscow was building communism "in a complex international situation. Revolutionary imperialist groups in the USA have openly embarked on a course of confrontation. They are increasing tension in literally all sectors of the struggle between the two opposed social systems." It was not by coincidence that

Kryuchkov's report focused on the three central strands of the Reagan administration's policy. The KGB leader warned that the military technological competition was intensifying and that tracking U.S. technological breakthroughs was critical: "It is important not to allow any alteration in the existing strategic parity or permit the adversary to gain military superiority through any scientific or technical breakthrough." He expressed serious concern about the U.S. strategy of "economic warfare." "International economic problems are becoming increasingly important in the information gathering field. This is due on the one hand to the need to counteract the adversary's designs to undermine the economy of the countries of the socialist community by means of 'economic warfare,' and on the other hand, the need to make use of economic facilities of capitalism in the interests of the economy of the Soviet Union." Finally, Kryuchkov expressed concern about American geostrategic "designs," particularly in Afghanistan and Poland.

For the stern KGB chief, the U.S. strategy warranted a powerful KGB response. He concluded, "The main problem in this field is to achieve more active participation by our partners in the struggle against the main adversary. Great tact must be displayed here. We must recognize that their interests do not always coincide with ours. Therefore in cooperation it is above all essential to define the range of common interests, and to be purposeful and tactful in making the heads of security agencies understand how vitally important it is for them to combat the subversive activities of the American special services."

Throughout October and early November, senior KGB officials formulated the service's "Work Plan for 1984." The International Department of the Central Committee outlined Soviet objectives and goals, and Boris Ponomarev, member of the Politburo, relayed them to Kryuchkov. Like the earlier meeting, the work plan reflected a Soviet preoccupation with the three strands of the secret U.S. strategy. In particular, it stated emphatically that collecting "the following is essential":

> Plans and subversive actions by the main adversary directed toward weakening the unity of the countries of the socialist community, to destabilize the situation in individual socialist countries (especially in Poland), and in

particular, the use of economic levers and ideological diversion.

Countering the USA's attempt to curtail commercial, economic and scientific contacts between developed capitalist countries and the Soviet Union.

In reviewing the work of KGB agents in previous years, Kryuchkov made special mention of the U.S. effort to curtail Soviet access to high technology: "Taking into account the additional measures adopted by the adversary, in the first place the USA, to reinforce control over observance of secrecy and the embargo on export of commodities, scientific and technical intelligence, we must analyze the existing situation in greater depth and discover fresh resources for dealing with scientific and technological intelligence."[23]

1. Sergei Fedorenko, "Roots and Origins of the Protracted Soviet Crisis," in *The Soviet Union After Perestroika: Change and Continuity* (Washington, DC: Brassey's, 1991), p. 87.
2. Vincent Cannistraro, interview with the author; Mohammad Yousaf, interview with the author.
3. Mohammad Yousaf, interview with the author.
4. William Clark, interview with the author.
5. Mohammad Yousaf, interview with the author.
6. Interview with U.S. intelligence official; John Fullerton, *The Soviet Occupation of Afghanistan* (London: Methuen, 1984), p. 96.
7. Caspar Weinberger, interview with the author.
8. U.S. official, interview with the author.
9. *Daily Telegraph*, December 3, 1981.
10. Glenn Campbell, interview with the author.
11. U.S. official, interview with the author.
12. Pope did not know specifics, from John Poindexter, interview. Details of Casey meeting, from U.S. official, interview.
13. Stef Halper, interview with the author.
14. Caspar Weinberger, interview with the author.
15. Caspar Weinberger, interview with the author.
16. William Casey, *The Secret War Against Hitler* (Washington, DC: Regnery, 1988), pp. 58–59.
17. U.S. official, interview with the author.

18. Herb Meyer, interview with the author.
19. Don Oberdorfer, *The Turn* (New York: Poseidon, 1991), p. 64.
20. Yevgenny Novikov, interview with the author.
21. Aleksandr Bessmertnykh, comments at Princeton University conference, "A Retrospective on the End of the Cold War," May 3, 1993.
22. KGB report no. 84/KR, January 6, 1984, in Christopher Andrew and Oleg Gordievsky, *More Instructions from the Centre: Top Secret Files on KGB Global Operations, 1975–1985* (London: Frank Cass, 1992), pp. 122–24.
23. KGB report no. 2126/PR, November 11, 1983, in Christopher Andrew and Oleg Gordievsky, *Instructions from the Centre: Top Secret Files on KGB Foreign Operations* (London: Hodder and Stoughton, 1991), pp. 16–22.

12

The year 1984 brought a national election in the United States, and in Moscow special attention was being paid to the tone of the campaign. It was pivotal for the Kremlin. Faint hope that Reagan might turn out to be an anticommunist Republican in the mold of Richard Nixon, who had instituted détente and warmed relations with the communist Chinese, was gone. Reagan had deeper ideological commitments and a strategic agenda that went beyond realpolitik. In the name of his cause, the administration was waging an economic war against the Soviet bloc and conducting covert operations in key Soviet zones (Poland and Afghanistan). At the same time, an enormous and intense high-tech defense buildup was being orchestrated. Reagan not only spoke of the "evil empire" and Marxism-Leninism's ending up on the "ash heap of history," he believed it.

Soviet officials were quite open with the American press about their assessment of the Reagan agenda. Radomir Bogdanov, deputy director of the USA and Canada Institute and a former senior official with the KGB, told Don Oberdorfer of *The Washington Post*: "You [Americans] are trying to destroy our economy, to interfere with our trade, to overwhelm and make us inferior in the strategic field." Valentin Falin of the Central Committee told the same reporter that

Reagan did not want conciliation with Moscow but rather "the circumcision of socialism."[1]

Concerns in the inner sanctum of the Kremlin led to a KGB active measures operation designed to undermine Reagan's reelection prospects, which was well under way by January 1984. L. F. Sotskov, the first deputy head of the KGB's Service A (Active Measures) was in charge of the fairly amateur plot. Around the globe, KGB residences were tasked with disseminating forged documents and hostile propaganda about the Reagan administration, all zeroing in on the theme "Reagan Means War."[2] On a more quiet front, the KGB was working earnestly to figure out how to exploit partisan political differences in the United States for its own ends.

Viktor Chebrikov, the new chairman of the KGB, had written a hand-signed letter to General Secretary Yuri Andropov in May 1983 about the possibility of working to weaken American political resolve by manipulating the opposition. Specifically, Chebrikov wrote concerning indirect dealings he claimed to have had with U.S. Sen. Edward Kennedy on May 9 and 10, 1983. Former U.S. Sen. John Tunney of California was the alleged go-between. "Using confidential contact, the Senator had asked him to bring the following to the attention of General Secretary Andropov." In his memo, Chebrikov alleged that through Tunney, Senator Kennedy wanted the Kremlin to know that he blamed Ronald Reagan's intransigence for the poor state of U.S.-Soviet relations. Chebrikov summarized this view by writing, "The principal danger was that Reagan refused to correct that policy." According to Chebrikov, Tunney also told him "that in the interest of world peace it would be useful and timely to take a few extra steps to counteract the militaristic policies of Ronald Reagan." What Kennedy wanted, according to Chebrikov, was an invitation for face-to-face talks with Andropov. "The Senator considers that would equip him with Soviet positions in arms control and add conviction to his own appearances on the subject in the U.S."

In the end, no action was taken on the alleged contacts. Andropov appeared unimpressed with Chebrikov's report, writing it off as an exaggerated description of a conversation, designed to impress the Politburo. Any signals from Kennedy were by no means clear, even if Andropov had taken the Chebrikov memo at face value. While the senator from Massachusetts did work for a more accommodating policy toward the Soviet Union, he publicly criticized the Soviet record on human rights and the repression in Poland. However, even if Andropov was not persuaded that Kennedy might unwittingly serve Soviet ends, he did like the idea of working to undermine Reagan. The Chebrikov report inspired some thoughts. In a typed note to Foreign Minister Gromyko, Andropov indicated that he wanted to turn Reagan's tough anti-Soviet positions into a campaign liability. He wrote, "The question of receiving Kennedy raises doubts in my mind. If the time ever comes to talk to the Democrats, then it would be better to meet one of the presidential candidates."[3]

As Andropov mulled over ideas to undermine Reagan's political position, his physical constitution was rapidly worsening. Toward the end of January, the gradual decline in health that had characterized his entire tenure as general secretary suddenly intensified. His internal organs were failing him one after another. Ever committed to the cause, Andropov was reportedly working on a memo when he died in his hospital room at 4:50 P.M. on February 9.

Days after Andropov's heart stopped beating, Bill Casey was on a plane for a secret thirteen-country journey. He was continuing to serve as a chief implementer of the strategic offensive that placed a heavy emphasis on covert operations. On this trip, Casey would make progress on every aspect of the anti-Soviet strategy, by now largely in place. He would visit Pakistan and put in motion one of the most sensitive and secret operations of the Cold War—the Afghan war would be taken into the Soviet Union; cooperation with China would evolve into efforts to destabilize Soviet Central Asia; the U.S.-Saudi relationship would be solidified; and the network in Poland would be expanded as supplies flowed with greater frequency.

Usually the DCI's black spy plane headed east through Europe for initial consultations. But this time his travels took him west, with Honolulu as the first stopover. Registered at a hotel under the name Mr. X. Smith, Casey had a good night's sleep and departed early the next morning. He worked the phone a bit, then read some reports.

The second stop was Tokyo, where he consulted with Japanese officials and discussed international oil pricing. The National Security Council staff members, particularly Roger Robinson and Bill Martin, were concerned about a possible jump in market prices. Robert McFarlane asked Robinson and Martin (an energy expert) to outline an alliance-wide strategy that would send the right signals to the market and prevent a sudden rise. Weeks later, Robinson and Martin coauthored a document on restraining oil price increases. It became a national security decision directive, signed by the president in April. Among other things, it called for the early, coordinated release of allied oil stocks if prices started creeping up. It directed the NSC to gain the cooperation of American allies—West Germany, France, Japan, and Britain. Robinson traveled to several foreign capitals campaigning for a concerted response. He and a small U.S. delegation succeeded in getting quiet agreements from several allied governments, including the Japanese, for an early release of oil stocks in the event of any significant price rise. "We sent a message to the market that if oil prices began to rise, the U.S. and its allies were going to flood the world with oil," recalls Robinson. "Speculators were going to be thrashed this time around."[4] And the Soviets were not going to profit. Casey, under the guidance of the White House, reinforced that theme in several meetings with government officials in Tokyo.

From Tokyo, Casey proceeded to Beijing, a destination he looked forward to eagerly. An avid reader of Chinese history, he was somewhat of a lay expert on Christian missionaries in China. Along with Caspar Weinberger, George Shultz, Robert McFarlane, and George Bush, Casey held firmly to the view that the Chinese were an enormous counterweight to the Soviet Union. They had fewer illusions about Moscow than just about anyone. Since the earliest days in 1981, the administration had been quietly flirting with Beijing, interested less in a marriage than in a courtship of convenience.

The DCI would spend several days in Beijing, covering with his hosts a constellation of issues, all of which had been discussed in White House meetings before his departure. There was intelligence sharing and fine-tuning the management of the electronic eavesdropping facilities along the Soviet border; the war in Afghanistan; the Vietnamese invasion of and civil war in Cambodia; and general discussions about the possibility of joint operations.

One night the Chinese foreign minister threw a private dinner for the director in a palatial and ancient dining hall. The foreign minister sat on Casey's right, while Ling Yun, the minister for state security, sat on his left. Directly across from Casey sat Ted Price, the CIA station chief. There was an enormous feast—duck, pork, chicken, and fish, covered with a variety of sauces and spices. Casey dug in for several helpings of just about everything. His hosts were amused and pleased at the zeal he displayed in consuming the food, all the while traveling the globe verbally with them. The Chinese listened politely but had trouble understanding most of the rhetorical flourishes their interlocutor threw out.

Near the conclusion of the dinner, the Chinese agreed to up their support for the mujahedin in Afghanistan. Someone offered a toast to the joint venture turning back Soviet adventurism. It ended up being an enjoyable evening for all. Throughout Casey displayed the constitution of a college student, staying up until the early morning, despite having traveled almost 12,000 miles.[5]

From Beijing Casey flew to Islamabad. He arrived at night, which among CIA and ISI officials was becoming a tradition. Pakistan was still being squeezed by Moscow. Verbal threats were being made, and aircraft were crossing the frontier with greater frequency than ever before, strafing mujahedin targets. In late January, two MIG jets had bombed and rocketed a remote Pakistani border village, killing forty civilians and injuring sixty.[6] The aggressive scorched-earth policy being carried out in Afghanistan continued to send refugees by the millions into Pakistan for sanctuary.

The meeting was a warm reunion of compatriots. Joining the two was the Pakistani foreign minister, Yaqub Khan, a brilliant man who waxed philosophical on a wide array of political and world issues. He could think around most corners that other leaders did not even see, and like Zia he was staunchly pro-Western and anti-Soviet. Casey brought words of encouragement and support. The administration was going to push for more aid to deal with the refugee problem. Efforts in Congress to reduce military assistance to Pakistan would be beaten back. "Keep the Afghan pipeline open, and the aid will continue," he said happily. Zia had a tungsten spine when it came to fighting the Soviets. He probably needed it.

There was also the nasty business of the threat to Zia. A U.S. diplomat in Moscow had been told at a diplomatic function that the

Kremlin would "get even" with Zia for his unwavering support for the mujahedin.[7] It was a pretty veiled threat, but Casey was taking it seriously. He offered additional CIA protection for the president and his closest advisers. Agency officials would be brought into Islamabad to beef up security and assess the procedures being used to protect Zia. Casey also brought another stack of valuable satellite photos.

He then turned to what he wanted. On January 24, Afghan guerrillas operating out of Meshed, Iran, had launched attacks across the border into the USSR, he told his hosts. The guerrillas had crossed into Turkmenistan, laying mines on roads, attacking isolated military posts, and ambushing Soviet border patrols. There was quite a large assault on a customs post at Torghondi, and guerrilla forces killed several guards and captured some arms and ammunition. This was something Casey wanted to do—take the war into the Soviet Union. "Casey had no problem going into Soviet Central Asia," says Fred Ikle. "He simply told Zia and Yaqub Khan, this is something that should be done." Zia nodded his approval. "Raise this matter with General Akhtar" was all the president said.[8]

From Zia's presidential office, a heavily guarded motorcade of bullet-proof sedans took Casey to an ISI command office. There he met with Brig. Mohammad Yousaf, director of the ISI's Afghan Bureau, and General Akhtar. The three sat down informally over some Afghan tea and light delicacies.

At a simple worktable they started out discussing the conduct of the war in Afghanistan. The arms pipeline was now working with only a few glitches, and the quality of arms arriving had improved. The mujahedin leaders had finally agreed to some sort of unified political structure, thanks to the hard work of General Akhtar. Now it was only a question of getting greater cooperation on the battlefield.

When discussions turned to the Soviet side of the war, there was an air of concern. Intelligence sources in Kabul were telling the Pakistani ISI that Moscow was actively considering the division of Afghanistan, with the north becoming part of Soviet territory. "The Soviets could not control Afghanistan, so they made a plan to divide Afghanistan into two halves," recalls Yousaf. "They planned on exploiting the north-south rivalry within Afghanistan, and claiming the north as their own."[9] To counter the move, the ISI was planning to further enlarge operations in the northern provinces. Akhtar wanted to train thousands of additional mujahedin on an emergency basis and send them to the northern reaches of Afghanistan. But he needed extra funds. Could the CIA help?

As he always did, Casey agreed to come up with the money to train an additional 6,000 mujahedin for the north. But then the DCI raised the notion of pushing even farther north, into the Soviet Union itself.

Casey went toward the wall map in the office. In rolled up shirt sleeves and loosened tie, he began. "The Soviet Union is vulnerable to ethnic tensions. It is the last multiethnic empire and eventually will face national challenges. Northern Afghanistan is a springboard to Soviet Central Asia." Pointing to the map and then looking at his hosts, he said, "This is the soft underbelly of the Soviet Union. We should smuggle literature, to stir dissent. Then we should ship arms, to encourage local uprisings."

The room was completely silent. It was a shocking suggestion. Yousaf recalls being a little surprised at the bluntness of Casey's tone and suggestion. "Mr. Casey was conscious of this Soviet weakness and grave vulnerability. And Mr. Casey was the first one to have openly pointed out this vulnerability. I can vividly remember that he used this phrase 'soft underbelly.' As you know, Mr. Casey was a highly diplomatic, secretive, and intelligent man, who would never easily give away his true feelings. But surprisingly, he never tried to hide his built-in hatred for communism and in particular the USSR."[10]

Putting together a military operation and carrying it into the Soviet Union had never been done. There had been no combat on Soviet territory since the Second World War. The diplomatic and military repercussions could be colossal. Pakistan as a sponsor of the mujahedin could be a target for military retaliation. But so could its sponsor, particularly if it became known in the Kremlin that this was a Reagan initiative. Yet the strategic opportunity was hard to pass up. How better to punish Moscow for its aggressive actions in Afghanistan than to bring the war to its soil?

People living in northern Afghanistan and Soviet Central Asia had much in common ethnically; they had more common blood than did the people of northern and southern Afghanistan. They shared religion, culture, and history. Since the late 1970s, Moscow had become particularly concerned about the spread of Islam in Soviet Central Asia. Units of the KGB in the Asian republics were tasked with aggressively clamping down on the flourishing underground Islamic revival. The Iranian revolution and the jihad in Afghanistan were encouraging acts of defiance throughout the republics.

The next morning, having discussed several ventures in detail, Bill Casey boarded his plane. He left behind the embryo of perhaps the most bold covert operation of the Cold War era. Pakistan had consented to plans to attack targets inside the Soviet Union.

The Pakistani ISI began almost immediately exploring how the secret war inside the communist superpower should be launched. Several possibilities were being considered. Casey had suggested sending books and literature in first, along with exploratory teams to get a feel for the local situation. Mohammad Yousaf began discussions with a CIA psychological warfare expert about what sort of literature might be distributed. An Uzbek who had been working for the CIA since the late 1940s, he suggested the Koran and several obscure books describing Soviet atrocities against Uzbeks. The CIA paid to have tens of thousands printed and brought to Peshawar.

Weeks later Yousaf summoned a number of mujahedin commanders from the northern provinces to his office. A comprehensive screening process soon began. Candidates for the supersecret probes into the Soviet Union would have to be completely trustworthy, in both temperament and politics. The operations would require dexterity and courage, subtlety and discretion.

After completing the screening, Yousaf asked several commanders to make contact with Soviet citizens across the Amu River and do some investigating. Would the Koran be welcomed? Would any locals be willing to participate in future operations or share intelligence on Soviet troop movements or industrial installations? Could some locals act as guides? He wanted more information before any operations were started.

At the same time, Yousaf summoned an outsider to his office. Wali Beg (a pseudonym) was fifty-three but looked much older. He had an ivory white beard and worn, tired skin. He was a farmer and an Uzbek who had lived much of his life in Afghanistan, on the southern banks of the Amu. His house was near the northern tip of Kunduz

Province, near the ancient Afghan port of Sherkhan. As a boy, Beg regularly crossed the Amu with his father to meet relatives—aunts, uncles, cousins, and grandparents—living on the other side. They used a traditional ferry, a flat-bottom boat pulled by two swimming horses. He was familiar with the area. The Soviets had driven Beg from his home, killing two sons and a daughter. He was now living in Pakistan as a carpet maker. Beg had great knowledge of the area and would provide independent analysis of the situation. "For our purpose Wali's knowledge of the border region, coupled with his oath of vengeance against the Soviets, made him an ideal mujahedin to carry the war over the Amu," recalls Yousaf.[11]

From Pakistan, Casey ventured to Saudi Arabia for secret meetings with King Fahd and Prince Turki. Despite having circumnavigated half the globe, Casey was bubbling with enthusiasm as he landed in Riyadh. After a morning mass, arranged in secret by his Saudi hosts, he prepared for his meetings. The Afghan program was running smoothly, which would please Fahd. The king enjoyed getting updates on the war and hearing news of great victories. And the Saudi security program was progressing nicely. The agency had been able to tip the Saudis off about several potential threats.

Casey entered the Royal Palace and was greeted warmly by the king. It had been a hard few months since their last meeting. At that time, Fahd had been somber, even slightly depressed. The Saudi economy was in a tailspin, with oil revenues down sharply. Production had been cut back to stabilize the world price. Natural gas was an inviting alternative, replacing oil in a growing number of industries around the world. The Saudi role as swing producer had worked well when the market was solid. But with rampant overproduction by a number of countries, that role was becoming very costly. Along with these economic woes, the tempo of Iranian intrusions into Saudi airspace was rising. And the visit paid by President Hassani of South Yemen to Moscow in November reignited lingering paranoia about Soviet designs in the region. Members of the Reagan administration, particularly Caspar Weinberger and Bill Casey, were quick to allay such fears as they ensured the Saudis of the U.S. commitment.

The most immediate security concern was Iran. At the suggestion of the NSC, President Reagan had requested that the CIA launch a covert operation to overthrow the Ayatollah Khomeini. The program was just beginning and was pretty mild. The CIA was establishing a chain of covert sanctuaries in Turkey for anti-Khomeini exiles. Distributing leaflets and making propaganda broadcasts was the extent of the activity. It was not expected to do much to the mullahs' hold on power and would do little to offer comfort to King Fahd. At the same time, Operation Staunch, a worldwide campaign to persuade countries not to sell arms to Iran, was in full swing. Pushed by Secretary of State George Shultz, Staunch could be devastating to Tehran if all the pieces were brought into place. The diplomatic side was being handled by State, but the CIA was taking care of the more delicate covert aspects of the operation. Agency officials were secretly working with government officials around the world, trying to persuade them to cut their exports.

Staunch would take time, something Fahd believed was in scarce supply. He was worried about the immediate military challenge. In early 1984, the Iranian army was launching a number of attacks against the Iraqis as the bloody, stalemated war continued. Perhaps ominously, the Revolutionary Guards were making their most aggressive push in the south, near the town of Basra. Wave after wave of raw recruits were being tossed at Iraqi fortifications. If they somehow succeeded in breaking through, Iranian forces would be only a few hundred miles from Saudi oil fields. King Fahd did not put much faith in diplomatic campaigns that could yield results in the medium to long term or in minor covert operations. He needed reassurances that the United States would stand by him and provide the military hardware necessary.

Casey reminded Fahd that the president would never let the royal family fall. Reagan had said publicly in 1981 that there would be no replay of Iran in Saudi Arabia with the king playing the role of the shah. The development of USCENTCOM was part of that commitment, Casey reminded Fahd. It was genuine muscle to protect Saudi territorial integrity.

Fahd, deeply naive in some ways but intensely shrewd in others, did not want just talk. He wanted something tangible from the president that let him know he could rely on Washington. Prince Bandar was asking Secretary of State Shultz for a formal written clarification on the president's commitment. Fahd also wanted the Stinger missiles he had asked for. Numerous requests had been made, and the administration appeared to be balking.

The Stingers were a very sensitive matter, Casey told Fahd. It needed to be handled even more delicately than the AWACS sale. Fahd agreed, but the sale was a test of America's real commitment to the royal family. Close friends and allies do not fail to support one another, he told Casey.

Fahd then suggested that the United States consider an approach to the Iranians. The Saudis had historically tried to maintain relations even with their enemies. Fahd thought there might be benefits in dialogue, particularly with Iranian moderates. Casey gave a muted response to the suggestion.

He then pulled out some folio folders and placed them before the king. They were intelligence updates on the Afghan project, and on the decision reached with Zia to take the war into Soviet Central Asia. This was about throwing off the Russian yoke and freeing the passions of millions of devout Muslims, Casey told Fahd. It would also convince Moscow to reconsider its commitment to Afghanistan by substantially raising the stakes. Casey wanted to bring the Saudis in on the deal and perhaps convince Turki to commit his resources in the region to a joint operation. It wouldn't be too blatant or large, just something to stir the pot. Fahd agreed in principle to cooperate but wanted more specifics. Casey agreed to relay the plans through Turki as soon as they were developed.

The two discussed several other joint operations, including destabilization operations against two Saudi foes, Libya and South Yemen. The CIA had excellent electronic intelligence on the leadership in South Yemen. If there was any more plotting against Riyadh, it was hoped the Americans would know about it.

From Saudi Arabia, Casey flew to Israel and Turkey, then on to Western Europe to review the Poland operation. In Rome he met in secret with Archbishop Luigi Poggi, a Vatican diplomat who handled contacts with the Polish government. Casey had hoped to meet the pontiff again, but the archbishop sat across the table instead. Poggi had just returned from meetings in Warsaw with Polish Foreign Minister Stefan Olszowski, with whom he had discussed the possibility of exchanging ambassadors. Poggi, a whiz at Latin and church history, looked like a simple parish priest. But he was a sharp political thinker and had a solid grasp of the nuances of diplomacy, as well as a tough streak that could reveal itself all too quickly.

Poland was not far off in the discussion. The administration was concerned because U.S. intelligence sources in the Polish Ministry of Defense had reported that a renewed "silent offensive" against the underground was being organized by the Interior Ministry. It was going to take several forms, the most sinister to include the killing of certain activists to sow fear in the hearts of anyone considering anti-State activities. A wave of mysterious murders was already passing through Poland. Grzegorz Przemyk, the nineteen-year-old son of the dissident poet Barbara Sadowska, was beaten to death by police. Andrzej Grzegorz Gasiewski, a Solidarity activist, was seized by the police and several days later turned up dead on a railroad embankment. Jan Samsonovicz, another activist, was found hanging from a wall in the Gdansk shipyards.

The Reagan administration was worried about the survival of the underground leadership—Bujak, Kuron, and also Lech Walesa. Church leaders were probably also targets, Casey told Poggi. He asked the archbishop to relay a warning to his contacts in Poland and have them spread the word. Unable to restrain or contain the underground, the martial law government would no doubt try to decapitate it.

Poggi then shared his reflections on the situation in Poland. It was not very positive. The Church itself was divided between radicals who wanted to back the opposition fully and those who favored a more accommodating approach to the government. It was an extraordinary admission about internal church matters from an archbishop, but perhaps he was returning what he saw as Casey's honesty about American limitations and weaknesses. The division within the Church was exposed in the small industrial suburb of Ursus, when more than 2,000 Poles packed into a Roman Catholic church to challenge the Polish primate, Jozef Cardinal Glemp. The primate had reassigned Rev. Mieczyslaw Nowak of Ursus, an outspoken supporter of Solidarity, to another parish. It was a squabble that was being replicated throughout Poland. The Jaruzelski government and its masters in Moscow no doubt enjoyed the spectacle.

At the same time the Church was experiencing division, the Polish economy was in bad straits. Poggi wanted the Reagan administration to know that sanctions were costly ($12 billion by one Polish government estimate), and Jaruzelski was of the clear opinion that the economic deterioration was to the advantage of his opponents on both sides, Solidarity and hard-liners who believed he had not been brutal enough against domestic enemies. Poggi advised Casey that the administration should keep the sanctions in place because Jaruzelski would eventually seek some sort of compromise.

The health of the underground was mixed. The government was holding about 1,000 activists in all, the most important a group of leaders at Mokotow prison on Warsaw's Rakowiecka Street. The group included Jacek Kuron, Adam Michnik, Zbigniew Romaszewski, who had set up Solidarity's clandestine radio network, and Henryk Wujec, a Catholic intellectual.

But the defiant courage of the detained leadership was not contained by the bars and prison walls. Michnik had just written a letter that had been smuggled out of prison. He was a true believer, who by sheer force of will felt compelled to resist communist rule. The letter showed the inner rage of a defiant activist, full of nerve and pluck. Jaruzelski had offered Michnik and other imprisoned Solidarity leaders asylum in France in the hope of exporting his chief opponents. Michnik's letter was a public response to the offer: "The very idea that there are people who associate Poland not with a ministerial chair but with a prison cell, people who prefer Christmas under arrest to a vacation in the South of France troubles you profoundly," he wrote to the Polish general. He called his jailers "scoundrels" and "vindictive, dishonorable swine." The letter had circulated in copied form among a few thousand activists, then fallen into the hands of officials from Voice of America and Radio Free Europe. The text was promptly broadcast throughout Eastern Europe.

Casey reiterated to Poggi the president's position on sanctions: they would not be relaxed until there were internal reforms in Poland and political prisoners were released. Lech Walesa had in recent weeks expressed his view that the sanctions should end immediately, but the administration's position was not changing. Casey asked the archbishop to pass that news along to his contacts in Poland.

In a very real sense, covert U.S. support to Solidarity was helping the underground survive the long, harsh winter of martial law.

The material pipeline was running from Brussels through Stockholm to Gdansk. There goods were dispersed by an extensive underground distribution system. On February 23, Radio Solidarity went on the air for the first time since October of the previous year. Using new radio and electronic equipment, Zbigniew Bujak encouraged resistance to the regime and called for a boycott of local government elections in June. The broadcast was brief—only six minutes—to avoid detection by the government's monitoring equipment. But it was a significant moral victory.

Contacts between antigovernment activists in Poland and Czechoslovakia were continuing on an informal basis. The Catholic Church, with a small presence in Czechoslovakia, was asked to help. Did the Church have any contact with opposition groups in Czechoslovakia? Would Western "encouragement" help? Poggi offered to make inquiries and get back to Casey.[12]

1. Don Oberdorfer, *The Turn* (New York: Poseidon, 1991), p. 76.
2. Christopher Andrew and Oleg Gordievsky, *KGB Instructions from the Centre* (London: Hodder and Stoughton, 1991), p. 97.
3. See the London *Times*, February 2, 1992, p. 2, and *Izvestiya*, June 24, 1992, p. 5.
4. Roger Robinson, interview with the author.
5. U.S. official, interview with the author.
6. *The New York Times*, January 29, 1984, p. 5.
7. Mohammad Yousaf, interview with the author.
8. Fred Ikle, interview with the author.
9. Mohammad Yousaf, interview with the author.
10. Mohammad Yousaf, interview with the author; interview with U.S. intelligence official.
11. Mohammad Yousaf, interview with the author.
12. U.S. official, interview with the author.

13

One of the most important priorities for the Reagan administration was collecting more accurate and relevant intelligence on the Soviet Union. Military intelligence was fairly reliable. But the president, the National Security Council, and the CIA felt they lacked pertinent information on Soviet political and economic developments. That meant primarily recruiting human sources behind the Iron Curtain. Over the first several years of his tenure, Bill Casey had paid substantial attention to the problem, in recognition of President Reagan's fondness for raw intelligence on the Soviet Union. Good intelligence was critical in determining the next move in the Reagan strategy, particularly one which hoped to capitalize on Soviet economic, technological, and psychological vulnerabilities.

But by April 1984, it had become clear that something was terribly wrong. Intelligence assets in Moscow were drying up. Sources that had been secure for several years had been arrested and taken away. Three human sources, cultivated over years, had recently been executed by Soviet officials for treason. Agency officials working out of the embassy were being tracked; their covers had been completely blown. It was as if the KGB had been given a list of every source for the station and the name of every CIA official in the embassy. On top of that, long-established and highly successful technical collection projects were going silent. Electronic intercept programs were jammed.

But there was a flash of good news to go with the bad. A senior officer on the Soviet General Staff had approached the CIA station and offered to be "helpful." He did not want money; his reasons for collaboration were strictly personal. The CIA station established a string of elaborate codes to contact and receive information from the agent. In a park on the outskirts of Moscow, he would walk his dog after work. He would change the dog collar to notify his contacts.

The source was such a big prize and came at such an unusual and difficult time that there was plenty of suspicion that he was a plant. But the prospect of such a high-ranking official passing information was just too tempting, and Casey favored continued work with him. In the end he provided extremely valuable information. "There was a very large effort to recruit informants and gain human intelligence in the Soviet Union," recalls John Poindexter. "I think we had some very good intelligence on the Soviet Union, particularly on the Politburo and leadership."[1]

In keeping with the Reagan administration's interest in economic and technology issues, American businessmen conducting business with the Kremlin became important sources for intelligence. They had a working knowledge of those subjects and radically different contacts than CIA recruits. Some old Casey friends in the business world like Stuart Jackson volunteered their services. Others, like Archer-Daniels-Midland chairman Dwayne Andreas, had to be persuaded. Businessmen who cooperated were given code names and briefings by the agency.

Perhaps more than anyone, American executives dealing with Moscow knew what Soviet economic requirements were. They could discern which technologies the Soviets needed most desperately, and which foreign sources they had developed for blacklisted American products. Particularly good sources, like Jackson and Andreas, would write out reports on their return from the Soviet Union, then call a special number at the agency. A courier would come, seal the report, and take it to the National Collection Division (NCD). Executives usually got a brief note of thanks from Casey in return. Especially important intelligence was forwarded to the NSC, or even the president.

The National Collection Division was a large operation, with thirty offices in major American cities. Agents contacted corporations doing business abroad and asked them to cooperate. Many business-people who assisted the agency were invited to Langley for "executive briefings." In 1984 almost 200 came to CIA headquarters to attend small-group information seminars and hear an address by Casey. After speaking about the dangers of the modern world, the DCI would make his pitch: "Corporate executives have been invaluable to the Agency. Not only have they provided information, but they have also given us leads to foreign nationals who might be working to make available information that might be critical to our national se-curity interests." He ended by stating forcefully, "You have my per-sonal promise of confidentiality."[2]

In addition to sharing information, nearly 200 major U.S. corporations were providing cover for CIA agents. This had been a key objective for Casey. These agents proved invaluable to conducting certain overseas operations. Some agents working in Poland were under business cover to avoid tracking from the embassy. Every month a summary of NCD success was forwarded to Casey.

Collecting information was necessary to understand and pin-point Soviet vulnerabilities. But the Reagan administration also had an important weapon in manipulating the flow of information to Moscow. In early 1984, a secret disinformation program to disrupt the Soviet economy was launched by the CIA and the Pentagon. It targeted the nucleus of the Soviet economy and its reliance on Western technology and know-how. This was a widespread program, including altered or fabricated technological information in both civilian and military areas. Middlemen were used to pass the information to Soviet technicians. "Basically, you provide the Soviet Union with false or partly false data and information, and it forces them to make the wrong technological decisions," says one official involved in the program. "In short, it really screws them up and confuses them."[3] The idea had first been suggested by members of the NSC staff and Pentagon in the wake of the Soviet pipeline fight. In its full form, the disinformation program exacerbated Soviet economic inefficiencies and deficiencies.

The CIA coordinated the release of incomplete and misleading technical data through various channels. Some CIA dummy companies overseas actually sold distorted information to Soviet officials, including blueprints for gas turbines, oil-drilling technologies, computer chips, and chemical compounds. The information was a mixture of truth and fiction: enough truth to get Soviet engineers to take the bait and begin digesting the information and using it in their own designs, mixed with enough fiction to make their efforts ultimately fail. The difficult issue was determining which information to share. The project had a number of notable "successes" in the first several years.

- A chemical facility in Omsk used misleading information in its expansion plans. Designs led specialists through a labyrinth of technical zones before proving completely worthless. The venture cost the facility an estimated $8 to $10 million before the problems caused were corrected.
- A tractor factory in the Ukraine tried to manufacture machinery using blueprints provided by the CIA. The factory ran at half capacity for sixteen months until engineers finally gave up on the "new automated systems" the plans were supposed to represent.
- Blueprints for gas turbine components were passed to the Soviets in early 1984. Some of those built were placed on the natural gas pipeline. But the blueprints included an engineering flaw. When brought on line, the turbine would fail. As a result, the pipeline suffered even further delays.
- Sabotaged computer chips sold through middlemen ended up in equipment at several Soviet military and civilian factories, where it took months before the problem was uncovered. Assembly lines stayed shut down for weeks.

While the agency was manufacturing disinformation on civilian projects, the Pentagon was doing the same on military technologies. Moscow had saved years in research and development and substantial resources annually by stealing Western defense technologies and applying them to Soviet weapons systems. The Pentagon disinformation effort covered six or seven sensitive military technology projects that the Soviets were expected to have a great interest in. These included stealth technologies, the Strategic Defense Initiative, and advanced tactical aircraft. The activities involved all operational levels, including the briefing of foreign journalists. False information was planted on development schedules, prototype performance, testing results, production schedules, and operational achievements.

In early 1984, Casey received an internal memo on the disinformation program that noted its great success. In addition to pointing out obvious problems created for the Soviets, the memo noted the debilitating effect the program was having on the entire Soviet foreign technology acquisition effort. "Unable to delineate between real and inaccurate data and information, the Soviet ability to absorb and apply western technologies in a fairly good pace has declined dramatically."[4]

To avoid problems that might develop at home, the disinformation program was tightly handled. "Disinformation was only spread outside the United States," recalls John Poindexter. "But it proved to be a powerful weapon against the Soviets. It had them scrambled and confused."[5]

At the end of April, the president called a meeting of the National Security Planning Group. Near the top of the agenda was the U.S.-Saudi relationship and the requests by King Fahd for Stinger missiles and some sort of written guarantee of Saudi security. Casey and Weinberger were pushing for a stronger U.S. commitment to Fahd. "Something that will reinforce the relationship and let them know we stand firmly behind them is what we need," Weinberger said. That meant first and foremost securing Stinger missiles as a tangible symbol of U.S. support. Secretary Shultz wanted to go slowly and not do anything that might shift the balance in the region too dramatically. The president was noncommittal.

Prince Bandar heard about the meeting and was quite upset. The Saudis only grew more frustrated and nervous about U.S. commitment. Iran was continuing to threaten Persian Gulf shipping, and the Saudis were perplexed. Weinberger met with Bandar and received a stern warning about the importance of the Stinger sale. Congress was threatening to block any sale, so something needed to be done. Weinberger arranged for Bandar to meet with the president in the Oval Office in the middle of May, to plead his case directly. Bandar brought with him a secret seven-page letter from King Fahd. The president read it, then looked serenely at the Saudi prince. "We don't put conditions on friends," Reagan said softly. "You will get your missiles and our support." Several days later the president dispatched a letter to King Fahd affirming U.S. military support for the royal family. It was very personal in tone, saying in effect, "You have my word, I will stand by you."[6]

Several days later, the president fulfilled his promise, invoking emergency procedures to bypass Congress. He used this extraordinary means claiming that the Saudis needed the missiles immediately to protect itself from possible Iranian air strikes. Over Memorial Day weekend, 400 Stingers were flown secretly to Saudi Arabia. They were not the 1,200 that Fahd had hoped for, but he was extremely pleased and sent a personal note to thank the president.

Two special national intelligence estimates (SNIEs) on the Soviet Union were completed in May 1984. They were extensive surveys of Soviet attitudes toward the United States. At the request of National Security Adviser Robert McFarlane, Casey had ordered the reports drawn up in 1983 in the shadow of the Korean Air Lines 007 disaster. They were based in part on information being provided by Oleg Gordievsky, the deputy KGB resident in London, who was secretly working for British intelligence. There was additional input from two other recent KGB defectors. Vladimir Kuzichkin had left the Soviet embassy in Tehran on October 25, 1982, and fled to the Americans. Anatoli "Boris" Bogaty had done the same in Morocco one month earlier.

The reports intimated that the Soviets were increasingly frightened by the Reagan administration. The Kremlin had actually instituted a series of special nuclear war alerts—Raketno Yadernoy Napadenie—because it feared that the United States might launch a first strike.[7] These had first been called by Yuri Andropov in 1981, while he was still chairman of the KGB, on the ground that a surprise nuclear attack by the Reagan administration was a serious possibility. That was by no means the consensus viewpoint at the senior levels of the Soviet regime, but enough of the Kremlin guard believed it to raise concern in the White House. The SNIEs also pointed to a more profound phenomenon. The Soviet leadership was psychologically shaken by the events of the last several years.

McFarlane remembers the SNIEs and the Soviet psychological position: "One of the surprises on the Soviet side that ran counter to their own portrayal of the capitalist system was the recovery in the

American economy. Having been so public about the decline of the American economy, they became buoyant in the 1970s. The contrast for them was when we began to recover. It was psychologically devastating for them. They began to lose their confidence. And of course we wanted to use that to our strategic advantage."

The SNIEs also noted that the Soviet leadership was beginning to fear that the correlation of forces was beginning to shift against them. As McFarlane recalls, "Being challenged in ways you have not been challenged before can be psychologically devastating. The process of having to deal with many crises can scare the leadership of a close political system unaccustomed to such a situation."[8]

The correlation of forces did appear to be shifting. The American military was building, particularly a new generation of high-tech, expensive weapons. By the mid-1980s, U.S. military expenditures exceeded those of the Soviet Union for the first time since the late 1960s. In the first six years of the Reagan presidency, the Pentagon purchased nearly 3,000 combat aircraft, 3,700 strategic missiles, and about 10,000 tanks, a procurement rate roughly double that of the 1970s. Most important, perhaps, these new systems were more sophisticated than ever. On the periphery of the Soviet system—in Poland and Afghanistan—there were visible cracks in the foundation. And it was becoming increasingly difficult for the Soviets to get access to Western technologies, so the rigidities in the command economy were having an even more difficult time coping. According to Yevgenny Novikov, "There was a strong belief inside the Central Committee and senior officers of the KGB that external pressures were destroying the economy. Some were saying, 'We cannot compete, we must cooperate.' But there was a fear that Reagan really wanted to undermine our system."[9]

Despite the shifting sands in the superpower competition, the Kremlin in early 1984 believed that Afghanistan was the one place it could win. The Soviets controlled the tempo of the war and held an overwhelming superiority on the battlefield. The mujahedin had managed somehow to contain sporadic attacks on Soviet and Afghan installations. But it was still not clear how they would be able to take advantage of any temporary gains.

That spring a senior general from the Soviet General Staff was flown from Moscow to a Soviet command post in Termez. Just across the Amu River from Afghanistan, this city was the main artery supplying Soviet forces in Afghanistan; 75 percent of all supplies went through Termez. Major General Saradov, commander of the Soviet 108th Motor Rifle Division (MRD), was there to greet the senior officer. Saradov was in charge of a massive offensive planned in the Panjsher valley. An airborne command post was sent up, packed with senior staff officers to monitor the attack. The offensive was to be the largest Soviet operation in Afghanistan to date.

On April 20, planes from air bases in Soviet Central Asia headed for Afghanistan. Dozens of Tu-16 Badger high-altitude bombers began carpet bombing the valley. On the ground, mujahedin under the command of the legendary Ahmad Shah Massoud hid in caves. The Soviets were using 500- and 1,000-pound bombs that violently shook the ground. But the narrow valley offered plenty of cover for the resistance. After two days of bombing, columns of tanks and armored personnel carriers began making their way through the valley. At the same time, Soviet airborne units, transported by helicopters, were dropped just north of the Panjsher. Saradov was no doubt happy that the operation had been launched smoothly. But the results were at best mixed. Soviet forces did take much of the Panjsher; the mujahedin managed to escape to fight another day. The senior Soviet general returned to Moscow to consult with the chief of the General Staff. His recommendation: that the Soviet Union escalate the war and try to bring maximum firepower into force so they could declare victory in Afghanistan.

The Soviets were dramatically raising their mortal commitment to the war. The Afghan army in 1979 had numbered about 80,000 men; it was now down to 30,000, despite numerous recruiting drives. The war was being "Sovietized" as more Soviet forces were doing the bulk of the fighting. There was a buildup in Soviet Central Asia of Soviet airborne troops, who were being shuttled into Afghanistan to attack insurgents, then returning across the border. They were the best-trained Soviet forces and were much more effective than the Afghan army had ever been.

It was against this backdrop in April 1984 that U.S. officials groped with what to do next in Afghanistan. A rising Soviet commitment would expose the Soviets to more losses, and the administration could choose to raise the burdens of the war. Clearly on the ascendancy was the view that the war might prove a powerful hammer to drive against the Soviet psyche. On the National Security Council, Donald Fortier believed that the Soviet Union was overextended, and that major fissures existed. The occupation of Afghanistan meant a Soviet commitment of greater and greater force levels. If the administration could develop a strategy not only to beat back the Soviet challenge but actually to win, it could have a devastating effect on the Kremlin. He looked to history for parallels, reminding Robert McFarlane that a loss in the 1905 Russo-Japanese War and the devastating losses suffered during the First World War had had revolutionary consequences in Russia.[10]

As Reagan administration officials debated the next step in Afghanistan, Wali Beg made his first foray into Soviet Central Asia. Recruited by the Pakistani ISI to gauge the situation in the area, he headed for the village of his childhood and much of his adulthood. He was hoping that two families he knew well were still living there. Once in Afghanistan's Kunduz Province, he had the difficult task of making it across the Amu onto Soviet soil. The area around Sherkhan, his hometown, was not safe. The busy Soviet port Nizhniy Pyandzh was on the other side and full of security personnel. So he chose an area west of Sherkhan where there was heavy cover on both riverbanks and plenty of reeds to conceal him in the water.

Beg chose to swim across the almost 700 yards of icy water instead of risking detection by using a boat. So he acquired a dried goatskin, inflated it, and worked his way across. He reached Soviet territory, wet and cold.

He walked to his destination during the early morning hours, eventually finding his old friends. He spent two days in the village, and indications of support for anti-Soviet operations were very encouraging. Two villagers asked for guns to fight the Soviets. Many others requested literature and materials. A number showed a willingness to serve as guides or provide food and shelter. Beg brought all the news back to Brigadier Mohammad Yousaf. "I was impressed by the number of reports of people wanting to assist," recalls Yousaf. "Some wanted weapons, some wanted to join the mujahedin in Afghanistan, and others wanted to participate in operations inside the Soviet Union."[11]

With the encouraging report from Yousaf based on Beg's expedition, the CIA immediately purchased several hundred Zodiac rubber boats to transfer mujahedin and literature across the Amu. But the United States balked at providing satellite photos of Soviet Central Asia to plan attacks and identify targets. The president and the administration did not want American fingerprints all over the operation. Attacks that were too precise, that surgically hit obscure targets of military significance, might tip Moscow off to U.S. involvement. No intelligence north of the Amu became the canon of the secret war on Soviet territory.

That spring, while the Afghan war began to infect Soviet Central Asia, the Pentagon was working to squeeze the flow of technology. Through a series of bilateral and multilateral agreements a variety of countries were being brought into the technology control alliance. At the same time, the list of technologies restricted for export was being lengthened. Illegal exports no doubt were still finding their way to Moscow. But it was getting increasingly difficult for the Soviets to access Western know-how simply by purchasing it. The tightening grip was causing serious resource allocation problems for the Kremlin, forcing officials to be especially creative to get around the restrictions. A common tactic included transshipping advanced Western technologies through neutral third countries.

Recognizing this tactic early on, a group of officials at the Departments of Defense, State, and Commerce decided to attack the problem on two fronts. The United States would pressure these neutral countries to stop such practices in exchange for greater access to U.S. markets and technologies. Sweden and Austria had already been romanced in such a fashion. On another level, U.S. officials wanted to force Western companies to police themselves and the companies in foreign countries they traded with. This meant using the Export Administration Act much as the administration had during the 1982 European pipeline fight.

In the spring of 1984, the Senior Interagency Group on the Transfer of Strategic Technology, headed by Undersecretary of State William Schneider, developed a new set of restrictions on technology exports to cut off the Soviet transshipment scheme. The proposal was to tighten the distribution of licenses that controlled the reexport of U.S. high technology. That meant, for example, that if any company in a NATO country wanted to reexport a U.S.-controlled item to any non-NATO country, it would have to furnish the American government with a customer list to certify that the product would not later be shipped to Moscow. The policy would apply to all U.S.-controlled commodities that were reexported under a distribution license by the West to neutral or third world nations.

The United States was using a broad definition for "American technology," which gave Washington substantial control over the flow of technology around the world. Europe was not pleased. As one German trade official put it, "We find it unreasonable for example, that a European company which develops computer software utilizing U.S.-origin technical data subjects itself to U.S. export regulations, regardless of how insignificant the U.S. contribution may have been."[12]

The squeezed Soviet technological base was coming under further strain as the administration pressed to broaden the high-tech defense buildup. In particular, the stress on emerging technology was reflected not only in procurement but increasingly in NATO alliance policy and doctrine. This would compel Moscow to expend a greater portion of its limited resources on weapons research.

In May 1984, Caspar Weinberger was in Brussels for a regular meeting of NATO defense ministers. They assembled in a private room and began their discussion of alliance strategy and policy. For two years Weinberger had been quietly courting his European counterparts to adopt a plan focusing NATO energies on emerging technology weapons systems. The U.S. military had already made significant changes in its outlook. In 1982 the army adopted the AirLand Battle doctrine, which augured an era of active defense that would include deep strikes against enemy targets, making maximum use of advances in electronics and communications equipment. Its leitmotivs included mobility, maneuver, and combined arms (the use of various services together). It rested on the premise of surprise to disorient the enemy and assumed that if the defender merely defended he would lose. It went so far as to envision counterthrusts by U.S. ground forces into Warsaw Pact territory. Weinberger was hoping to make the American commitment to advanced technologies and a new strategy a NATO-wide commitment.

In December 1983, the secretary of defense had proposed the alliance give high priority to thirty emerging technology weapons systems. But his proposal was broadly rejected by the alliance leaders, who either lacked faith in the concept or did not want to commit themselves to an expensive reorientation of their defense budgets. But Weinberger was persistent. He lobbied his counterparts in secret.

At the May meeting in Brussels, there was considerable movement. The controversial proposal was ratified. The ministers directed the Independent European Program Group to organize Europe-wide cooperation on the development of emerging technologies. The significance of the agreement was not in the initial financial commitment to the projects, but in the ratification of the overall concept.

The NATO agreement emphasized building onto or accelerating projects that were already being pursued in one or more of the allied nations. If successful the plan was expected to have a dramatic effect on the battlefield. As one NATO report put it, "On the basis of preliminary studies, NATO nations believe that technologies in sensors, signal processing and data processing can be used along with communications advances immediately to provide powerful force multipliers through emerging technologies."

But NATO ministers also enshrined the commitment to emerging technologies in doctrine when, in 1984, they approved a new strategy that incorporated many of the principles in AirLand Battle. Less ambitious and aggressive than AirLand Battle, Follow-on Forces Attack (FOFA) was nevertheless a dramatic change in NATO strategy. And it was not well received in the Soviet Ministry of Defense.

While NATO was formally adopting this shift to emerging technologies, Marshal Ogarkov was calling for a renewed Soviet effort to keep pace with the United States. As he told a Soviet military paper, "The rapid development of science and technology in recent years creates real preconditions for the emergence in the very near future of even more destructive and previously unknown types of weapons based on new physical principles. Work on these new type of weapons are already in progress in a number of countries, most importantly the United States. Their development is a reality of the very near future, and it would be a serious mistake to not take account of this right now."[13]

The Kremlin was determined not to fall behind in this crucial technological race. American defense procurement allocations rose by 25 percent per year in each of the early Reagan years, doubling the budget between 1980 and 1985. Of even more concern for Soviet military officials was the rapid rise in Pentagon research and development, the birthing ward for new technologies. Between 1980 and 1985, spending on R & D almost doubled.[14] The Soviet defense budget was set to rise 45 percent between 1981 and 1985, but Soviet officials deemed this increase insufficient to match the American high-tech challenge. So in the spring of 1984 General Secretary Konstantin Chernenko announced that "the complex international situation has forced us to divert a great deal of resources to strengthening the security of our country."[15] It was a shift that further weighed on the already sickly Soviet economy.

The diversion entailed committing even more resources to the high-tech military sector. Moscow spent tens of billions of dollars it could ill afford responding to SDI, according to Roald Z. Sagdayev, who headed the Soviet Space Research Institute in the 1980s. "This program became priority No. 1 after Mr. Reagan's announcement of the 'Star Wars' in 1983." He believes the spending weakened the Soviet Union and may have contributed to its demise.[16] Funds were allocated to develop scientific-industrial facilities from scratch. Sixteen inter-branch complexes were to be created by 1986, dealing with technologies such as lasers and genetic engineering. A new bureaucracy was erected to manage the "diversion." Glavkosmus, the awkwardly labeled Chief Administration for Development and Use of Space Technology for National Economy and Science Research, was born overnight. By the fall of 1984, the Soviet Academy of Sciences had announced a $100 million research effort to develop its advanced computer technology in an attempt to leapfrog a technological generation and establish itself at the forefront of international research in the field. Staff and funds were beefed up for

- Particle beam weapons research being conducted at Sarova, near Gorky, under H. I. Pavlovski
- Research on proton beams and near IR-laser beam research being done at Krasnoyarsk, Tyuratam, Semipalatinsk, and Krasnaya Rechka
- Fusion reactors at the Sefremov Institute in Leningrad[17]

But beyond the shift in resources, the technological challenge posed by the American buildup would eventually compel the Kremlin to make structural changes to the economy in a desperate attempt to keep pace. Moscow could compete in a race that placed a premium on quantity. But a technological challenge, which placed a premium on innovation and quality, was another matter.

The Soviet economy offered few incentives and suppressed creativity, producing goods that were of poor quality. Much of the technology incorporated in Soviet military weapons was acquired from the West. To the Soviet Ministry of Defense, the poor performance of the domestic economy was manageable so long as it did not infringe upon the relative power of the military. But with the Reagan administration's commitment to high-technology systems such as the Strategic Defense Initiative, economic reform became a necessary evil. As early as 1981, the Soviet Ministry of Defense had produced a monograph noting this necessity. Entitled *The Economic Basis of the Defense Might of a Socialist State*, it noted that the continued decay of the Soviet high-tech industrial sector "could decelerate the development of the very basis of military power—the economy—and therefore inflict irreparable damage on the defense capability." A backward economy now meant not only shabby consumer goods but a second-rate military. In short, in the intensive high-technology defense environment, the rules of the game had changed. As Eduard Shevardnadze so eloquently put it, suddenly "it is not so much a state's stock of weapons which are of decisive significance for its security as the ability to create and produce fundamentally new weapons."[18]

In a strange way, the birth of perestroika was a consequence of Reagan policy. "Perestroika was in many ways a military initiative," recalls Yevgenny Novikov. "They spoke about it as early as 1982, and saw it as necessary to preserve Soviet military capability, particularly in light of the American buildup."[19] Or as Soviet member of Parliament Ilya Zaslavsy prefers to put it, "Ronald Reagan was the father of perestroika."

1. John Poindexter, interview with the author.
2. Joseph Persico, *Casey: The Lives and Secrets of William J. Casey* (New York: Penguin, 1991), p. 456; U.S. official, interview with the author.
3. Interview with the author.

4. Directorate of Intelligence internal memo [1984].
5. John Poindexter, interview with the author; U.S. officials, interviews with the authors; "U.S. Using Disinformation Policy to Impede Technical Data Flow," *Aviation Week and Space Technology,* March 17, 1986, pp. 16–17.
6. U.S. official, interview with the author.
7. See Christopher Andrew and Oleg Gordievsky, *KGB: The Inside Story* (New York: HarperCollins, 1990), pp. 583–85.
8. Robert McFarlane, interview with the author.
9. Yevgenny Novikov, interview with the author.
10. Robert McFarlane, interview with the author.
11. Mohammad Yousaf, interview with the author.
12. "Export Control Shift Worries Europeans," *Aviation Week and Space Technology,* April 30, 1984, p. 59.
13. *Krasnaya Zvezda,* May 9, 1984.
14. Caspar Weinberger, Annual Report to the Congress, FY 1986.
15. *Krasnaya Zvezda,* March 3, 1984.
16. *The New York Times,* August 18, 1993, pp. A1, A15.
17. *Literaturaya Gazeta,* June 20, 1986; *Pravda,* October 28, 1985.
18. Eduard Shevardnadze, quoted in *Mezhunardnaya Zhizn,* no. 11, 1988.
19. Yevgenny Novikov, interview with the author.

14

The summer of 1984 was long and hot. In July COCOM completed a review of the international embargo lists on technology exports to the Soviet bloc. The three lists—munitions, atomic energy, and international—were revised and expanded. Added were computer software, telecommunications equipment, and small military-relevant computers. The parameters of enforcement were tightened up, particularly in the area of halting the transshipment of goods through third countries. Members of COCOM agreed to coordinate efforts to halt third-country shipments. Acquiring Western technology was becoming more difficult than ever before.

In Moscow, the nervousness about Reagan had not abated. On June 21, Vladimir Kryuchkov informed KGB residences that obtaining more intelligence on the United States was critical. "The deterioration in the international situation and the growing immediate threat of war on the part of the United States means that our service is confronted ever more urgently with the task of operating against the USA as the main adversary," he said in a memo. Because of the special international situation the Reagan administration had created, a schedule for operational reporting by KGB residences abroad was adopted. It laid down a strict requirement that all stations overseas report on the work against the United States twice a year. (Previously this procedure was only in force for certain stations.)[1]

The Soviets were not naive about their ability to influence American elections, but they clearly wanted to do whatever they could to hurt Reagan's chances. "The clear and widespread belief was anyone was preferable to Reagan," recalls Yevgenny Novikov.[2] In the hope of somehow swaying public opinion, Soviet officials were making known in public their views about the administration in Washington. A prominent role in this effort was played by Foreign Minister Andrei Gromyko, a nearly permanent fixture in the Soviet diplomatic machine and a recognizable face to many Americans. On July 27, Gromyko, on vacation in Yalta, received former Senator George McGovern as a visitor. The presidential candidate from 1972 had given it another shot in 1984, but a poor showing in the primaries forced him to drop out. The visit was a personal gesture of peace by McGovern. The two men met for three very candid hours, in which Gromyko opened up to his American visitor.

Gromyko told McGovern that he expected Reagan to be reelected. But he did not foresee any letup in the administration's "anti-Soviet" policies. Reagan and his aides "want to cause trouble," he said. "They want to weaken the Soviet system. They want to bring it down."[3]

Plans were in the works for Gromyko to visit Washington in late September or early October, just before the election. He dismissed an invitation from the White House as a ruse to paint Reagan as a more peaceful statesman and to blunt attacks from the Democrats that he was moving the superpower competition dangerously close to war. For measure, Gromyko planned to meet with Walter Mondale, the Democratic nominee, the day before he went to the White House.

On September 23, Gromyko addressed the United Nations General Assembly in New York. It was a high-profile speech that outlined the three central elements of the secret Reagan strategy to weaken the Soviet Union. Gromyko pointedly attacked Washington for "interference in the internal affairs of Poland." Speaking as if he had just read NSDD-32, Gromyko claimed an attempt was being made "to shake loose the socialist foundations of the Polish state." He accused the administration of engaging in economic warfare, by "putting pressure on other states, particularly in Europe, to curtail their ties with the socialist countries." Finally, he accused Washington of whipping up the "arms race." In particular, he singled out American concentration on the emerging technology systems that threatened Soviet systems with obsolescence. "Who would believe that it is concern for peace that motivates the accelerated pace of the development of newer weapons?" he pointedly asked.[4]

Five days later, Gromyko took the same script to the White House. At one point he told Reagan, "Behind all this lies the clear calculation that the USSR will exhaust its material resources before the USA and therefore be forced to surrender."[5] Reagan was characteristically low key, fending off Gromyko's charges with humor and a smile.

While senior administration officials were concerned with the next step in American foreign policy, it was the domestic economy that garnered the most interest and attention. To sustain the economic recovery, a consensus emerged that bringing down international energy prices was an important objective. This would be unambiguously good for American industry. A few of the more strategically oriented Reagan officials—Caspar Weinberger, Bill Casey, John Poindexter, and others on the National Security Council staff—recognized that lower prices would also deliver a devastating blow to the Kremlin. Casey and Weinberger had made known to Saudi officials the American preference for lower and stable oil prices. But in late 1984 the campaign to secure them would become more direct and focused.

The Reagan administration had invested serious political capital in the Saudi royal family. "The Saudis were one of the most important components of the Reagan strategy," recalls Alan Fiers. In addition to supporting the United States on several important regional issues, Riyadh was providing financial support for the Nicaraguan contras and the mujahedin. But influence over oil pricing was part of it, too.[6]

The administration had secured for the Saudis the purchase of AWACS and advanced fighter aircraft and most recently shipped Stingers using extraordinary presidential authority. A new military command, USCENTCOM, had been created to meet the specific security needs of the Persian Gulf. The president had even sent a personal note to King

Fahd spelling out his commitment to the House of Saud. In early 1985, the U.S. Air Force would break ground on Peace Shield, which would be the most technologically advanced integrated air defense system outside NATO. It was a computerized command, control, and communications system that would link Saudi AWACS planes with five underground command centers and seventeen long-range radar stations.

Peace Shield was designed to deter any regional threat. If deterrence failed, the system would coordinate a Saudi air force response, to include a barrage of air to surface missiles. It was hoped that Peace Shield would hold off any attack for ten days, until American help arrived. It would also further solidify the U.S. military commitment to Saudi Arabia. It would include a permanent staff of 400 to join the 1,700 American military personnel already stationed in Saudi Arabia. The command post would maintain constant contact with the USS *La Salle*, the flagship of the fleet of six American combat ships in the Gulf and the command post for USCENTCOM forces stationed in the United States.

While never providing this security commitment as a prid quo pro, the administration was clearly hoping that it would influence Saudi oil pricing. According to Weinberger, "One of the reasons we were selling all those arms to the Saudis was for lower oil prices."[7]

In the fall of 1984, a few days before a scheduled trip to Saudi Arabia, Bill Casey pulled aside Glenn Campbell, the chairman of the President's Intelligence Oversight Board. Casey preferred working with Campbell and this smaller board rather than the much larger President's Foreign Intelligence Advisory Board. They talked about several issues; then Casey made clear the administration's intentions. "He was going to approach the Saudis about reducing prices," recalls Campbell. "He didn't offer too many details. He just mumbled after that."[8]

Throughout 1984 the Reagan administration conducted a rhetorical campaign in favor of lowering international prices. On August 1, Sheik Zaki al-Yamani, the Saudi oil minister, had negotiated with the British energy secretary and several major oil companies to stop the price of oil from falling and defended $29 per barrel. This was an attempt to prop up prices, something that did not sit well in Washington. Two weeks after the British-Saudi announcement, Treasury Secretary Donald

Regan sent a memo to Energy Secretary Donald Hodel, advocating a U.S. push for lower prices by "resist[ing] any pressure on us to prop up oil prices."

Shortly thereafter Hodel asked rhetorically in a public speech at an oil conference in London: "Are [oil] customers seeing prices that are low enough?" He didn't answer his question directly, but the implication was that they were not. Several weeks later, Hodel took the highly public and unusual step of sending telexes to major oil companies in the United States criticizing OPEC's efforts "to manipulate the market by setting artificially high prices or by seeking to fashion arbitrary restrictions on production." The administration seemed to be "talking down" oil prices.[9]

That the U.S. economy would benefit greatly from a reduction in oil prices was very much on the minds of senior officials. A confidential State Department memorandum to Secretary George Shultz reiterated the findings of the 1983 Treasury Department interagency report on international oil prices. "The prospect of somewhat lower oil prices has prompted Treasury to review the 1983 Interagency study on subject. The conclusion remains that lower oil prices would be beneficial for the world economy, and problems that such a development might create for oil exporters do not present a threat to the world trading or financial system."[10]

This effort did not go unnoticed by Sheik Yamani. In private consultations with U.S. and foreign officials, he pointed to "evidence of a conspiracy by the United States Government to drive down the price of oil," according to State Department cables. Some European officials were drawing the same conclusions. Jean Syrota, a high-ranking French energy official, told one U.S. official that Hodel's comments were the first time a top U.S. energy official had so specifically addressed the oil price issue in public. The U.S. official cabled back to the State Department that "without directly saying it, Syrota implied that the U.S. may be behind a move to drive oil prices down. . . ."[11]

In September, Bill Casey was in Saudi Arabia to meet with King Fahd. The U.S.-Saudi relationship had never been stronger. At the Royal Palace, Casey and Fahd reviewed the strategic situation in the Gulf as they had time and time again. The Afghan war was going well, and Casey brought the king up to date on some of the more important aspects of the administration's Afghan policy.

Casey then raised the subject of international oil pricing. The price was much too high, he told Fahd. If prices remained high, they might strangle the U.S. economic recovery. And the royal family was suffering by cutting production. The only beneficiaries were Saudi enemies—Iran, Libya, and the Soviet Union, who were pumping as much as possible at a Saudi-maintained price. The financial harvest was paying for the Soviet presence in South Yemen, Syria, Ethiopia, and Afghanistan. Natural gas was replacing oil because prices were just too steep.[12]

Fahd heard Casey out, nodding occasionally. He said that he generally agreed with the administration's assessment, but he did not tip his hand. The response was encouraging. Fahd apparently used the expression "fee al-wakea," an Arabic declaration to emphasize that Casey was speaking the truth.

What Casey was doing was only the crescendo of American diplomacy with the Saudis to lower oil prices since the earliest days of the Reagan administration. "I raised the issue in general discussions with Saudi officials—the defense minister, Prince Bandar, and King Fahd," recalls Caspar Weinberger. "They knew we wanted as low an oil price as possible. Among the benefits were our domestic economic and political situation, and a lot less money going to the Soviets. It was a win-win situation."[13] As part of the general strategy to restrict Soviet hard currency earnings the effort became particularly necessary after the first strand of the Soviet gas pipeline deal went ahead in September 1982. "It became even more important to bring oil prices down because the price of natural gas was based on the price of oil," says Weinberger. "The lower the oil price, the less financial benefit that would come to the Soviet Union from the export of either oil or gas."[14]

In late 1984, Reagan administration officials were growing impatient with the war in Afghanistan. There was an unspoken but well-entrenched assumption in many circles that the Soviets would eventually win the war, and that the best American aid could do was prolong the

Soviet agony. Officials at the NSC such as John Poindexter and Robert McFarlane were more optimistic, believing that perhaps Moscow could be forced out of Afghanistan. But it had been a hard year for the resistance. The fighting had intensified as the Soviets made greater use of airpower, pounding mujahedin targets more heavily than ever before. The large-scale Soviet offensives launched in the spring were replicated throughout the summer. Even though Moscow was no closer to winning the war on the battlefield, the campaigns were putting a strain on the resistance. Casualties were much higher than they had been in 1983. The strategy of massive bombardment was thinning out the civilian population as people fled to Pakistan or Iran. The support base that was so important to the mujahedin was evaporating. More and more supplies had to be brought in overland from bases in Pakistan, making logistics a nightmare. Anticipation of even more intensive Soviet operations next spring was greeted with a deep sense of foreboding by General Akhtar of the Pakistani ISI. He was telling Washington quite clearly: the mujahedin could win, but only if they had the necessary material support.

Reagan administration officials, in cooperation with sympathetic members of Congress, were working hard to sustain the resistance. Reagan had asked National Security Adviser Robert McFarlane to give Afghanistan high priority for 1984. Aid to the mujahedin would be doubled, thanks to broad-based support in Congress.

Akhtar and Mohammad Yousaf had been running parts of the war on a shoestring. At $100 million per year, this was the largest covert war in American history. But the Soviet presence was massive and the tactics brutal. Yousaf had wanted to conduct a series of attacks on Kabul during the winter of 1984–85. The plans were militarily feasible and strategically sound, but they were never executed. "In the end it came down to the money," recalls Yousaf. "Did we have sufficient funds for the extra transport costs to pre-position stocks or for warmer clothes? Regrettably the answer was no." Many of the fighters were going without winter clothing. Money constraints were forcing Yousaf to make critical trade-offs every day, between purchasing clothing or weapons. The latter, it was always decided, was more important.[15]

Akhtar had told Washington that a window of opportunity might exist. The change in Soviet strategy was a reflection of a renewed commitment. But it was also a sign of desperation. The losses that the Soviets had been able to sustain were no longer sustainable. A dramatic increase in CIA funds would translate into more weapons and ammunition, as well as training and supplies. It was hoped that the new resources would raise the stakes for Moscow. The Soviets' casualties were way up because of their heightened involvement in the fighting.

The additional funds that Casey had procured earlier in the year for training were already being put to good use. The strategy of concentrating mujahedin activities in the northern provinces was giving the Soviet army fits. Thousands of troops were bogged down trying to keep supply lines secure. And the mujahedin were knocking on the door of Soviet Central Asia.

The specially trained mujahedin had some notable successes only months after the training began. A series of attacks were launched on Bagram Air Base, a well-protected facility with a large garrison. Some twenty aircraft were destroyed on the ground using 107-mm rocket launchers donated by the Chinese.

Trained units were also targeting the Soviet high command in Kabul. Seven senior Soviet officers were reported killed in Kabul in 1983. In 1984 that figure almost doubled. In addition mujahedin commanders were being trained and organized to hit Soviet military targets in the capital city. The CIA was providing all the tools, with the help of the ISI. Using Chinese rocket launchers with an effective range of four to six miles and detailed U.S.-supplied satellite photographs, thousands of rockets were by mid-1984 raining down on Soviet and Afghan military installations, as well as the offices of the KGB and the Afghan KHAD. As a consequence, morale was very low among senior Soviet military officers.

But the Pakistanis wanted to ensure that the Soviet officers in Kabul remained uncomfortable and nervous, so they forwarded to Casey an unusual request. General Akhtar wanted sniper rifles ("packages") so the mujahedin could target Soviet commanders and generals. The CIA had already pinpointed the homes and offices of leading Soviet generals and was tracking their movements. Visiting commanders from Moscow and Tashkent were also being monitored. Hitting them would be a formality, given all the intelligence available. Casey liked the idea on military grounds, but the subject was sensitive: the guns would be used for assassination, and a presidential executive order prohibited the U.S. government from involvement in the assassination of foreign officials.

Casey took the matter to CIA lawyers and the NSC in early 1985. The lawyers balked; the stench of "assassination" was too strong. Casey was confused. This is a war, he boomed, what's the difference between supplying rockets to kill officers on the battlefield and supplying these rifles? The difference is intent, the lawyers told him. If the rifles are provided with the intent to kill Soviet generals, we would be violating the presidential directive on assassinations. You could go to jail.

Reportedly Casey waved off those concerns. Well then, if anyone asks, don't tell them these are sniper rifles for assassination, tell them they are hunting rifles; that is our intent, he said. What they choose to hunt is their decision, not ours.[16]

Senior officials and the NSC staff debated the proposition for months. Finally approximately one hundred "packages" were sent, and mujahedin were trained in how to use them. But the United States would not be sharing any intelligence on the movements of Soviet military officers.

To further its objectives in Afghanistan, the Reagan administration at the close of 1984 launched an intense propaganda campaign in Soviet Central Asia. It worked with Pakistan, China, and Turkey to encourage local citizens to counteract Soviet rule. "It was an effort to distribute literature across the border in Soviet Central Asia to sow dissent," recalls John Poindexter.[17] The United States was responsible for conducting operations from Pakistan using the Afghan resistance and the ISI. "We played a role in supporting anticommunist movements in Soviet Central Asia," recalls Mohammad Yousaf. "Besides smuggling propaganda, we had clandestine radio stations. The CIA provided the broadcast equipment, and broadcast material."[18] The administration was stirring the boiling pot, hoping to create more domestic problems for the Kremlin.

1. Christopher Andrew and Oleg Gordievsky, *More Instructions from the Centre: Top Secret Files on KGB Global Operations, 1975–1985* (London: Frank Cass, 1992), p. 2.

2. Yevgenny Novikov, interview with the author.

3. Don Oberdorfer, *The Turn* (New York: Poseidon, 1991), p. 89.

4. *The New York Times*, September 24, 1984, pp. A1, A14.

5. Andrei Gromyko, *Memoirs* (New York: Doubleday, 1989), p. 307.

6. Alan Fiers, interview with the author.

7. Caspar Weinberger, interview with the author.

8. Glenn Campbell, interview with the author.

9. Treasury Department and Energy Department memos.

10. Department of State information memorandum to Secretary of State George Shultz (confidential), October 25, 1984.

11. State Department cables.

12. Interview with two intelligence officials.

13. Caspar Weinberger, interview with the author.

14. Caspar Weinberger, interview with the author.

15. Mohammad Yousaf, interview with the author.

16. Interview with U.S. officials.

17. John Poindexter, interview with the author.

18. Mohammad Yousaf, interview with the author.

15

Six weeks after winning reelection decisively, Ronald Reagan received a good friend and ideological soul mate as a visitor. British Prime Minister Margaret Thatcher arrived in Washington to discuss a myriad of issues. Events in the Soviet Union were near the top of the list.

They met with a few select aides at the presidential retreat at Camp David, amid the lush hills of rural Maryland. The two were quite informal, talking on a first-name basis. Thatcher briefed the president on talks she had held on December 16 with a rising star in the Soviet hierarchy named Mikhail Gorbachev. He was an impressive man, she told Reagan. Unlike any other Soviet leader she had ever met. Gorbachev had expressed concern that the U.S. National Security Council believed that Soviet economic stagnation was in the American interest, citing newspaper accounts of leaked documents. He also raised concerns about the Strategic Defense Initiative, indicating in Thatcher's words that Moscow "wanted it stopped at any price." Reagan listened and learned, as always giving Thatcher's views an extra thought.

Soon the discussions shifted to SDI and the administration's plans. Thatcher had her first opportunity to hear Reagan speak directly and candidly about SDI. She noticed immediately the passion and dripping idealism that attached itself to almost every sentence he uttered about the program. He explained that SDI was ultimately an international system that could eventually be shared with Moscow; it was for the good of the entire globe. Thatcher, not as interested in the vision, nonetheless expressed support for the American program. She then asked a few questions about the research program and the consequences the system might have on the strategic nuclear balance.

The president, off his lofty perch, admitted that he was not certain where the research program would lead, or whether it would yield a workable system. But it did warrant investigation. And besides, he told the prime minister, even if was never developed, it would be an enormous economic strain on the Soviet Union. "[The president] argued that there had to be a practical limit as to how far the Soviet government could push their people down the road of austerity."[1]

The visit offered the administration an opportunity to make progress on its attempts to include the major Western allies in the SDI research program. Of the allied leaders, Thatcher was the closest to Reagan philosophically and shared in general terms his vision for a strategic defense system. Caspar Weinberger, ever the Anglophile, Robert McFarlane, and George Shultz felt a statement of support from Thatcher would begin the process of gaining broad acceptance of SDI in major foreign countries. Working with McFarlane over pen and paper, the prime minister outlined four points that she felt were crucial to getting European cooperation on SDI. The United States needed to ensure the Europeans that (1) SDI was not designed to achieve superiority in the superpower balance; (2) SDI deployments would be negotiated given existing treaty obligations; (3) the objective was to enhance, not undermine, deterrence; and (4) superpower negotiations would continue to seek a reduction of offensive weapons systems on both sides. In exchange for agreement on these points, Thatcher issued a statement declaring that it was her "firm conviction that the SDI research program should go ahead."[2]

The vocal and public support of Margaret Thatcher proved central to moving SDI from a president's dream to a research program pursued by leading scientists across the Western world. Weinberger would work hard in the next several years sealing agreements with America's closest allies to conduct research on the new system.

*   *   *

In January 1985, the administration received detailed knowledge of Soviet plans to dramatically escalate the war in Afghanistan. The intelligence came largely from the CIA source on the Soviet General Staff. It was detailed, direct, and substantial. Officials at the CIA had the materials translated and placed in folders. Bill Casey took them immediately to the NSC and Weinberger at the Pentagon.

There were dozens of pages from reports, translated by agency linguists, minutes from a General Staff meeting, and a report on military policy dealing with Afghanistan. They all pointed to a renewed push by the Soviet General Staff to win the war quickly. Soviet military commanders were planning to expand the war rapidly by shifting to more belligerent methods and sophisticated tactics. More specially trained Soviet commandos (Spetsnaz) would be brought in to fight the mujahedin, using advanced techniques and night attacks with special equipment. Almost one quarter of the Soviet army's special commandos would be assigned to Afghanistan. At the same time, the KGB presence would be dramatically increased to assist the special forces and regular troops. "Omsk vans," mobile sophisticated and integrated battlefield communications centers, would be deployed to intercept mujahedin battlefield communications. Coordinated aerial attacks on rebel targets would become a regular occurrence, in the hope of further demoralizing the enemy.

Special weapons including camouflaged mines and liquid gas explosives would be employed. Perhaps the most significant sign of this phase in the Soviet war effort was the assignment of a new commanding officer. General Mikhail Zaitsev was one of the wonder boys of the Soviet armed forces. At a relatively young age he had been given the prestigious command of Soviet forces in Germany. His presence alone suggested the heightened vigor with which the new strategy would be carried out. The documents indicated that the General Staff was being pressured by Soviet hard-liners to win the war and fast. The goal was an outright military victory in two years.[3]

The enormous rise in American aid flowing to the mujahedin would provide more weapons and supplies. But strategy and war aims needed to be radically shifted if the Soviet onslaught were to be turned back. Moscow had apparently decided that not losing did not mean winning. If Washington failed to do the same, defeat for the resistance might become a quick certainty.

Days after this information came from CIA, officials at the NSC and Pentagon were at work. A secret team of military officers and specialists began dissecting the Soviet battlefield strategy and developing effective countermeasures. A summary of the intelligence information went directly to the president, part of his regular Friday packet of Soviet intelligence information, and he digested it quickly. Casey, Weinberger, and McFarlane wanted to move fast. "The president wanted to move even faster," recalls McFarlane.[4]

In late January 1985, a meeting of the National Security Planning Group was convened. Issue number one was Afghanistan and recent Soviet plans to escalate the war. The president, who usually sat back amicably to listen to his aides debate, started the meeting forcefully. "Do whatever you have to to help the mujahedin not only survive, but win," he said sternly.[5] National Security Adviser Robert McFarlane was tasked with developing a new U.S. strategy and codifying it in a secret directive for the president to sign.

Working with NSC staff members Vincent Cannistraro, Donald Fortier, and Adm. John Poindexter, McFarlane put together a document that radically remade U.S. objectives in the war. Signed by President Reagan in March 1985, NSDD-166 articulated for the first time specific objectives with regard to the Afghan war and put them in a strategic context. And the entire government foreign affairs apparatus would be directed to support the effort. "We all at the NSC felt we had to alter the approach to the war in Afghanistan," recalls McFarlane. "We felt that we had created a stalemate. If we could defeat the new challenge and up our support, we could win."[6]

The new directive had several key elements. First, there was to be more effective supply and distribution of weapons to the mujahedin. Special attention would be paid to supplying more advanced high-tech weapons systems. At the same time, the U.S. intelligence community was directed to put more resources into collecting intelligence on the Soviet war effort. Particular attention would be paid to Soviet order of battle, tactics, and force structure. The political and military intentions of the Soviet High Command would also be assessed and monitored.

A third key element was heightening the international political costs of the war. Working through organizations such as the United Nations, the United States would exert maximum political pressure on the Soviets to withdraw. There would also be a linkage between the Soviet occupation of Afghanistan and improved relations with the United States.[7]

But the most significant paragraph in NSDD-166 came in a long annex to the document, which articulated Reagan administration objectives. When the Carter administration had launched the mujahedin covert aid program in 1980, it had issued a top-secret intelligence finding describing U.S. goals and objectives in Afghanistan. The aim was to "harass" the occupying Soviet force. Victory was not just a far-off fantasy but a cruel joke. But the administration was also nervous about angering Moscow by being too aggressive in Afghanistan. The modest covert aid program with vague objectives was the result. For five years the Reagan administration had labored under the same finding. But the new annex changed the U.S. goal. The new goal was victory, the outright defeat of the Soviet armed forces in Afghanistan.

Because of that radical shift, NSDD-166 proved a major watershed in the effort to expel Soviet forces from Afghanistan. "You didn't have a major coordinated [covert] program until President Reagan came into office," says Vince Cannistraro, who served in the CIA in the 1970s and 1980s. "You didn't have a coherent response until 1985. NSDD-166 was the turning point in the war. It is hard to overestimate, to err on that side. If you look at the military situation on the ground prior to 1985, you had a stalemate. But all they could do was wage a hit-and-run guerrilla war. They didn't have the high-tech weapons to turn back the Soviets. That soon changed with NSDD-166." With the new policy objective in Washington, things began to change on the ground in Afghanistan.[8]

Afghanistan was one of two geopolitical challenges Moscow faced in early 1985. The war was costing the Soviets $3 to $4 billion per year, largely because of the arms and equipment the West was providing the mujahedin. "We always had a sense that this was big money from Moscow's perspective, money that had to be specifically allocated for the war effort at the expense of their economy," recalls Roger Robinson. "Siphoning off precious Soviet hard currency resources in Afghanistan and elsewhere complemented our success with the strategic trade triad."[9] United States sanctions against Poland were forcing Moscow to prop up the Jaruzelski government with an emergency infusion of $1 to $2 billion per year. In both these outposts in the Soviet empire, American policy was contributing to the crisis.

But Moscow could cope with these challenges, or so it was believed. The duel was manageable. It was assumed that the resistance movements in Poland and Afghanistan would eventually succumb, or at least wither into irrelevant nuisances. What was of most concern in early 1985 was SDI. While many Western scientists remained skeptical about the ability of such a scheme to work, Moscow was acting as if success was a given. It had made large-scale resource shifts to the military industrial sector in a desperate attempt to maintain Soviet competitiveness in the arena.

The Reagan administration was well aware of how concerned the Kremlin was about the program. Oleg Gordievsky, a KGB officer in London and a double agent for British intelligence, provided reports on their reactions. Summaries of his reports were circulated among senior U.S. officials. According to Gordievsky, Col. A. I. Sazhin, a military attaché at the Soviet embassy in London, told a group of diplomats and intelligence officers that military officials believed the SDI system might prove 90 percent effective. And Sazhin saw little chance of the Soviets' being able to keep pace with the United States.[10]

Soviet concerns about SDI were also evident in a February 1985 KGB report Gordievsky provided to his handlers. The Reagan administration was "striving to gain military superiority over the Soviet Union," the KGB warned. The Strategic Defense Initiative was "widely publicized as an effective method of defense of the whole population of America in a nuclear war." But there was also the possibility that the United States was hoping "to draw the USSR into a costly arms race in areas where according to American estimates it is lagging behind the USA." Alarmed about the system, the report listed a number of important responses for the KGB, including "possible active measures on the Soviet side designed to promote opposition to American 'star wars' plans and support for the attitude of the USSR at the Geneva talks."[11]

By early 1985, the secret economic war against the Kremlin was beginning to bite as well. Expected credits, hard currency, and technology from the West were drying up or being cut back. The Siberian gas pipeline, so critical to the Soviet hard currency earning structure, was proceeding, but its size had been cut in half and it was two years behind schedule. Although U.S. sanctions had been rescinded, they had caused major disruptions in the construction schedule. "Intelligence indicated that sanctions cost them a minimum of two years," recalls Roger Robinson.[12] Oleg Tikov, a specialist formerly with the Soviet Oil Ministry, concurs: "It was not an excuse when we blamed American sanctions for the delay. It was the truth. Everything was chaotic. First we had no turbines, then we tried to make our own, then we could get them again. What chaos, what disruptions. Two years, and billions of dollars it cost us."[13]

The Reagan administration had managed to further complicate the construction process through the technical disinformation program it was running. "Bill Casey had told some of us on the NSC not to worry unduly about the pipeline, even after full construction resumed," recalls Roger Robinson. "They had a lot of problems over there with pipelines and turbines breaking down, fires in control facilities, and so forth. Was it all a function of Soviet incompetence or bad luck? We had reason to doubt it."[14]

The delay was an enormous blow to the Kremlin. The Siberian gas pipeline was supposed to be a cash cow, to help Moscow get through difficult economic times. In 1980, it was projected that perhaps $8 to $10 billion in hard currency could be generated per year by as early as 1985, and $15 to $30 billion or more later in the 1990s, after the second strand was fully subscribed (depending on oil prices). But because of the Reagan administration's unyielding stance, there would be no second strand. And because of the sanctions, Moscow was having to wait two extra years to see extra hard currency, with the economy in a tailspin. In addition, they were already out perhaps another $15 to $20 billion because of the delay in the first strand.

At the same time, the infusion of Western technology that had been so central to keeping the Soviet economy afloat and developing had declined precipitously. While it was impossible to calculate the complete cost that tightening technology transfer laws was having on the Soviet economy, some reports were offering evidence that the bite was in the order of billions per year. A formal report entitled "Total Effect of Technology Transfer on U.S./Western Security, A Defense Department Overview," informally called the Aggregate Assessment, was issued in December 1984. A team of engineers examined seventy-nine technology export licenses that had been denied over the last year and tried to determine the value the exports would have to the Soviet industrial economic base. The estimated price tag for those technologies alone was between $500 million and $1 billion per year for twelve years in additional research and development costs and manpower. The government was denying thousands of exports per year, so the total cost was much higher.[15] "We were just doggedly roughing ahead with this policy," recalls Stef Halper. "It became clear that they could not acquire the technologies they needed. They might need some machine tools from the West, and we would squelch the deal. So a factory would sit idle for months. We felt we had our fingers on the pulse."[16]

Only one track of the economic war against Moscow had yet to be fully implemented. Lower oil prices became a key administration objective in 1985. For many the main advantage was to the United States. "We wanted lower international oil prices, largely for the benefit of the American economy," says Edwin Meese, then the White House counsel. "The fact that it meant trouble for Moscow was icing on the cake."[17] But some individuals recognized the gravity of the subject as it related to Moscow's precarious economic position. Roger Robinson recalls, "Bill Casey was keeping an eye on oil prices almost daily, and so were we. It was the centerpiece of the Soviet hard currency earnings structure and principal funding source of its military industrial complex."[18] Some believed that lower oil prices would happen simply by letting the market process run its course. Others, like Casey and Weinberger, thought the world's largest oil producer, Saudi Arabia, needed some encouragement and support from the United States.

It was against this backdrop that unusual import was given to an official state visit in early 1985. One of the first foreign heads of state to visit President Reagan at the start of his second term was King Fahd. For the Saudis, raising oil production dramatically was not difficult. And production was relatively cheap. It cost the Saudis only $1.50 barrel to extract oil from the desert floor, so they could turn a healthy profit at a lower market price than just about any other world producer.

The administration had quietly been campaigning for lower oil prices. Weinberger had raised the subject generally with the Saudis, and Casey had been even more pointed during his September visit. Energy Secretary John Herrington had been publicly trying to coax the price down by arguing that it was artificially high as a result of OPEC policies that no longer reflected market realities.

Getting the price of oil down would have an immediate stimulative economic impact. A $5 drop in the price of a barrel of oil would increase the U.S. gross national product by about 1.4 percent, reduce inflation, and increase disposable income. Lower oil prices would also directly reduce the U.S. trade deficit. "It was to our advantage all around," recalls Adm. John Poindexter. "It was in our interest to drive down the price of oil as low as we could. We saw it as a very important objective to keep the price of oil down."[19] Oil pricing was part of the overall strategy and was apparently codified into policy. Poindexter says, "I would be surprised if in NSDD-75, an NSDD after that, or a covert action finding about Saudi Arabia if there wasn't something that in a general way addressed that issue. Something like 'It is the objective of the United States to reduce the foreign price of oil because of the effect that it has on the free world economy but also the impact on the Soviet Union.' "[20]

The visit of King Fahd would include multiple secret meetings. While the king met with the president, Sheik Yamani, the Saudi oil minister, would have consultations with Shultz, McFarlane, and Energy Secretary Herrington. Yamani had been hearing for months the American drumbeat for lower prices. The meetings in Washington were no different. A secret briefing memorandum prepared for Shultz on February 9, 1985, outlined the issues and positions of the United States. Implicit in it was the assumption that world oil prices were too high and that the U.S. would benefit from a reduction. The key objective of the meeting listed in the memo reads: "Discuss the present world oil price situation: OPEC/Saudi efforts to defend OPEC's system of official prices and production ceilings and allegations the U.S. is manipulating oil markets." The memo noted, "OPEC ministers including Yamani have accused the U.S. of engineering a plot to drive down oil prices to some pre-conceived level." Yamani was only half wrong: the United States had no preconceived price.[21]

The Fahd visit had enormous symbolic and political implications. Robert McFarlane met several days before the king's arrival with Prince Bandar to assure that Fahd would be afforded special attention and the respect he deserved. The king would be getting a one-on-one meeting with the president for as long as he liked, as well as several private meetings with other U.S. officials.

On February 12, the king's motorcade arrived at the White House. Surrounded by aides in traditional garb, Fahd was escorted to a private room to meet the president. Reagan greeted him warmly. No aides were present, and no notes were taken.

King Fahd had several concerns of note, as did the president. The two leaders had mutual admiration, each believing the other to be a quite courageous figure. To the president, Fahd was standing by the United States in an increasingly hostile and turbulent region. He was also providing tens of millions a year to the mujahedin in Afghanistan and the contras in Nicaragua, two of the president's favorite foreign policy projects. Fahd saw in Reagan someone who had fought hard for Saudi interests on a number of occasions.

The two discussed the problems of the region, particularly the continuing—indeed mounting—threat posed by Iran. At one point Reagan looked the Saudi king straight in the eye and gave him his absolute assurance that he would do whatever was necessary to ensure the integrity of Saudi Arabia. It was something Reagan excelled at—a personal diplomatic gesture pregnant with meaning. Fahd was very pleased.

The two also discussed international economic issues, the problems caused by the strength of the dollar and the U.S. deficit. Then President Reagan raised the subject of international oil prices. The economy of Saudi Arabia's chief protector, the United States, greatly benefited from lower oil prices, Reagan told Fahd. A strong America was in the Saudi interest. Saudi Arabia's chief enemies—Libya, Iran, the Soviet Union—benefited from high oil prices. The United States hoped for a cooperative relationship with the royal family, Reagan said.[22] He was reinforcing and echoing some of the themes that Weinberger and Casey had articulated in previous meetings with Saudi officials. The sensitive issue was handled by the president with characteristic verve. No quid pro quo was ever presented and no specific price ever suggested. Instead the issue was managed as a spouse might seek to change a partner through a kind missive denoting the benefits of the marriage union. But the message to Fahd was unambiguous—the president who had demonstrated his commitment to Saudi Arabia wanted oil prices down for the benefit of both countries and the injury of their common enemies.

Two days after his meeting with the president and a series of other meetings with senior administration officials, King Fahd hosted a feast for 600 of his closest friends and supporters at the J. W. Marriott Hotel in downtown Washington. Fahd invited corporate CEOs, government officials, and others who had significant dealings with Riyadh. The gala did not go off without a hitch: someone had mixed up the seating charts, and guests were forced to find their own tables. But the spread was lavish and the atmosphere affable. Fahd reportedly spent nearly $300,000 on the food for the event. Administration officials were on hand to join the festivities and celebrate the warm relations between the two countries.

1. Margaret Thatcher, *The Downing Street Years* (New York: HarperCollins, 1993), p. 467.
2. Ibid., p. 468.
3. Robert McFarlane, interview with the author; Vincent Cannistraro, interview with the author.
4. Robert McFarlane, interview with the author.
5. Robert McFarlane, interview with the author.
6. Robert McFarlane, interview with the author.
7. Vincent Cannistraro, interview with the author.
8. Vincent Cannistraro, interview with the author.
9. Roger Robinson, interview with the author.
10. Interview with U.S. intelligence official; see also Christopher Andrew and Oleg Gordievsky, *Instructions from the Centre* (London: Hodder and Stoughton, 1991), p. 107.
11. Ibid., pp. 112–13.
12. Roger Robinson, interview with the author.
13. Oleg Tikov, interview with the author.
14. Roger Robinson, interview with the author.
15. "U.S. Tallies Cost to Soviets of Technology Transfer Rules," *Aviation Week and Space Technology*, December 10, 1984, p. 67.
16. Stef Halper, interview with the author.
17. Edwin Meese, interview with the author.

18. Roger Robinson, interview with the author.
19. John Poindexter, interview with the author.
20. John Poindexter, interview with the author.
21. State Department internal memo.
22. U.S. official, interview with the author.

16

Poland, at the heart of the Soviet empire, was a continuing battleground between the two superpowers in 1985. Moscow was supporting the Jaruzelski government with economic aid and the other tentacles of the Soviet state, intelligence and raw military power. Washington was continuing its covert financial and material support for the underground, as well as passing along critical intelligence that might prove useful.

The Jaruzelski government's declared amnesty of July 22, 1984, had a mixed effect on the underground. Several hundred activists had been freed, but there was continued—even heightened—police harassment. The government was trying to lure away support for the opposition. If citizens ended their antigovernment activities immediately, they would be spared prosecution. Failure to do so would mean arrest. By the January 1, 1985, deadline, approximately 350 activists had taken the government up on its offer. But the core leadership was intact and undaunted. As Lech Walesa promised in a New Year's Eve address, the underground would "continue their struggle until a final victory."

The general failure of the amnesty gambit led government authorities to redouble their efforts to stamp out the opposition through force. Police conducted sweeps looking for underground print shops and secret organizing meetings. On February 13, twenty plainclothes policemen forced their way into an apartment in the Zaspa district of Gdansk, where Lech Walesa was meeting with several underground leaders. Diligent intelligence work had paid off. Among those arrested were five regional leaders of the Solidarity movement: Bogdan Lis of Gdansk, Wladyslaw Frasyniuk of Wroclaw, Stanislaw Handzlik of Krakow, Janusz Palubicki of Poznan, and Adam Michnik of Warsaw. The group had been meeting for two hours, discussing strategy and the possibility of organizing another major strike. Two days later police held Michnik, Lis, and Frasyniuk in custody. By November 1985, they had a total of 340 underground activists under lock and key.

In early 1985, the security personnel pressed their war against the underground. Polish and Soviet intelligence officials were desperately working to expose and shut down the financial and material pipeline running from the West to the underground. The KGB directed its gaze at the CIA but also at the Vatican. Its concerns were apparent in an early 1985 top-secret memo prepared by KGB Director Viktor Chebrikov and sent to the director of the Polish Interior Ministry. In it Chebrikov ordered the Interior Ministry to maximize its efforts to "expose material support coming from imperialist circles in the West." The stern KGB chief chided Poland for being the "weakest link" in the Soviet bloc and for tolerating subversion. He encouraged the Polish secret police to infiltrate the underground and to bribe activists to pass along information. He also committed more KGB resources to uncovering "provocateurs" who were menacing Poland and "funding subversion."

The KGB also deemed that the Vatican required increased observation. Officials of Soviet intelligence accused the Holy See itself of subversion in Eastern Europe. One report noted, "The anti-socialist bias of the Vatican's activity has become particularly marked with the arrival on the papal throne of John Paul II, whose hostility towards the countries of the socialist community is conditioned both by his personal anti-communist and anti-Soviet convictions and by the influence exerted on him by the most conservative representatives of the Catholic clergy and reactionary political figures of the West, especially the United States." The KGB charged that the Vatican was seeking to expand its influence in Eastern Europe. "The Vatican's principal interest is concentrated on the most 'promising' countries of Eastern Europe, from its

point of view: Poland, Hungary and Yugoslavia." In view of the
Church's political predispositions and its work in Poland, the KGB
made a priority of "uncovering and exposing cooperation between
representatives of the Vatican and organizations of the Catholic Church,
and the CIA."[1]

Reagan administration officials with knowledge of the covert aid
program were always mindful that if it were exposed by Moscow, there
would be serious and possibly dramatic repercussions. A below the
surface distress emanated from the White House when complications
arose. Such was the case in late February 1985, when Polish exile Jacek
Knapik was returning home from the West. He was an activist and
Solidarity sympathizer, so when he arrived at airport customs after
landing, his belongings were thoroughly searched. Among them police
found items they claimed "show[ed] the ties of Solidarity abroad" with
the Solidarity underground in Poland and "Western intelligence services." Police displayed a letter written by Jerzy Milewski, head of
Solidarity's Brussels office, to Bogdan Lis, the leader of the Solidarity
underground in Gdansk. The letter supposedly described contacts between Solidarity officers and officials of the State Department's Eastern
European section. Knapik denied the charges that he was involved in any
sort of subversive activities and denounced the whole thing as a frame-
up. Nothing ever came of the arrest.

But the incident demonstrated how a courier might be vulnerable to interception by authorities. Solidarity offices in the West, the
AFL-CIO, and the agency had been using couriers to transfer information and funds to the underground on a regular basis. The process
usually worked because of sympathetic customs officials who could
make the proper arrangements. Couriers remained an important tool,
but beginning in 1985 much greater use of Radio Free Europe and
Voice of America was made to convey intelligence to the underground.

The Polish Interior Ministry saw American diplomatic posts in
Poland as links in the chain, so diplomatic personnel in Warsaw and
those at the U.S. consulate in Krakow became targets for even greater
surveillance. "They were convinced it was being run from the embassy,"
recalls one intelligence official. "They were following everyone and
going through everything that went in and out of the embassy, including
the trash. They were really frustrated."[2] In February, the U.S. defense

attaché at the embassy in Warsaw was expelled by Polish authorities on allegations of spying. In early May, two U.S. diplomats assigned to the consulate in Krakow were roughed up and declared persona non grata, for alleged involvement in antigovernment activities. In a desperate attempt to disrupt support from the West, the Interior Ministry also shut down the air courier for the U.S. embassy. The U.S. Air Force had for years flown periodically into Warsaw, usually carrying mail and foodstuffs.[3] Polish officials thought perhaps it was carrying more than provisions for the embassy. The action proved more an act of frustration and intimidation than anything else.

By early 1985, the cash flow to Solidarity was running at a peak of $8 million. It was sustaining the underground. Much of the leadership was back in jail by the early spring, but the resistance activities continued. On May I, while the government celebrated the official May Day holiday, more than 15,000 people in Warsaw and 2,000 in Gdansk took to the streets in support of Solidarity. It was the largest display of defiance since the declaration of martial law in 1981.

At the same time, a secret literary movement was flourishing. The underground was publishing thousands of newspapers, books, and monographs. One publication was entitled "The Small Conspirator." Written by an outspoken and wily architect named Czeslaw Bielecki, who was combative and aggressive in all he did against the government, it told how to conspire against the government, even in minor ways, without compromising and without being arrested. Writing under the pseudonym Maciej Polecki, the six foot five Bielecki had established a clandestine publishing house called CDN—the Polish initialism for "to be continued." It produced a variety of pamphlets and monographs, even a Solidarity newspaper for the army. Unbeknownst to Bielecki, U.S. government funds provided some of the equipment and supplies that had helped launch the enterprise and later sustained it. The covert pipeline was bankrolling similar projects by the thousands across Poland.[4]

In March 1985, Secretary of Defense Caspar Weinberger was in Luxembourg to attend a series of meetings with NATO defense ministers. The alliance was in reasonably good shape, having survived the storm over the deployment of the Pershing II and Cruise missiles and the pipeline fight of 1982. Weinberger had worked hard since the earliest days of his tenure to move the Europeans closer to the U.S. position on weapons systems and alliance strategy. Now he had his toughest sell yet—convincing his European counterparts to support the Strategic Defense Initiative (SDI) and even participate in the research program. Support from Margaret Thatcher had been helpful in preventing the issue from becoming a debate between the two sides of the Atlantic.

During the meeting, Weinberger was passionate about the potential benefits of the strategic system. It would not decouple Europe (remove it from the American nuclear umbrella); SDI would enhance deterrence, not undermine it; the system would encourage superpower stability, not impair it. But perhaps the most persuasive argument was based on economics. The Reagan administration was planning to allocate research and development contracts that could prove quite lucrative to a number of European manufacturers and scientists. In addition, research on the system would lead to multiple scientific and technological spin-offs. Did Europe really want to lose so much in terms of economic and technological benefits? Weinberger's face-to-face lobbying in Luxembourg added considerable momentum to secret bilateral talks the administration was pursuing with a number of key allies. Eventually a series of SDI collaboration agreements were signed. Britain (December 1985), Germany (March 1986), Israel (May 1986), Italy (September 1986), and Japan (July 1987) added their considerable scientific and technical abilities to the research program. The Strategic Defense Initiative was quickly becoming an international research program, something Moscow could never hope to match.

As Weinberger lobbied in Luxembourg, intelligence coming out of Moscow indicated that there was a cloud of uneasiness hanging over the Kremlin. For months intelligence analysts and NSC officials had been tracking the health of Konstantin Chernenko, the tired, decrepit general secretary, who was fighting an array of maladies. In mid-January, a Warsaw Pact meeting had been scheduled for Moscow. It was expected to be a tense and important session that would include encouraging the Eastern European satellites (particularly Poland) to seek out and destroy their domestic enemies. But the gathering was canceled at the last minute because of Chernenko's poor health. Some American intelligence analysts were taking bets on the date he would expire.

Analysts at the CIA at one point informed Bill Casey that Chernenko was already lifeless and that the Kremlin was delaying the announcement until a new leader was chosen. By special courier the report was sent immediately to National Security Adviser Robert McFarlane and to Caspar Weinberger at the Pentagon. Three days later, at 6:00 A.M., Chernenko's death was formally announced, and his heir was displayed for all the world to see. Mikhail Gorbachev, age fifty-four, was the new general secretary. The fact that the death of Chernenko and the elevation of Gorbachev were announced almost simultaneously indicated that the analysts' hunch had been correct.

Gorbachev inherited an empire in veiled crisis, facing geopolitical challenges in Afghanistan and Poland. The hard currency earning structure that had sustained the rickety economy was twisted and tangled by what cumulatively amounted to an economic war. And Gorbachev faced an economy that was not up to an American high-tech defense drive that would compel him to expend even greater resources for the military. As he began mastering the controls of the Soviet ship of state, senior administration officials worked hard to press their advantage.

During the late spring, Casey set out on a series of trips to check the operation of several initiatives. He began with a swing through Europe to look into the Solidarity operation and to search for new opportunities in Eastern Europe. Then he flew on to Pakistan and the covert supply line running to the mujahedin in Afghanistan. There the new U.S. strategy and greater supplies meant that the tempo and nature of the war were going to change. Casey wanted to assess the progress that was being made on the battlefield and the effort to take the war into the Soviet Union. The final port of call was Saudi Arabia, where he would follow up on a number of subjects, including oil pricing.

In Frankfurt, Casey met with some of the European field officers to talk about a wide array of issues. He also had lunch with an official from the Swedish prime minister's office, to whom he extended the administration's thank-you for serving as a conduit to Solidarity. Contrary to early concerns, the Swedes were proving quite adept at masking the supplies going into Poland. Polish officials were trying to monitor all shipments coming from Western Europe, but they had failed to expose the supply path. Rewarding the Swedes' cooperation, Casey promised more naval intelligence, particularly in the areas where Soviet submarines were operating. Before the meeting broke up, he asked the Swedes to step up their medical aid to Afghan refugees in Pakistan.

While in Frankfurt, Casey also received interesting reports about Czechoslovakia. Western intelligence officials had identified several antigovernment underground organizations that might benefit from American covert assistance. The president had always envisioned U.S. support being funneled to underground movements in several Soviet bloc countries. His NSDD-32 had explicitly cast a wide net when it came to where the United States would consider supporting such movements. Identifying the organizations was the easy part; figuring out how to get assistance to them was another matter. Casey had the reports sent to the White House, then put some people to work on the problem.

Casey's plane left Frankfurt early the next morning for the long flight to Islamabad. Onboard he read a five-inch stack of intelligence reports concerning Afghanistan. The administration was gravely concerned about the situation there. The level of Soviet military activity was rising fast. In particular there was a concerted effort to cut mujahedin supply lines from Pakistan. Soviet force levels were growing and were now estimated to number some 120,000 troops, with more than 30,000 just across the border being ferried over for special attacks on mujahedin targets in the northern provinces. The attacks were also becoming more sophisticated. There were additional night assaults, with Spetsnaz forces surprising mujahedin units, who were unable to respond in the darkness because the resistance lacked night vision equipment. Seismic mines and other new explosives were being introduced. Mujahedin casualties were almost double the rate in previous years.

But amid the pessimism and concern, some administration officials had a flicker of hope. Reports from the Soviet Union indicated that the war was becoming increasingly unpopular. Polls of Soviet citizens overseas indicated that 25 percent opposed the war, a remarkably high rate given that only the politically reliable elite had the opportunity to travel. The cynical Soviet populace appeared to believe that losses were much higher than Western estimates. Robert McFarlane in particular thought that even a small increase in expenses and losses could have disproportionate political effects on the Soviet commitment.

When Casey arrived in Islamabad, the city was perhaps more tense than at any previous time. The Soviets were escalating operations along the Pakistani border, trying both to cut off the mujahedin supply routes and to intimidate the Zia government. Random bombings in Peshawar, the border town that served as a base for the muj, were becoming all too common.

Pakistani intelligence had evidence of Soviet-sponsored subversion directed against the mujahedin supply base. The Pakistan Progressive Party (PPP), factions of the Movement for the Restoration of Democracy (MRD), the Baluch Students Organization (BSO), and the Pakistan National Party (PNP) were all receiving Soviet funds to encourage dissent. The Al Zulfikar terrorist organization, based out of Afghanistan, was sending personnel into the country to terrorize the civilian population. The KHAD and KGB had apparently approached two border tribes, the Afridi and the Shinwari, and offered them arms. Unruly and mercenary, the tribes were hostile to any central authority. Soviet air incursions were also on the upswing.

President Zia and Director Casey sat down as they had many times before. But times were more difficult now for Zia. Domestic political opposition was growing, and critics of the army had somehow lost their fear. Zia was the key to the Afghan project, and keeping him in power was critical. Most of the political opposition groups were against cooperating with the United States.

The CIA was running several programs to help keep Zia in power. He was receiving plenty of intelligence, including highly prized satellite photos and electronic communications intercepts on his enemies. The CIA had also organized and was advising the security team around the Pakistani president. To reward Zia for his commitment to the Afghan cause, a new military and economic security assistance package for Pakistan was being put together in Washington. It would be worth almost $1 billion more than the previous one. Several administration officials were also working on Zia's request for high-tech weapons such as the Stinger. But there was always the chronic trepidation that

Soviet threats and mischief would wear Zia down and that he might be tempted to reach an accommodation with the USSR.

That was especially the case in 1985, as the war was about to enter a new, even more dangerous phase. Hundreds of mujahedin were being specially trained by the ISI to run military operations deep inside Soviet territory. It would be only a question of time before Moscow would discover the gambit. Then the temperature would rise to precarious levels.

From General Zia's office Casey took a bullet-proof CIA car with armed agents in tow to a military facility outside the city. Waiting were General Akhtar and Brigadier Yousaf, eager to discuss the American revision in policy toward Afghanistan. Covert assistance was about to balloon—basically doubling in size. That would solve a lot of the logistical problems the resistance was facing, but there would be more sophisticated equipment as well: advanced night vision technology, special explosives, and precision guided munitions. Perhaps the most important contribution to the war effort was plans to raise mujahedin access to high-tech American intelligence.

The United States had the best technical intelligence apparatus in the world, hands down. The new administration strategy, as detailed in NSDD-166, was to devote a large share of that system to winning the war in Afghanistan. It was a valuable resource that had been utilized only sparingly. A KH-11 spy satellite was being redirected from its regular orbit to gather more intelligence on Afghanistan. The satellite intelligence would come weekly, to keep the Pakistani ISI aware of Soviet maneuvers and operations. It would help in identifying targets and planning actions. Complex operations—coordinated and precise—had become possible for the first time. By midsummer the trickle of satellite photos became a stream.

At the same time spy satellites had their gaze redirected, the American worldwide net of electronic intelligence was collectively shifted to gather information relevant to the war effort. The National Security Agency (NSA) was recasting its electronic eavesdropping assets to concentrate for the first time on Afghanistan and Soviet Central Asia. By the summer of 1985, specialists from the NSA arrived in Islamabad to establish a team to cull information, classify it, and bring the relevant intelligence to Yousaf. The intelligence web was so great that few aspects of the Soviet war effort avoided American exposure. For example, NSA technicians were monitoring military aircraft communications all around air bases in the Soviet Union. Every pilot was given a "signature"—which identified him by accent, tone of voice, or speech pattern. The signature was placed in a computer so that if it was later detected in Afghanistan, the NSA would know which military units had been rotated in, and what their capabilities were.

American expertise in the form of military specialists and analysts was another resource the NSC wanted involved in the war. By mid-1985 officials at the Pentagon and CIA were analyzing photos and offering assessments to Pakistani military and intelligence officials about Soviet order of battle and tactics. As a consequence, the Soviet army and commanders would become well known to the resistance, even predictable. Resistance commanders could anticipate a Soviet move with regularity.

Under the new NSC strategy, the CIA would also supply the ISI and mujahedin with an array of advanced burst communicators—virtually impossible for the Soviet army to intercept. Communication on the battlefield (or rather the lack of it) had been a chronic problem. It was taking weeks, sometimes months to get information to commanders. Mujahedin units only miles apart had difficulty relaying information with any sort of accuracy. The new equipment would greatly aid in the coordination of resistance operations.

In keeping with the objective to raise precipitously the costs of occupation for Moscow, General Akhtar and Brigadier Yousaf outlined to Casey the shift in targeting and methods that they planned. A series of attacks on Soviet natural gas and oil facilities in Afghanistan would begin in earnest. Sabotage was not popular with the mujahedin. It was not glorious to blow up a pipeline. The practice was anathema to a people who, having declared a holy war, found the highest honor in dying for their cause. Nonetheless, Yousaf saw to it that acts of sabotage increased. The major natural gas pipeline from Shibarghan to the Soviet border was a particularly inviting target. Buried three feet underground and submerged under the Amu River, it was an enormously important economic target because it was fueling Soviet industries in Central Asia. The mujahedin exposed the pipe and blew it up in several places. There were also rocket attacks on several natural gas facilities, which started two fires that burned for days. "Reportedly," according to Yousaf, "all the industrial units using gas were closed for two weeks."[5]

When the discussion of tactics was complete, Akhtar, Yousaf, and Casey turned their attention to hardware. The sniper rifles had been procured, and more advanced artillery was on the way. But one problem remained. The mujahedin lacked an effective response to Soviet air attacks. Surface to air missiles provided in the past had proven totally ineffective. The SAM-7 was awful, and the British Blowpipe and Chinese Red Arrow only slightly better. All the major systems tried were ill suited to the guerrilla war the muj were fighting. Over 90 percent of Soviet aircraft losses occurred when they were attacked on the ground. Failure to counter Soviet airpower would put the new strategy of victory in jeopardy. The one system that might do the trick was the "wonder weapon," as Akhtar called it. Islamabad was going to get its first shipment of Stinger missiles in July. What about giving some to the muj? Casey saw the need for the Stinger and had been pushing it for months. Hitting Soviet airpower was the next logical step up the ladder of escalation. "When we start knocking $20 million planes out of the sky, the Kremlin will get nervous," Casey told aides. Yet there was resistance from the State Department and some elements of Defense, which feared the missiles might fall into hostile hands.

Casey assured Akhtar that there were many in the administration, including the president, who would seriously consider the matter. He promised to raise it directly with National Security Adviser McFarlane and the president.

The next element of the Reagan strategy was explored when Casey flew to Saudi Arabia. The kingdom now was very different from the one he had visited in 1981. Oil production had plummeted from a high of 10 million barrels a day that year to 2 million. Oil revenues were off $70 billion from three years ago. In Riyadh, office buildings were only 60 percent full.[6]

The internal threats to the regime were violently displayed in mid-May, when Muslim extremists set off a series of bombs in Riyadh. The bombings had been executed by Islamic Jihad, a group committed to both the Iranian revolution and the overthrow of the Saudi royal family. A mystery caller had told one news agency: "Our cells acting in Saudi Arabia have started carrying out the operations assigned to them in order to shake the reactionary Saudi dynasty." The caller had charged that the House of Saud had "seized by force and trickery the holiest land of Islam, and we shall therefore plot earnestly with other Muslim believers to regain power and oust the despots." The attacks played on the royal family's worst fears.

Casey and the king spoke at length about the new U.S. commitment in Afghanistan and the contra war in Nicaragua. They also discussed the Iran-Iraq War and prospects for a settlement. Saddam Hussein seemed genuinely interested in a peace agreement with Khomeini, if only because he was doing poorly on the battlefield. But Tehran was exhibiting little interest in peace. The mullahs appeared to want nothing less than Hussein's total humiliation and defeat.

The fire of Iranian radicalism was not burning out; the mission of undermining the conservative monarchies of the Persian Gulf remained firmly in place. Casey told Fahd that the president was very concerned about continued Soviet involvement in the region, particularly in South Yemen and Syria. In light of the recent terrorist bombings in Riyadh, he offered the assistance of the CIA's Office of Technical Services to provide additional internal security for the royal family. Fahd thankfully accepted.

At the twilight of the conversation, Casey yet again raised the administration's view that stable and ultimately lower oil prices would be an extremely favorable development. He even offered Fahd a bit of information that would prove helpful to the Saudis. The former international banker told Fahd that the Treasury Department was planning over the next twelve months or so to slowly devalue the dollar. The scheme was part of a campaign to boost U.S. exports by making them cheaper when sold in other currencies. This news was invaluable to Fahd because many Saudi foreign assets were in nondollar currencies. When the dollar did decline, these assets would suddenly be worth more. The information would go far in boosting the kingdom's difficult financial condition. As was Saudi fashion, Fahd apparently did not directly address the subject of oil pricing and production. But it was clear that the Saudis were now indebted to the United States for security as well as some economic help.

✻　✻　✻

On July 29, Casey was in New York City for a secret meeting with several dozen American CEOs. They all had significant business interests in the Soviet Union. Included in the group were Dwayne Andreas of Archer-Daniels-Midland, Edgar Bronfman of Seagram, Martin Davis of Gulf & Western, Donald Kendall of PepsiCo, Laurance Rockefeller, Rawleigh Warner of Mobil, and George Champion of the Chase Manhattan Bank. The venue was the upscale Link Club at 36 East Sixty-second Street.

It was an informal gathering, one which senior Reagan cabinet officials periodically held with corporate America. The topic was the relative health of the USSR. Casey's prognosis on the political situation in the communist superpower could have an enormous impact on East-West trade, by either shaking or building American business confidence. Andreas greeted Casey in the lobby, and they went to the third-floor dining room and a U-shaped table. Andreas and Casey were on a first-name basis, and the ADM chairman had been a good source of intelligence on the Soviet Union. Some of the executives Casey had known for years, well before he became DCI. All had been more or less cooperative in sharing their views on the Soviet Union with the National Collection Division. Several executives were allowing the agency to use their corporations for cover both in the United States and overseas.

After lunch, Andreas stood up at the head of the table with Casey seated beside him and gave the guest of honor a glowing introduction. He highlighted Casey's service in the OSS during World War II and his work in New York financial circles. There was mention of his tenure at the SEC and at the State Department as head of economic affairs. "Currently you know him as the director of the CIA. I present to you Bill Casey." There was excited applause as Casey went to the podium. Even for corporate executives of Fortune 500 companies, there was giddy intrigue about hearing a private presentation from the director of the CIA.

Casey began by giving his reading of the new Soviet general secretary. These were businesspeople, so Casey spoke most about Gorbachev's economic and political program. The new general secretary was committed to fixing the faltering Soviet economy. He was going to try some radical solutions, but they would most likely fail. The party bureaucracy was against him, and so was the military, Casey somberly told the crowd. The Soviet economy was chaotic, and there were acute resource crises and structural problems. There would be attempts to make the business climate more hospitable to Western companies, but they would be largely a facade. Casey reminded his audience that in February Moscow had had to temporarily suspend payments to its foreign suppliers because of a currency shortage. Companies doing business with the Soviets would be leery. It was a pessimistic message on the economic side.

In the political sphere Casey was more optimistic. Soviet expansion would slow because making continued probes and extending the empire was too expensive; Moscow was out of money. The empire was proving a financial drain, not an economic benefit. Gorbachev just might be compelled to reduce military spending to deal with the economic crisis.

In conclusion, Casey made the pitch that he usually did to closed meetings with business executives: share information with the administration. "I look to you for clues as to what's happening in the Soviet Union. You can take the pulse of the Soviet economy—and give us the heart rate."

After the speech and a few questions, his audience gave him an ovation. As he left, Casey slapped a few backs and shook some more hands.[7]

In the summer of 1985, Washington was abuzz about the new Soviet general secretary. Mikhail Gorbachev was an enigma. A full generation younger than Chernenko, he had traveled extensively in the West during his youth. His mannerisms were more Western than his predecessors', and he was already projecting quite vocal opinions on their tenure, during the so-called years of stagnation.

On June 25, 1985, the NSC assembled in the Old Executive Office Building to discuss a multitude of security issues. With vigor and intellectual intensity, the staff verbally wrestled over what changes if any the Gorbachev era would bring for the Soviet Union. Someone quoted Andrei Gromyko's quip that Gorbachev had a nice smile, "but iron teeth," and noted that from a protégé of the steely KGB chief and General Secretary Yuri Andropov nothing dramatic could be hoped for.

Another emphasized that Gorbachev was a survivor. He had been the agriculture minister, the political graveyard of Soviet political life, and still managed to become general secretary. President Reagan apparently even chimed in with "Gorbachev's a new type of Soviet leader—he's the first who actually weighs more than his wife."

As the focus turned to issues of American policy, Reagan sat back, as usual, and listened to the discussion unfold. His view of the Soviet Union had changed somewhat since he had taken office. He understood the value of communication and diplomacy and had come to believe that there was some truth to the cliché "Soviet paranoia." He had ordered the probing military flights along the Soviet periphery dramatically reduced in light of this reality. After twenty minutes or so, Reagan intervened. "Mr. Gorbachev may or may not be a new type of Soviet leader," he said. "Time will only tell, and it may not be for a decade. But I want to keep the heat on the Soviets. I don't want to let up on anything we're doing."[8]

George Shultz was to continue in his efforts to foster a diplomatic dialogue, and even a superpower summit, which had first been proposed by Vice President Bush to Gorbachev at the Chernenko funeral. But everything else was to stay on course.[9] "The president understood the value of both diplomacy and a strategic offensive," recalls John Poindexter.[10]

By late summer, two important economic policies were enacted that would create dire economic problems for a Soviet economy already in a tailspin. The first came from Washington. Under the direction of Secretary of the Treasury James Baker, the dollar began its gradual movement down in what would become a one-quarter devaluation over the next twelve months. The motive was almost entirely domestic. Devaluation was expected to boost American exports by making goods less expensive on foreign markets. But at the same time the devaluation in effect cut the value of Soviet exports by one quarter in real terms. Moscow usually sold its energy exports in foreign currencies but exchanged them for dollars, its currency of preference. That policy was beneficial when a strong dollar allowed the Soviets to maximize their purchasing power in Europe and Asia. But a weaker dollar meant the reverse was true. By agency estimates, the cost of devaluation for the Kremlin was on the order of $1.5 billion.[11]

The other policy change—ultimately of fundamental import to the demise of the Soviet economy—came out of Riyadh. In the late summer of 1985, Saudi officials alerted the Reagan administration that they should expect an increase in Saudi oil production, and as a consequence a precipitous decline in international oil prices. "They told us in advance that we could expect a sizable jump in production," recalls Weinberger.[12] For a variety of security and economic reasons, the Saudis were electing to do what the administration had counseled for some time. The decision to alert Washington stood in stark contrast to the surprise Saudi production decision in the 1970s, and was a testament to the level of U.S.-Saudi cooperation and shared goals.

Without any knowledge of the financial cyclone that was about to hit, Mikhail Gorbachev was in Moscow meeting with his key advisers and allies to work out the economic reforms that he wanted to institute in the next five-year plan. The problems of the Soviet economy were abundant and had for too long been ignored. The centerpiece of the new general secretary's first reform package was to accelerate growth and bring the Soviet Union into the next century as a reinvigorated superpower. Modernization was the new goal, not production, as it had been for decades. It was to be achieved through a sharp investment increase in machine building, particularly technology—instruments, robotics, electronics, computers—and through rapid replacement of obsolete capital. To make the plan work, Gorbachev needed several critical ingredients that only a change in Reagan administration policy could deliver—Western technology, hard currency, and an end to the geostrategic challenge.

Gorbachev issued an aggressive appeal to Western policy makers and businessmen to expand trade. He did so by linking technology trade with political cooperation. "In this dangerous world we simply cannot, we have no right to, ignore such a stabilize [sic] of relations as trade and economics, scientific and technical ties," he told his audience. "If we want really solid and stable relations of ensuring reliable peace, their foundations must include developed business relations."[13]

One priority for Gorbachev was the oil and gas sector. It was the chief generator of hard currency, and hard currency was paying for grain and other imports from the West. The goals set by the new general secretary called for gas flow to increase from 22.59 trillion cubic feet per year in 1985 to 30.00 by 1990. Most of the increase would be for export. The gains would come from new fields in western Siberia that had only recently come on line. Oil production was also supposed to jump. During the next five-year plan (1986–1990), Gorbachev authorized that the oil industry receive an infusion of $51.5 billion, to upgrade oil production facilities and to bring a record sixteen new oil fields on stream in 1986 alone. Gorbachev was looking for the energy exports to earn billions in extra hard currency.

But in addition to Western inputs—technology, hard currency, and credits—Gorbachev was also looking for relief in the military sphere. By the end of 1985, the U.S. was producing more weapons than Moscow for the first time since the 1960s. More important perhaps, the doubling of the American research and development budget worried the Soviet military brass and Gorbachev. According to a former member of the Central Committee at the time, "We very firmly believed that the correlation of forces were shifting against us. In the military-technology sphere, in the ideological sphere, and in the economic sphere. Something had to be done to arrest these developments, to correct the American challenge."[14]

Soviet military officials such as former Defense Minister S. L. Sokolov were threatening to match American military developments with those of their own.[15] Gorbachev painted an ominous picture of the shifting nature of the military competition, which perhaps outlines why SDI would become an obsession for him. The central problem in the world, as he saw it, was that "the development of science and technology has reached a level where the broad-scale introduction of new achievements, particularly in the military field, can lead to an entirely new phase in the arms race." The fear was that Moscow was facing a technological challenge that it could not answer. According to Aleksandr Bessmertnykh, "the economic element" of the military burden posed by the American buildup was "the number one preoccupation of Gorbachev."[16] Anatoly Chernayaev, personal adviser on foreign affairs to Gorbachev, recalls: "[It was] an imperative for Gorbachev that we had to put an end to the Cold War, that we had to reduce our military budget significantly, that we had to limit our military industrial complex in some way. For him, it was absolutely clear that he would have to negotiate with President Reagan and he would have to go very far in negotiating very significant reductions with President Reagan."[17] Of perhaps greatest concern was the Strategic Defense Initiative. Bessmertnykh says: "When we were talking about SDI, just the feeling that if we get involved in this SDI arms race, trying to do something like the U.S. was going to do, to do space programs, space-based weapons, et cetera, looked like a horror to Gorbachev."[18]

In June 1985, Gorbachev convened a special conference on scientific-technical progress. As its centerpiece was a look at accelerating the development by updating the machine tools industry and moderniz-ing computer technology, instrument-making, and the electro-technical and electronics industries. These were the "catalysts" of acceleration (*uskoreniye*), and critical sectors in keeping the Soviet edifice in place. At the conference the new general secretary declared that scientific and technology progress was his most important mission. What did it mean to change the economy, he asked? "It means above all, the scientific-technical renewal of production and the attainment of the highest world level of technology."

The eleventh five-year plan that was being developed by the CPSU reflected this preoccupation and concern. It gave a very high priority for overcoming the perceived lag with the West in electronics. The plan called for a rise in output of industrial robots from 13,000 to 28,000 and machine tool development centers from 2,500 to 10,700. In the first two years of the new plan, investment in engineering-sector facilities for research and development, testing, and evaluation was said to be 50 percent above the funding for the whole of the previous five years. And R & D funds were to be especially concentrated on high-tech projects.

The trouble was that the best Soviet resources in the field were being directed toward the military-industrial base. Half of the machine tools were going to defense enterprises, which also employed the best scientists. At least half of all research and development expenditures were for the military. And the Reagan defense buildup—particularly its emphasis on emerging technologies—meant that more resources needed to be shifted to defense.

The Soviet General Staff was painting an ominous picture of the Reagan administration's commitment to emerging technologies, in both conventional weapons and the Strategic Defense Initiative (SDI). The

Soviet military establishment was confronting a new stage of technological development. General Yevseyev wrote in one Soviet military journal that the threat posed by emerging technologies would give the capitalists a surprise-attack capability, similar to the one posed by the Nazis when they invaded the Soviet Union in June 1941. Deputy Defense Minister General Gareyev, in another article, held out Popkov, an old worker and a hero in Simonov's *The Living and the Dead*, as a model for the Soviet citizen. Facing a new capitalist threat, the public, it was hoped, would lament as Popkov did: "In the last resort I would have even given up this flat and lived out my life in a single room on bread and water . . . so that the Red Army could have everything it needed."[19] The party had promised never to let the capitalists regain military superiority, but by keeping their word they would pay dearly.

And Gorbachev wanted to stick to that pledge. For his part, falling behind the United States in the military technology sphere threatened the superpower status of the Soviet Union. "There is no other way," Gorbachev told the party faithful. "The competition that has grown more acute under the impact of scientific and technological progress is affecting those who have dropped behind ever more mercilessly."[20] For Gorbachev, SDI was an American plan to further burden the Soviet economy. "The U.S. wants to exhaust the Soviet Union economically through a race in the most up-to-date and expensive space weapons," he told people on Moscow television. "It wants to create various kinds of difficulties for the Soviet leadership, to wreck its plans, including the social sphere, in the sphere of improving the standard of living of our people, thus arousing dissatisfaction among the people with their leadership."[21]

The temper of the times meant that Gorbachev would be devoting even more to defense than had been the case in the past. The new five-year plan called for more spending on advanced weapons. As Gorbachev would later admit, the planned rate of growth for defense in 1986 through 1990 was almost 8 percent per year, twice the rate of national income growth.[22] All told, defense expenditures would rise an astonishing 45 percent in the next five years.

Gorbachev was looking to the West, in particular an anticommunist U.S. president, to ease up on the campaign against the Soviet Union.

1. KGB cable no. 2181/PR, December 19, 1984, in Christopher Andrew and Oleg Gordievsky, *More Instructions from the Centre: Top Secret Files on KGB Global Operations, 1975–1985* (London: Frank Cass, 1992), pp. 48–52.
2. Interview with the author.
3. *The New York Times*, May 3, 1985, p. 1; *The New York Times*, May 7, 1985, p. 7.
4. U.S. official, interview with the author.
5. Mohammad Yousaf, interview with the author; Vincent Cannistraro, interview with the author.
6. *The New York Times*, April 26, 1985, p. 1.
7. Joseph Persico, *Casey: The Lives and Secrets of William J. Casey* (New York: Penguin, 1991); U.S. official, interview with the author.
8. Edwin Meese, interview with the author.
9. Edwin Meese, interview with the author.
10. John Poindexter, interview with the author.
11. U.S. official, interview with the author.
12. Caspar Weinberger, interview with author.
13. *Pravda*, December 11, 1985.
14. Interview with the author.
15. *Krasnaya Zvezda*, May 5, 1985.
16. Aleksandr Bessmertnykh, remarks at Princeton University conference "A Retrospective on the End of the Cold War," February 26, 1993.
17. Anatoly Chernayaev, comments at Princeton University, February 26, 1993.
18. Aleksandr Bessmertnykh, remarks at Princeton University, February 26, 1993.
19. See both Yeveseyev and Gareyev in *VIZh*, no. 11, 1985.
20. Mikhail Gorbachev, *Political Report of the CPSU Central Committee to the 27th Party Congress* (Moscow: Novosti, 1986), p. 19.
21. Mikhail Gorbachev, Soviet television, October 14, 1986.
22. Mikhail Gorbachev, "Speech to Nizhniy Tagil Workers," Moscow Domestic Services in Russian 1545 GMT, April 27, 1990.

17

August 1985, a stake was driven silently through the heart of the Soviet economy. Although the effects would not be felt immediately, the Saudis opened the spigot and flooded the world market with oil. The difficult and in retrospect momentous decision by the Saudis came after Oil Minister Sheik Yamani had repeatedly declared to fellow OPEC members that Saudi Arabia wanted a larger share of the world oil market. Six months after the president had mentioned it, four months after development of the ambitious Peace Shield had begun, Saudi production jumped dramatically. What factor lay most heavily on the minds of the Saudis when they made the decision is anybody's guess. As Caspar Weinberger puts it, "It was an internal Saudi decision to increase production and cause the price of oil to drop in 1985. But it was a decision that they knew would sit very well with the United States."[1]

In the first few weeks of the Saudi push, daily production jumped from less than 2 million barrels to almost 6 million. By the late fall of 1985, crude production would climb to almost 9 million barrels a day.

For the United States, the coming drop in oil prices was a boon—the equivalent of tens of billions of dollars being given to

American consumers. For the Kremlin, any drop in oil prices was damaging to the economy. But in 1985 it was cataclysmic. Soviet hard currency reserves were strapped. Gold sales had been doubled in 1985 to keep hard currency coming in at the necessary level. Energy, being the bread and butter of the Soviet hard currency earning machine (almost 80 percent), mattered more than any other commodity to the health of the economy. A top-secret CIA report on the Soviet economy issued in July 1985 already indicated weakness in export earnings. The Soviet trade balance with the West had moved from a $700 million surplus in the first quarter of 1984 to a $1.4 billion deficit in the first quarter of 1985.

More important perhaps, Mikhail Gorbachev was counting on hard currency generated by energy exports to finance the purchase of technology and consumer goods to make his reforms a reality. They were supposed to pay for imported Western goods and foodstuffs. "The drop in oil prices was devastating, just devastating," says Yevgenny Novikov. "It was a catastrophic event. Tens of billions were wiped away."[2]

Shortly after Saudi oil production rose, the international price of oil sank like a stone in a pond. In November 1985, crude oil sold at $30 a barrel; barely five months later it stood at $12. For Moscow, over $10 billion in valuable hard currency evaporated overnight, almost half its earnings. And the Soviet economy began breathing even more heavily.

As Moscow braced itself for the financial cyclone, attentions turned to the upcoming superpower summit in Geneva. George Bush had proposed a summit to Gorbachev during Konstantin Chernenko's funeral. The new Soviet leader had warmly accepted. The Reagan administration had extended the invitation in the hope of building confidence between the superpowers. The president and Secretary of State George Shultz believed that a face-to-face meeting might spur progress on arms control. Ronald Reagan, no conventional advocate of arms control as an end in itself, did have an idealistic obsession with eliminating nuclear weapons. Along with rolling back communism, dramatically cutting nuclear arsenals on both sides was one of his passionately held goals.

If Reagan proposed a summit to soothe a Soviet leadership

concerned about his assertive policies, Gorbachev seized it as an opportunity to seek relief for an economy in a tailspin. The American pressure on the Soviet system was enormous. In Afghanistan and Poland, the Soviets were unable to solidify their grip on power. Opposition to the war in Afghanistan was growing, and Gorbachev knew well the corrosive effect it was having on Soviet society. In Poland the underground was not only surviving but thriving. Morale in the Jaruzelski government was declining almost as quickly as the economy. In addition to bankrolling indigenous forces in Afghanistan and Poland trying to shake off Soviet hegemony, the Reagan administration was making the task of reorganizing Soviet society insurmountable by tightening the noose of technology restrictions, limiting Soviet energy exports, and increasing the pace of the superpower military competition. In particular the Strategic Defense Initiative had Gorbachev painted into a precarious corner.

Senior Reagan administration officials worked on initiatives and responses that could be used to advance the president's agenda in Geneva. They wanted to make sure that the summit did not have a singular focus on arms control, as so many superpower parleys had in the past. In keeping with NSDD-75 and the administration's goal to "roll back" Soviet power, National Security Council staffer Donald Fortier devised a "regional initiative." The proposal would focus attention on five regional hot spots where Soviet-backed regimes were fighting anticommunist insurgents. The United States would propose that the warring sides negotiate among themselves with superpower support and supervision while joint efforts were made to eliminate foreign military aid. Economic aid might also be provided. Fortier was under no illusions that Moscow would entertain such a proposal. But it was a useful counterstroke to lay on the table, preventing Gorbachev from banging the SDI drum throughout the summit.

On SDI, Bill Casey and Arms Control and Disarmament Agency Director Kenneth Adelman proposed a similar kind of initiative, which would go nowhere but at the same time prove very useful. The two suggested that the president propose "open labs" for SDI research. Akin to the "open skies" proposal made by Dwight Eisenhower thirty years earlier, "open labs" would commit the two superpowers to making their research labs accessible to each other. Moscow, of course, would never go along with it, but it would blunt the expected Soviet onslaught.

Before the Geneva summit, the president studied more raw intelligence on the Soviet economy. "He just loved reading that stuff," recalls Don Regan. "He would take the big stack and read them one by one over the weekend. He understood a lot more about the Soviet economic and military situation than most people gave him credit for."[3] This material pointed to a weakening situation, with shortages becoming more chronic, production facing more bottlenecks, and a tightening hard currency crisis. Reagan understood that he held if not all the cards at least those that mattered most.[4]

In 1985 the superpowers were two tectonic plates colliding, the rumbling and moving ground a production of opposition on a variety of subjects. Geneva, Switzerland, a solemn city with a taste for hospitable importance, was the backdrop for the first summit for both leaders. Reagan and Gorbachev would face each other, searching for an advantage, each contentious and clearly trying to grab the upper hand. A series of diplomatic sessions involving Secretary of State George Shultz and Soviet Foreign Minister Eduard Shevardnadze were planned, covering Afghanistan, human rights, arms control, and SDI.

Gorbachev began almost immediately pressing on SDI. It would lead to a new spiral in the arms race, he told the president. It would bankrupt both countries and prove destabilizing. Looking Reagan squarely in the eye, the general secretary warned that he could and would do everything necessary to counter SDI with more offensive weapons. The Strategic Defense Initiative was evidence that the U.S. sought strategic superiority and a first strike capability, he continued. Gorbachev then issued a veiled threat: unless the correct decisions were made on SDI in the next eighteen months, the consequences could be grave.

Reagan countered forcefully, speaking from his heart with the power of belief rather than the ramblings in his State Department briefing memos. Gorbachev responded briskly, and the verbal boxing match ensued. Try as he might, Gorbachev could not get Reagan to budge on SDI.

After a brief interlude spent on other subjects, Gorbachev pressed his case a second time. Granting that the president was committed to testing and developing a strategic defense system, Gorbachev was looking for some flexibility in its eventual deployment. The general secretary assured Reagan that banning SDI would not mean a "loss of face" for Reagan or his administration. The president tried to push the issue aside, saying that SDI was not negotiable, at which point Gorbachev acted indignant and claimed the president was not giving him adequate respect. Arms control would be impossible without a ban on SDI, he curtly told Reagan, who shrugged off the invective.

When the summit agenda shifted to regional issues, it was Reagan's turn to scold Gorbachev. In words more harsh than a president had ever spoken to a Soviet general secretary, Reagan launched salvo after salvo at Gorbachev concerning Afghanistan. Moscow was practicing genocide, said Reagan. The children of a poor, nonthreatening country were suffering because of booby-trapped toys Soviet aircraft were dropping. Elsewhere—Poland, Nicaragua, Angola—the Soviet Union was fighting national groups that simply wanted their freedom. Are you still trying to take over the world? he boldly asked a visibly upset Gorbachev.

The summit led to no major shifts in policy and ended with the typical pageantry of such events. Reagan, who had little interest in the diminutive details of diplomacy, headed home with confidence. Gorbachev had pressed extremely hard on SDI, revealing his desperation. And the president had made it very clear that when it came to issues such as Afghanistan, he would press right back.[5]

Having failed to accomplish his goals in Geneva, Mikhail Gorbachev returned to Moscow facing a bleak economic horizon. Recalls Aleksandr Bessmertnykh, "As for the Soviet Union, we were already feeling the pressure of the arms race. Gorbachev wanted to go on with the reforms, and the continued arms race was a tremendous hindrance to the future of those reforms."[6]

The gravity of the Soviet economic crisis was clear to Gorbachev, who understood the link between economic renewal and Soviet power. Economic strength determined Soviet geopolitical strength. On May 23, he told diplomats at the Foreign Ministry that "without an acceleration of the country's economic and social development, it will be impossible to maintain our positions on the international scene."[7] The economic crisis was becoming so fundamental that it would be impossible to continue international activities unless the economy turned around, he told them bluntly.

The Soviet military press was filled with reports concerning the impact that new Western high-tech weapons systems still in development would have on the battlefield.[8] Economic and technological prowess—possible only through radical reform—was a national security requirement. As one military journal put it: "Only a strong, modern economic base is capable of providing the opportunity for the maintenance and improvement of the armed forces, and for providing them with the necessary quantities of modern weapons, military technology, and all sorts of allowances."[9] Perestroika wasn't just about modernizing the Soviet civilian economy and alleviating the shortages in consumer goods that made the lives of ordinary citizens so miserable. It was about reversing the shift in the correlation of forces that was already under way. General Dmitri Yazov (later the defense minister) declared that perestroika was the "intensification of production based on the newest achievements in science and technology." He was backing reform as a military necessity.[10]

For those in Washington who took Gorbachev's reform efforts seriously, the program presented a vexing problem. A less monolithic society, more open and free and therefore less aggressive, was surely in the U.S. interest. But what if Gorbachev somehow managed to create a more efficient and technologically advanced empire that retained all the Marxist-Leninist trappings of the past seventy years? And what if his call for reform was nothing more than a ruse to secure Western credits?

As Gorbachev began his crusade to inject technological dynamism into the Soviet economy, the Reagan administration's efforts to erect a worldwide strategy of technology denial around the Soviet bloc were beginning to bear fruit. Since 1981 a number of structural and legal reforms had been made in the American export control regime. Enforcement was getting more attention than in any previous administration. Operation Exodus, launched with much fanfare, was more aggressive than ever. During the 1970s and early 1980s, only two or three technology theft cases were prosecuted. In January 1986 alone, the Department of Justice would prosecute more than one hundred. The Commodity Control List was being expanded throughout the administration. Twenty-six technology items were added to the list between October 1983 and September 1987.

But perhaps the most substantial change came in 1985, when through a bipartisan effort and with strong administration support, the

Export Administration Act of 1979 was amended. The amendments gave U.S. export enforcement officials the power for the first time to investigate illegal exports outside the United States. Agents could track technology exports in locales such as Hong Kong, Switzerland, and India. Bilateral agreements signed with several neutral foreign countries led these countries to police their own exports. Customs officials also received other additional powers. They could now search suspicious shipments without warrants and could seize suspect shipments. The penalties for illegally shipping goods became much more stiff: prison sentences instead of fines.[11]

The strategy of technology denial was in full force by 1986. The COCOM countries had tightened their control over exports, and the leaks in Sweden, Austria, and Switzerland were being plugged up. About 40 percent of all U.S. manufacturers' exports required an export control license of some sort, making the legal purchase of advanced U.S. high technology virtually impossible for Moscow. In four years, the Reagan administration had succeeded in establishing a security bureaucracy whose sole purpose was to track exports to the Soviet bloc. Using advanced computers to track technology shipments around the world, the Technology Transfer Committee at the CIA was engaged in unprecedented worldwide monitoring of high-technology trade flows. Constant pressure from Washington led several major Western allies to do the same, albeit on a smaller scale. In 1984, the British Ministry of Defense had created a technology transfer unit staffed by technical specialists to track high-tech exports. Similar programs had been launched in Paris and Bonn.

Moscow was hungry for Western technology and was not getting near the quantities needed. The smothering restrictions on exports compelled the Kremlin to take desperate measures. By 1986, the number of KGB and military intelligence (GRU) officers in the field trying to steal Western technology jumped dramatically. "Throughout the 1980s, as restrictions on exports tightened, their industrial espionage efforts jumped," recalls Stef Halper. But espionage was hardly an adequate alternative. Stealing technology—as opposed to legally purchasing it—was inefficient. Theft did not give Soviet technicians the training, instructions, or technical support that often accompanied sales.

Predicting that a desperate Kremlin might resort to greater

industrial espionage in the pursuit of Western technology, Casey and other senior U.S. officials expanded the technological disinformation program to throw sand in the gears of the Soviet economic engine. Intelligence analysts at Langley took Gorbachev's five-year plan apart piece by piece, identifying those sectors of the economy that would most be looking for Western technology inputs. Coupling this analysis with reports from defectors, technology experts compiled lists of technology that Soviet bloc agents would have the most interest in. Specialists then concocted faulty information in these targeted areas, which third parties in Europe and the United States would pass along, or even sell, to unsuspecting Soviet agents.

Oil and gas technologies, particularly new extraction processes, were an area of marked Soviet interest. Facing the U.S. embargo, Soviet oil and gas officials apparently tried to develop internal components for offshore oil drilling. Such component designs from the West were highly prized and became an acquisition priority. With the help of oil industry experts, the agency passed along some plans that seriously complicated Soviet efforts. Soviet engineers pored over the documents, packaged as complete plans for American offshore oil rigs being used in the Gulf of Mexico, for months, trying to imitate the American design. Perhaps tens of millions of dollars were wasted by engineers determined to copy the U.S. design, according to one estimate. "It worked like a charm," recalls one specialist. "We had them so confused on oil and gas technologies that they probably still can't figure it out."[12]

The CIA's National Collection Division convinced several small Silicon Valley companies to design flawed mainframe computers and advanced satellites. "The engineers had a ball with it," recalls one official. "To these guys working on a black project and purposefully screwing up designs was tantalizingly challenging." Using discarded designs from other manufacturers, engineers put together a series of "advanced designs" that were sold to Soviet agents for approximately $15,000. Rumor had it that some of the designs were still being analyzed and used as late as 1989. "Once you get garbage into the research and development cycle, it's hard to get it out," says one official.[13]

The Reagan administration was also turning to disinformation as a means of heightening Soviet concerns about SDI. Information provided by Oleg Gordievsky, the KGB official who defected in 1985 after having worked secretly for the British, indicated that there was a consensus developing among Kremlin leaders that SDI might really work, and could even pose a fundamental challenge to the Soviet strategic arsenal. Bill Casey, Caspar Weinberger, and John Poindexter wanted to use that concern to their psychological advantage. Essentially the campaign was designed to create the impression that much more substantial progress was being made by U.S. technical experts than was truly the case. Already a Gorbachev obsession, SDI loomed even larger as a challenge.

If the technological competition was straining the Soviets, the geopolitical challenges were risking to unhinge the empire from the Soviet frame. At the behest of the president, Bill Casey was managing a number of covert operations around the globe designed to roll back Soviet power. Casey, for one, was confident that in this game of chess he was not trying to take a few pawns; he was hoping for checkmate.

A few weeks after the Geneva summit, Casey was in his Langley office having lunch with Alan Fiers from operations. Fiers had spent time on the Saudi peninsula and was now assigned to Central America. The two were discussing the situation in Central America and the Casey vision of supporting anticommunist insurgencies around the world. The DCI wanted a victory somewhere. "When we win one," he told Fiers, "the whole house of cards will come tumbling down. It will set off a chain reaction throughout the empire." In early 1986, despite repeated setbacks and Soviet intransigence, no place offered a better chance for a Soviet rollback than Afghanistan.[14]

As the winter of 1986 descended on that war-torn country, the guns grew almost silent. As had been the pattern for the past six years, Soviet and Afghan army units had left the hills and valleys just as the snow arrived, electing to stay in fortifications or cities. The Soviet blitz, now under the direction of General Zaitsev, had yielded few results since it had been launched one year earlier. A major offensive in the east, including 20,000 men, failed to seal the border with Pakistan or cut the mujahedin off from their base of support. On the other hand, the dramatically heightened U.S. commitment to the resistance was beginning to pay dividends. The number of arms in the pipeline had jumped sharply: 10,000 rocket-propelled grenades and 200,000 rockets arrived for the mujahedin in 1985, more than for the entire five previous years. There were 50,000 tons in all arriving annually, compared with only 10,000 only two years earlier.

When he visited Pakistan in early 1986, Casey went over the war with General Akhtar and Brigadier Yousaf at a forward base near the Afghan frontier. They were looking at satellite photos and large maps of Afghanistan, checking deployments, casualties, and possible scenarios for the upcoming year. What was most striking was how the resistance had changed in five years. The mujahedin were now running sophisticated and large-scale operations, more effectively with each passing month. Mujahedin units that five years ago had been equipped with bolt-action rifles and marched into Afghanistan searching for soft targets were now using high-tech weapons and hitting Soviet air bases. New radio communications systems with effective ranges of up to 600 miles were now being used. With communications sites in the Afghan hinterland—at Parwan, Paghman, Mazar-i-Sharif, and Kandahar—regional bases for the Afghan resistance commanders were established. And a remarkably sophisticated process was in full swing. Satellites from the United States would blanket Afghanistan and send images down to U.S. analysts in Washington and Pakistani ISI officers near the frontier. Using the intelligence, ISI officers would send instructions to these regional bases. They, in turn, would pass along orders to commanders in the field by using frequency-hopping radios with a range of 20 to 30 miles.

Mujahedin fighters were also becoming more proficient thanks to numerous schools established in 1985 to train fighters in weapons use. Two-week courses in antitank and antiaircraft guns, mine laying and lifting, demolitions, urban warfare, and sabotage were offered for thousands of fighters. Twenty thousand mujahedin were being pumped out every year by these schools, dubbed "CIA U" by some wags.

The fruits of the U.S. commitment to victory were already apparent in 1985, a year of some spectacular successes by the mujahedin. Commander Ahmad Shah Massoud, the so-called Lion of the Panjshir Valley, seized the heavily defended post in Peshghor, which was held by a battalion of men in bunkers. Over 450 prisoners were taken.

Elsewhere mujahedin commanders were targeting Soviet airfields and the expensive aircraft parked on them. Kandahar airfield, rocketed heavily throughout the summer of 1985, was effectively abandoned when the Soviets moved the bulk of their planes to more distant facilities. Perhaps more ominously for Moscow, there was also plenty of activity in the northern provinces, along the Soviet frontier. Soviet transportation barges were being sunk as they crossed the Amu River. British intelligence (MI-6) had provided small limpet mines that could be clamped on the side of boats just below the waterline. Specially trained mujahedin would swim across the river, plant several mines, then swim back to Afghanistan.

But the most serious escalation came in the form of mujahedin attacks being planned for Soviet territory itself. The suggestion had originally arisen in the White House in 1983, and Akhtar and Yousaf had embraced it. But by late 1985, the administration was starting to get cold feet. While they wanted the attacks to proceed, Casey had decided that it was best if Washington did not share any satellite intelligence on Soviet territory itself. It would make such attacks all the more effective, which might directly implicate the United States. "If you had coordinated rocket attacks carried out with precision, the Sovs would have known that satellite intelligence would be used," recalls one official. "We were the only ones who could provide that sort of intelligence. That would have been too much, too visible. It could have meant Soviet retaliation."[15] Yousaf, when organizing the attacks, had to make do without American satellite intelligence.[16]

But the United States did contribute in other ways. The specially trained units working inside the Soviet Union would be equipped with Chinese rocket launchers and high-tech explosives provided by the CIA. They were to seek out Soviet civilian and military targets for sabotage. They would hit Soviet industrial sites, derail some trains, and fire rockets at Soviet military installations.[17]

The technical training provided by the CIA was also lending itself to a change in resistance tactics. In late 1985, the mujahedin almost succeeded in assassinating Mohammud Najibullah, the head of the Afghan secret police (KHAD). A muj commander, with the assistance of a sympathetic KHAD officer in Kabul, had dreamt up the plot. He used equipment provided by and skills learned from the CIA. Explosives and timing devices were smuggled into Kabul in August 1985. The KHAD agent purchased a used car under a false name and loaded it down heavily with explosives. In response to a tip that Najibullah would be visiting the Indian embassy in late November, the car was parked on the street in front. Lacking a remote control detonator, the conspirators used a timing device. Najibullah, however, was almost an hour late, and the bomb blew up harmlessly.

After analyzing maps and satellite photos, discussing the new strategy, and smiling about successes, the troika of Akhtar, Yousaf, and Casey steered the discussion to the future direction of the war. General Akhtar raised the subject of Stinger missiles. The request had in effect died of neglect, and the Pakistani general wanted an explanation. "It was the single weapon that could turn around the war," Yousaf recalls thinking about the request.[18] Casey responded that he was frustrated, too, along with other administration officials. But the corner was about to be turned. Robert McFarlane had taken the matter to the president in late 1985, and it appeared as if the request would be granted. Optimistically, the mujahedin might see some Stingers by the summer. Akhtar was elated. This could permanently change the course of the war, he told Casey.

Continued success in the execution of the war in Afghanistan depended on the support of Pakistan. A senior American diplomat in Moscow had been told by Soviet officials that the Kremlin intended to "teach Zia a lesson" for supporting the resistance.[19] Casey told Akhtar that the United States would do whatever it could to protect the Pakistani president. Security was already tight, but it would need to be notched up a point or two. Three years later, when a plane carrying President Zia exploded in midair, circumstantial evidence would point to a KGB or KHAD hand in it.[20]

After the meetings, Bill Casey went to see some firing demonstrations by mujahedin. The ISI had a fireworks display plan including guns, mortars, rocket-propelled grenades (RPGs), and recoilless rifles. By early 1986, some of the trainees would be in Afghanistan facing the Soviet army. It appeared as if it were going to be a good year. The mujahedin were beginning to take the initiative on the battlefield, the Soviet military situation looked more precarious, and the military probes into the Soviet Union itself would begin shortly.

1. Caspar Weinberger, interview with the author.
2. Yevgenny Novikov, interview with the author.
3. Donald Regan, interview with the author.
4. John Poindexter, interview with the author.
5. John Poindexter, interview with the author; Robert McFarlane, interview with the author.
6. Aleksandr Bessmertnykh, comments at Princeton University conference "A Retrospective on the End of the Cold War," February 27, 1993.
7. Quoted in Don Oberdorfer, *The Turn* (New York: Poseidon, 1991), p. 162.
8. V. Vorobyev, "Time in Battle," *Krasnaya Zvezda*, no. 233, October 9, 1985, p. 2.
9. *Voyenno-Istoricheskiy Zhurnal*, no. 4, 1986, p. 6.
10. D. T. Yazov, *On Guard Over Socialism and Peace* (Moscow: Voyenizdat, 1987).
11. Stef Halper, interview with the author; William Schneider, interview with the author.
12. Interview with the author.
13. Interview with the author.
14. Alan Fiers, interview with the author.
15. Interview with the author.
16. Mohammad Yousaf, interview with the author.
17. Mohammad Yousaf, interview with the author.
18. Mohammad Yousaf, interview with the author.
19. Mohammad Yousaf, interview with the author.
20. Mohammad Yousaf, interview with the author.

18

The Saudi decision in late 1985 to increase oil production rapidly, sending prices through the floor, did not go unnoticed in the halls of the Kremlin. In the face of an unprecedented drop in hard currency earnings, a strongly worded letter signed by Politburo members was sent to King Fahd in early 1986. Oleg Alekseevich Grinevsky, the head of the Middle East Department of the Foreign Ministry, and Geidar Aliyev, a Politburo member and Arabist, relayed the message to Fahd and worked to coordinate a response with Iraq and Libya, two other losers in the Saudi gambit.

The letter apparently warned against pushing prices lower and proposed secret meetings in Geneva to stabilize prices. Iran for its part made public threats, as the loss of oil revenue threatened to force an end to its planned offensive against Iraq. There were growing attacks in the Persian Gulf as both Iran and Iraq violated almost every time-honored law of war. Tankers were being hit along with oil refineries and drilling sites. The Iranian air force was beginning to crumble as a result of a lack of spare parts, so the Revolutionary Guards were perfecting a dangerous new technique to target the Iraqi oil trade: speedboats filled with zealous soldiers armed with rockets. There had already been several close calls on tankers in the Gulf.

The Saudis were looking for reassurances in early 1986 that the United States would continue to ensure the security of oil coming from the Gulf. While the threat of Iranian attacks affected the Saudis much less than it did other producers, such as Kuwait, King Fahd wanted the comfort of knowing that the United States would not allow Iran to dominate and intimidate Gulf shipping. Prince Bandar in Washington had communicated his concerns to Caspar Weinberger and Bill Casey. When Vice President George Bush visited the Arab peninsula in April 1986, there would be direct talks on the matter.

Saudi production in early 1986 was running at almost 10 million barrels a day. Prices continued their plunge. For the Saudis, the burst in production more than made up for the drop in price. Earnings were expected to be up by one third. Even if the price of oil dropped as low as $8 per barrel, the Saudis would still collect more than in 1985. And the decline in the U.S. dollar, to which Fahd had been alerted, was another enormous economic boost. According to a secret State Department memo, the Saudis "received a major windfall due to the recent decline in the dollar." For the last six months of 1985 alone, that windfall amounted to "as much as $10 billion." The Saudis were expecting a similar harvest in 1986.[1]

In February 1986, the U.S. effort to roll back Soviet power in Eastern Europe entered a new phase when funds began to flow to the underground in Czechoslovakia. In keeping with NSDD-32 and the president's wishes, contact had been made with Czech expatriates in the West, and a modest pipeline to the Czech underground was established. It was, however, nowhere near the Polish operation in size or scope, only a few hundred thousand dollars per annum. The Czech opposition was still in its embryonic stage, led mostly by intellectuals in human rights organizations such as Charter 77 or lay Catholics. Funds from the CIA were funneled through émigré organizations in the West, who were already smuggling private funds into the country. Although the amount was small, it was hoped that the sum of the two covert funding operations would be larger than the whole. Solidarity had taken the courageous step of supporting opposition movements throughout the Soviet bloc. There had even been collaborative consultations between the leadership of the opposition in both countries, held in remote sites in the forests along the Czech-Polish border. If the two underground movements were to join forces, the challenge to Soviet power in the region would become even more ominous.

Dealing with underground movements behind the Iron Curtain was risky business. Identifying avenues to funnel aid was not easy. Bill Casey sent a memo to Clair George, his new director of operations. He wanted some work done on identifying opposition movements and how they could best be helped. "Bill wanted to see what we could do to support opposition movements throughout the region, and encourage their cooperation," recalls one official with knowledge of the memo.[2]

There was the additional problem of exposure. The Soviet bloc intelligence services might uncloak the scheme and use it to destroy the underground. In the 1920s, the Bolshevik secret police had established several fictitious underground organizations as vehicles to hunt down true opponents of the regime. The best known of these was the Monarchist Association of Central Russia (MOR), better known by its code name, Trust. Trust successfully penetrated other anticommunist organizations and undermined several intelligence operations in Russia.

But if Poland was any example, external support could make an enormous difference. Solidarity was receiving some $500,000 a year in private donations from overseas in addition to the agency funds. Three hundred thousand dollars alone came from the AFL-CIO. But the flow was not uninterrupted. Several shipments from Stockholm and the port city of Ystad were intercepted in the early spring of 1986. Polish authorities were waiting dockside when the shipments arrived. These were not chance interceptions. Someone, somewhere in the pipeline, was tipping officials off. Dissecting the channel would disrupt the flow of goods, but there were few other options.

Most of the suspicions turned on the Swedish portion of the operation. Solidarity activists were handling the shipping up until goods reached Sweden. And while it was possible that Solidarity in the West had been penetrated by enemy agents, it seemed doubtful. Only the most trusted of Solidarity activists were involved in the clandestine supply operation. Newcomers were not brought in. But in Sweden the channel was dependent on reliable dockworkers and port officials. If someone uncovered the nature of the contents inside the crates, he might be tempted to alert Polish authorities in exchange for money. In mid-February, from his White House Office, Bill Casey apparently put in a call to a Swedish official with knowledge of the clandestine operation. There was a leak in the Swedish portion of the channel, and Casey asked him to plug it.

Some U.S. agents were dispatched to cooperate with a Swedish investigation. The joint team spent two and half weeks going over every inch of the Swedish portion of the operation—observing, checking records, and monitoring workers. They could find nothing. Finally, on a tip from a dockworker they had questioned, the team tailed a Swedish customs agent in Ystad and discovered that he was telexing messages to customs officials in Gdansk. By searching his bank records, the team discovered that he was being paid approximately $200 per tip.

Having found the culprit, the team was still in a quandary. Arresting or firing him might lead to press reports and expose the whole operation. The Swedes decided on a compromise solution: he would be reassigned, with more pay and benefits. It was perhaps the only time that a government employee saw his career get a boost from sharing information with a Warsaw Pact country. His job transfer went smoothly, and the leak was plugged.[3]

At the same time the Reagan administration was expanding its covert financial support to underground movements behind the Iron Curtain, Mikhail Gorbachev was taking the podium at the Twenty-seventh Party Congress in Moscow. For ten days Communist Party leaders from around the world assembled, trying to chart the future of their movement. At the presidium, Gorbachev sat next to Yegor Ligachev. Behind them were Gen. Wojciech Jaruzelski and Erich Honecker.

Gorbachev's speech was historic in that it broadened the discussion that was beginning to emerge about the sins of the past. He also offered a clarion call for restructuring Soviet society. As he spoke forcefully and energetically, elevating his voice to make a point, Gorbachev touched on a number of important themes. Technological progress was essential to the Soviet future, he told the crowd. Only technological development would allow the Party to achieve its goal of doubling the country's "economic potential." The new five-year plan called for a central emphasis on technology. "The Party requires funds and resources to be invested where the greatest return can be obtained in the shortest space of time; and not by increasing the number of workers, but by creating fundamentally new, highly efficient machinery and technology," he said.[4] The plan called for an investment policy heavily focused on what was termed the "high-technology sector." Over 200 billion rubles were to be allocated to this sector and for modernization of industry. That was more than had been spent in the previous ten years. Investment in high technology held the single greatest promise for economic growth and development.[5]

Gorbachev also issued a warning about American intentions. He spoke of his "sincere desire to throw off the burden of the 'star wars' and of the arms race in general." He warned that "the U.S.A. and its military-industrial machine, which so far does not intend to slow its pace, remains the locomotive of militarism." He also spoke of the "basic principles of economic security, which envisage a renunciation of any discrimination, blockades, and sanctions." And he denounced interference in the internal affairs of countries, particularly Poland and Afghanistan. Imperialist forces were attempting to "subvert Poland," he warned. "Counterrevolution and imperialism have transformed Afghanistan into a bleeding wound," he told the assembled faithful.[6]

In the spring of 1986, the downward plunge in international oil prices was causing serious worries around the world but also among some quarters in the Reagan administration. Vice President George Bush was preparing for a highly visible ten-day tour of the Persian Gulf area. A product of Texas oil country, Bush saw danger, not hope, in the dramatic and recent decline in oil prices. High prices were good for the southwest, his political base. And the vice president was being uncharacteristically public in expressing his views on the matter.

On April 1, before leaving for his trip, Bush told a Washington press conference that "stability in the market is a very important thing, and I will be selling very hard in terms of our domestic interest . . . and thus the interest of our national security. . . . I think it is essential that we talk about stability and that we just not have a continued free fall like a parachutist jumping without a parachute."

These comments went against the grain of everything else the administration had said and done. The president, Caspar Weinberger,

Bill Casey, and John Poindexter, not to mention domestic advisers, saw the drop in prices as a big plus. An unusual public retort came after Bush's remarks. "The way to address stability is to let the free market work," a White House spokesman said. He also pointedly stated that Bush would stress to King Fahd that market forces should determine price levels.[7]

Only a few days after the public flap, Bush was in Riyadh, dedicating the new U.S. embassy building. At dinner that evening, the vice president spoke with several Saudi ministers, including Sheik Yamani. They talked about a variety of subjects quite candidly and pointedly about the price of oil. Bush warned that if prices remained at rock bottom, U.S. oil producers would exert pressure on Congress for some sort of tariff or protection from imports. Yamani took the vice president's warning with more than an ounce of concern, and it added to Saudi confusion. For months senior administration officials had been talking down the price of oil. Weinberger, Casey, and finally the president had encouraged greater Saudi production and a halt to any efforts to prop up prices. Now Bush was in Riyadh saying the very opposite.

From Riyadh, the vice president proceeded to Dhahran, where King Fahd was temporarily in residence at the Eastern Palace. The king threw a large dinner, complete with waiters who wore rifle cartridges, swords, and pistols. Bush and Fahd spoke privately after the gala, and it quickly became a late-night session. Iranian vessels had just attacked a Saudi tanker, and Fahd was nervous about Tehran's seemingly increasing aggressiveness. It appeared quite likely that the Iranians were going to shore up their position in southern Iraq by capturing the Fao peninsula, the southernmost portion of Iraq, which borders Kuwait. Fao could be the path to tiny Kuwait and perhaps even the Saudi oil fields. Fahd was nervous, and Saudi forces were on a higher state of readiness. Bush reiterated that the United States would stand firmly by the royal family in the event of an Iranian assault. Iran would not be permitted to attack Kuwait or Saudi Arabia without inviting some sort of an American military response. American naval vessels in the Gulf were tracking Iranian operations, and Washington was well aware of Iranian military activities.

When the discussion turned to oil, Bush told the king that he was looking for "stability in the market." The price of oil had already plunged from $30 a barrel in the fall of 1985 to only $10 in April 1986 on the spot markets. Some were predicting that it might go as low as $5 a barrel. Bush told Fahd what he had told Yamani earlier: pressure would mount in the United States for quotas or tariffs on oil imports, so it would be best if the House of Saud worked to prop up prices. Fahd was visibly concerned. This clear departure from administration policy was quite unusual for Bush, who had proven to be a loyal, if quiet, vice president during the previous five years of the Reagan presidency. This was his first break from administration rank, but he was making it with a foreign head of state.

When word got back to the White House about what Bush had told Fahd, Reagan felt compelled to take some action. He did what he had rarely done before: "He gave Bush a real dressing down," according to an ambassador in the region. It did not look good when the president and senior cabinet officials were saying one thing and the vice president another, Reagan apparently told Bush.[8]

There was a clamor in some Western circles for intervention in the international oil market to enforce some sort of "stability." At a secret meeting of the International Energy Agency in the spring of 1986, several countries were pushing for a top-level gathering of member energy officials to prop up prices. The American delegation, in keeping with administration policy, declared that such an arrangement was unacceptable. They went so far as to excise any mention of "stability" from a draft of the gathering's statement on the impact of lower oil prices.

Just how the drop in oil prices was gutting the Soviet economy began to emerge in a May 1986 CIA secret report entitled "USSR: Facing the Dilemma of Hard Currency Shortages." The report summary noted: "Low energy prices, declining oil production, and a depreciating dollar will substantially reduce the Soviets' ability to import Western equipment, agricultural goods and industrial materials for the rest of the decade. The decline of Moscow's hard currency import capacity—most likely on the order of one-third or more—comes at a time when Gorbachev probably is counting on increased inputs from the West to assist his program of economic revitalization." The report continued: "The sharp drop in world oil prices this year has dramatically altered Moscow's earnings position. . . . As in 1985, oil exports to hard currency countries would probably bear the brunt of any production declines. With few short-term opportunities at home for stepping up the pace of energy conservation or oil substitution, reduction in deliveries to domestic consumers probably would disrupt production at a time when Gorbachev is placing a high premium on boosting economic growth." The report restated a calculation from an August 9, 1984, intelligence finding that for every one dollar drop in the price of a barrel of oil Moscow would lose between $500 million and $1 billion per year in critical hard currency. The calculated annual loss from the price drop was $13 billion. The price of natural gas was paralleling oil, so the revenues from natural gas exports were off by billions. At the same time, the devaluation of the dollar was estimated to cost Moscow approximately $2 billion per year, because Soviet exports were priced in dollars, and most imports in European currencies.[9]

But the full cost of the price plunge was only beginning to be tabulated. Arms, the number-two Soviet export behind energy, went mostly to Middle East countries once flush in petrodollars. Soviet arms sales to the Middle East had increased fivefold during the oil boom of the 1970s and had remained the most significant portion of the USSR's total sales throughout the early 1980s. But the most wealthy and steady Soviet arms clients were now cash poor because of the oil price plunge. Iran, Iraq, and Libya experienced a 46 percent cut in oil earnings during the first half of 1986. As a consequence, Soviet arms sales dropped 20 percent in 1986, another $2 billion in hard currency out of the Kremlin's coffers. Soviet losses were rising dramatically when hard currency was most needed. The timing could not have been worse.

The swing in Soviet financial fortunes, on the heels of the Reagan defense budget, was so dramatic that it is difficult to fathom. The high oil prices of the 1970s were an enormous blessing to the Kremlin. Between 1973 and 1982, Soviet earnings from energy exports increased fifteen times, while the volume of sales did not even double. The Soviet Union's "terms of trade" improved by 65 percent during the period, allowing it to import about two thirds more goods for the same quantity of exports. But the stunning decline in world oil prices reversed the process with a vengeance. Consequently, many imports from the West (foodstuffs, machine tools, consumer goods) that had allowed the system to limp along became prohibitively costly. By July 1986, it took almost five times more Soviet oil to purchase a given piece of West German machinery than it had a year earlier. Using hard currency for reform was no longer a viable option for Gorbachev.

The Soviet hard currency tempest brought a number of other repercussions. Dozens of large industrial projects in the USSR were canceled for lack of funds. Renault had a planned $1.2 billion project to refit car factories put on hold. At the Neryungri coal fields in Siberia, imports of Japanese and U.S. machinery were abruptly halted because they could not be paid for. Two chemical plants to be built by John Brown PLC and Chemical Industries PLC of Britain, at the cost of $1 billion, were also scrapped.

The plunge in oil prices led the Kremlin to lean even more heavily on Western credits as a source of badly needed cash. Some rather remarkable reports put together by Roger Robinson on the NSC staff early in the administration had pointed out that the Soviet Union and its client states were deriving tremendous financial advantages from being able to access Western interbank deposits. The process sort of served as a reserve checking account to meet the Kremlin's short-term cash requirements, allowing Moscow to stave off financial problems by juggling deposits. Interbank deposits were a well-worn banking tradition, and they could not be done away with overnight. But the administration on numerous instances raised the subject in banking circles, in the hope of somehow limiting this practice.

One such instance came when Bill Casey arrived in New York for a private (even secret) meeting with top bank officials. The gathering took place in a nondescript dining room near the financial district. Casey, himself an international banker, was at the luncheon to see old acquaintances, get and give advice. He gave the group his perspective on the dilemma facing Gorbachev. They know that to compete with us, they are going to have to make advancements in computers and communications technologies, he said. But in order to do that, they would have to lessen their political grip on the populace. The big question for official Washington was, Should America foster that process to encourage economic liberalization, or should it maintain its technological and economic lead? Casey didn't answer his question, but he went on the discuss the current financial situation in the Soviet Union. In bad economic straits and with its most important sources of hard currency—oil, gas, and armaments—worth substantially less, Moscow would press Western creditors for more loans, he said with intensity. But from one banker to another, he confided, it would be a poor credit risk. Because they were already having trouble paying their debts, and with hard currency earnings plunging, it would not make sense to advance the Soviets more credit. He then relayed to the financial titans the administration's concern about interbank deposits and other schemes the Kremlin might be using to draw on the pool of Western capital.[10]

As the financial core of the Soviet empire reached a meltdown, on the far-flung geographic periphery of that empire challenges to communist authority were growing, fed by a desire for independence and assisted by U.S. support. In both Poland and Afghanistan—the two greatest challenges—things continued to run against the Kremlin. On June 5, 1986, Polish authorities stumbled across Solidarity underground leader Zbigniew Bujak, whom they had been hunting for years. He ran the organization, oversaw the bank accounts that included donations from the West, and distributed resources. His capture could have presented an enormous setback for the resistance. He had managed to elude authorities by shifting locations and using disguises—hair, makeup, fake mustaches, hats—stolen from university theater departments by sympathetic students.

Three hundred and twenty other activists had been arrested in the first several months of 1986, but none had the stature of Bujak. There were still plenty of activists at the lower levels of the movement, but the command and control system that helped organize and manage the resistance was effectively severed. "The movement was still doing what it always did, but it was beginning to lack a national focus," recalls one official. "The loss of Bujak shattered the movement at the top levels."[11] Without Bujak the underground was in temporary disarray. The structure of Solidarity's Provisional Coordinating Committee had been such that few leaders knew the specifics of what the others were doing—their responsibilities, daily activities, and locations. Such an organization prevented infiltration and leaks, and assured that arrested leaders would not be able to reveal too much information to authorities. But it also made replacing Bujak an impossibility.

But the arrest of Bujak would not stand. Amid a deepening economic crisis, exacerbated by stinging American sanctions, Polish trade with the West had almost dried up. In 1980, this trade was $7.5 billion; by 1986, it had declined to $1.0 billion. Foreign credits from the West soon declined. Unable to export to the West, Poland could not get credit. Before 1980, Warsaw had been able to borrow up to $8.0 billion annually; by 1985 it was down to $300 million. As a consequence, Poland had been forced to borrow from other Soviet bloc countries, who could barely afford to make loans. The amount of debt to their comrades was rising rapidly—reaching close to 5 billion in transferable rubles.

The seizure of Bujak became a powerful symbol that underlined why American sanctions remained in place. Jaruzelski, fearing upheaval in light of economic conditions, called his advisers to his office and declared that Bujak would have to be released. In addition, the government would have to work to fulfill some of the Reagan administration's demands in order to have sanctions lifted. Washington had laid down three prerequisites: a real dialogue with the Church needed to begin; national reconciliation had to take place, with concessions granted to opposition groups; and political prisoners had to be released.

Such demands were hard for General Jaruzelski to swallow. But by the summer of 1986, ending American sanctions became critical to the survival of the regime. On July 22, barely a month and a half after Bujak had been arrested, the Jaruzelski government declared a general amnesty. All political prisoners were freed. The enemies of the regime were returned to the streets, free to rejoin the underground. The gambit to crush Solidarity had failed.

The response from Washington was muted. Warsaw was fairly close to meeting the three preconditions, but the mood in the White House was combative. Casey, Weinberger, and many on the NSC staff were advising the president to keep sanctions in place. Squeezing Jaruzelski further had its benefits. Perhaps more concessions could be extracted for the underground. The opponents of the Warsaw government were clearly picking up steam, and the economy was on the verge of collapse. Reagan asked for consultations with the Vatican to get its views.

For its part, the underground in Poland was eager to see sanctions end immediately. Lech Walesa and nine other prominent Solidarity leaders issued a statement asking Reagan to alter his hard-line stand because deteriorating economic conditions "threatened the rulers and the ruled, and future generations." Cardinal Casaroli was giving the same advice. The pope felt the people had suffered enough. The administration delayed a decision until January 1987, when the president heeded this advice. Covert funding of Solidarity continued.

The amnesty caused a surge of confidence in Solidarity ranks. The underground had survived. It was well funded, and the leadership was intact. Financial, logistical, and material support from the West was pumping nutrients into the body of the resistance. In early October, Solidarity leaders met in Gdansk for two days to reassess their strategy in light of the greater elbow room they now appeared to have. In simultaneous press conferences in Gdansk and Warsaw, the leadership made a dramatic declaration: they were going aboveground. "We do not want to act clandestinely," Walesa announced.

It was a bold and courageous move. The resistance was going to challenge the Polish central government in the daylight. Elements in the Solidarity leadership had tipped off the Reagan administration to their impending announcement, so Washington was prepared. National Security Adviser John Poindexter made sure that Polish authorities understood in no uncertain terms that a crackdown on Solidarity would mean continued U.S. sanctions and a tighter grip on credit. Jaruzelski, facing a Hobson's choice, relented. The strong crackdown that some anticipated did not come.[12]

Efforts on the part of Polish authorities to cut off clandestine Western aid to Solidarity continued. A shipment on the docks of the Swinoujscie ferry was impounded by Polish authorities. It was a big catch. A forty-ton truck was seized, including $200,000 in valuable equipment: twenty-three offset presses, forty-nine copiers, sixteen fax machines, several IBM computers, nine disk drives, and twelve printing calculators. But despite this and other hiccups, the supply effort continued.

Support from the CIA was also going to some Czech and

Hungarian émigré groups in Europe and the United States in the hope
that they might cooperate in providing intelligence on events in their
home countries. Reagan's NSDD-32 had called for a regionwide effort
to unshackle Eastern Europe from the Soviet bloc, so the subversion
campaign was broadened. In mid-1986 someone had alerted the NSC
to the fact that a letter was being drawn up and signed by dissident
groups behind the Iron Curtain. It would be a call for joint action to
fight Soviet oppression. Casey and NSC officials decided to help. About
$25,000 went to the organization working on the letter.

At the end of October 1986, a bold call for people across
Eastern Europe to throw off Soviet power was issued. It was only a
letter, a few words culled by lonely dissidents. But this was no appeal
for better treatment. This was a political earthquake, a joint appeal from
dissidents in Hungary, East Germany, Czechoslovakia, and Poland issued as Hungary quietly marked the thirtieth anniversary of the Warsaw
Pact attack on it.

Joint action by East Europeans was a Soviet nightmare. Uprisings in Hungary and Czechoslovakia had been easily contained because
they had come intermittently. But a regional crisis would be another
matter. Nothing had enraged the Kremlin more than when Solidarity in
1981 had called for other East European nations to organize their own
free trade unions. And the letter heightened fears of general unrest. The
122 signatures on the letter included the leading lights of the opposition: Vaclav Havel in Czechoslovakia, George Konrad in Hungary, and
Lech Walesa in Poland. The idea for the letter had originated with the
dissidents themselves. Western émigré movements that relayed information in and out of most European countries had circulated the letter in
Eastern Europe. It was eventually read on Radio Free Europe/Radio
Liberty.

The letter went to the heart of NSDD-32. Solidarity had
weathered the storm in Poland, and the second cash shipment (of
$50,000) into Czechoslovakia had been sent in early October and
arrived safely. The region was restless, and the Reagan administration
was encouraging that mood.

While Polish activists continued to nibble away at communist
authority with rallies, literature, and the politics of protest, Pakistani
soldiers at an air base outside Islamabad started unpacking some very

delicate cargo in early July. Inside the ordinary looking crates were the "wonder weapons" the mujahedin had been waiting for. The Reagan administration was fulfilling its promise—the first shipment of Stinger missiles had arrived. From the earliest days of the war, the Soviets had been bombing mujahedin targets heavily without any fear of air defenses. Few surface to air missiles in the mujahedin arsenal seemed to do anything but go off like roman candles. "That was the single greatest need the mujahedin had," recalls Vincent Cannistraro. "Strafing was the most effective Soviet tactic. The introduction of the Stinger was a qualitative change that changed the dynamic of the war. It put the Soviets on the defensive."[13]

The tides of war were constantly shifting in Afghanistan, and 1986 was proving costly but successful for Moscow. The new aggressive tempo of Soviet military operations led to the toppling of Zhawar, the mujahedin's most important guerrilla base inside the country. The resistance had been routed at Khoust. But these Soviet successes were in reality only temporary. The mujahedin were more effective than ever. And the widespread use of aircraft, which had proven critical at Zhawar and Khoust, was about to come to an end.

The Stingers are highly prized and safeguarded; few American allies have access to them. Quite simply the best surface to air missile system in the world, the Stinger is a fire and forget weapon, so there is no need to remain exposed to guide the missile to its target. It has an effective ceiling in excess of 15,000 feet, carries a high explosive war-head, and races at 1,200 miles per hour to its target. The missile uses a complex infrared, heat-seeking detection system that, once it locks onto its target, is virtually impossible to distract with countermeasures.

One chief concern in the decision to provide the Stingers to the mujahedin was that they might fall into the hands of terrorists and extremists. A civilian airliner in Western Europe or the Middle East would be easy prey with such a weapon. But the president himself decided to provide the weapon even with such risks.

With the arrival of the Stingers, Brigadier Mohammad Yousaf took personal responsibility for selecting which mujahedin should be trained in their use. Casey had hoped that the CIA might conduct the training, but the Pakistani ISI refused. A simulator was brought in by the U.S. Army, and, with the help of the local CIA staff, it was set up at Ojhiri Camp in Rawalpindi. Mujahedin commanders were brought in, and a three-week training course began immediately. Two hundred and fifty Stinger grip stocks were to be shipped per year, with 1,200 missiles.

Strike teams were organized to follow the new Stinger commanders. Once a plane was shot down, the strike team would finish off the pilot. It was a grisly task. After several months of training, the Stinger finally made its debut in the skies over Afghanistan.

On September 25, a group of mujahedin hid on a small hill only a short distance from Jalalabad airfield. Commander Ghaffar was giving the orders to his unit of three Stingers and an efficient strike team. The commander and his team sat quietly in the bushes, all eyes looking for a suitable target. By three in the afternoon, a group of eight Soviet HIND gunships approached Jalalabad for a landing. The HIND was a particularly despised aircraft, a common sight that had inflicted massive casualties on fighters and civilians alike.

The Stinger system was incredibly easy to operate. It would lock onto its target automatically and indicated its readiness with a light pinging sound. The Stinger specialists slowly pointed their grips at separate targets, and the targets were locked. Anxious fingers rested on the triggers. Another mujahedin sat in the bushes with a video camera, watching the momentous event.

As the HINDs hovered only about 600 feet above the airstrip, Commander Ghaffar gave the order. The three missiles, along with shouts of "Allah o Akbar," shot through the air. One missile malfunctioned and fell harmlessly to the ground. But the other two slammed into their targets. There were explosions, and two fiery mechanical carcasses plummeted out of the sky. In the excitement the mujahedin began screaming for joy and passing around the Stingers so others could have their turn. Two more missiles were fired, and both found their targets. The remaining gunships hastened away, the crews in horror over what they had witnessed. The mujahedin had demonstrated their new weapon, which would ultimately alter the course of the war. The potency of the "wonder weapon" was clear: of the first 200 Stingers fired, 75 percent hit aircraft.[14]

Several weeks after Commander Ghaffar first employed the Stinger, the mujahedin videotape made its way to the White House, where the president viewed it in private. It was largely a series of blurred images. The excited cameraman had been running around in celebration and took only steady footage of the smoke and wreckage. Along with the video, the president received the tube of the first Stinger fired in Afghanistan.

Within several weeks there were more Stinger attacks. Soon the news began to spread among Soviet pilots. American intelligence, which had been intercepting Soviet military communications in Afghanistan for several years, began to pick up frantic shouting matches. Pilots were refusing to fly certain attack formations and were being castigated by superiors for dropping their charges from extremely high altitudes. Pilots returning from missions or transports bringing cargo began adopting tight corkscrew approaches when landing. "They started to bomb from much higher altitudes," recalls Vince Cannistraro, who was viewing the intelligence. "That made their bombing ineffective. From that point on, they started taking losses that were unacceptable. From a low-grade infection, Afghanistan was being converted into a hemorrhage."[15] "The use of Stingers tipped the tactical balance in our favor," says Mohammad Yousaf. "As success followed success, so the mujahedin morale rose and that of the enemy fell."[16] The trauma that the introduction of the Stinger imposed on the Soviet psyche cannot be overestimated. Sergei Tarasenko, principal foreign policy assistant to Eduard Shevardnadze, recalls, "I went with Shevardnadze to Afghanistan six times . . . and when we were coming into Kabul airport, believe me, we were mindful of Stinger missiles. That's an unpleasant feeling. You were happy when you were crossing the border and the loudspeaker would say, 'We are now in Soviet territory. Oh, my God. We made it!' "[17]

Mujahedin Stinger strike units were deployed aggressively around Soviet air bases. The first were placed around Kabul and Jalalabad. The second were in the north, along the Soviet border. Mujahedin along the border were looking to hit not only aircraft in Afghan airspace but also those flying in the Soviet Union. To encourage aggressive use of the Stinger and avoid commanders' hoarding the missiles, the ISI came up with an ingenious incentive plan: for each confirmed hit, a commander would be given a bonus of two more Stinger missiles.

As the Stinger missiles threatened the skies over Afghanistan, the

United States was pressing for and threatening the expansion of the war into Soviet Central Asia. That fall Undersecretary of Defense Fred Ikle testified on Capitol Hill concerning U.S. policy in Afghanistan. Answering a question from a congressman, he set off a firestorm in Moscow. "I said that if the Soviets did not comply with U.N. resolutions, that the war might spread to Soviet Central Asia; after all, there were all these incursions," he recalls. The incursions had been encouraged by Casey, and Ikle was trying to cajole Moscow into withdrawal by the threat of a widening war on Soviet territory. A TASS reporter attending the hearings wired back his story to Moscow, and the Foreign Ministry issued a stiff protest to the U.S. State Department. They quickly got back to Ikle. "The State Department said it was too much, I had gone too far," recalls Ikle. "But we were acting on that threat. We tried all kinds of things. Passing literature into Soviet Central Asia, and other ongoing operations. Casey was very vigorous on this strategy, and we gave him full support."[18]

By late 1986, reports of mujahedin activity inside the Soviet Union began coming back to Washington. Mujahedin commanders in the northern provinces of Afghanistan were being issued Chinese 107-mm rocket launchers and 122-mm Egyptian rocket launchers with ranges of almost ten miles. By night the systems would be set up on the southern bank of the Amu to fire volleys across the river, bringing down a rain of explosives on Soviet soil. Teams specially trained by the ISI and equipped by the CIA were making their way across the Amu to hit Soviet border posts, lay mines, and knock down power lines. An airfield just north of the Soviet town of Pyandzh was repeatedly hit by mujahedin commandos. Strikes were secretly launched from Jowzjan and Badakhshan provinces. Once they crossed the border, Soviet citizens would occasionally meet them and join in the operation. In early December 1986, some thirty mujahedin crossed the Amu in Zodiac boats to attack two hydroelectric facilities in Tajhikistan. To get to the power stations, they had to knock out two Soviet guard posts. When the mujahedin struck, eighteen Muslim soldiers fled to join the resistance. The facilities were heavily damaged, leaving parts of the republic without electricity for several weeks.

During the last months of 1986, a series of further attacks inside the Soviet Union were being planned for the spring. These operations would be more ambitious, with specially trained forces probing even deeper into the communist superpower while making use of more sophisticated weaponry. The plans included a heavy rocket attack on an airfield called Shurbo East, near the Soviet village of Gilyambor. Then a party of twenty men would also ambush forces on a frontier road east of Termez, the ancient Asian city on Soviet territory. The men would be armed with antitank mines, rocket-propelled grenades, and machine guns. The group would mine the road, wait for military vehicles to arrive, and, after a mine was triggered, open fire. Another planned operation was even more ambitious. It called for a unit headed by Wali Beg to penetrate almost fifteen miles into the Soviet Union to strike an industrial target near a sensitive military air base called Voroshilovabad.[19]

For the Kremlin, these attacks were a direct assault on the territorial integrity of the Soviet Union and played to a grave fear. Nationalism and Islamic fundamentalism were a brewing tempest on the horizon. Shortly after the attacks on Soviet soil began, they started paying dividends. The rising human toll, the costly losses caused by the introduction of the Stinger and the operations on Soviet territory were enough to force a Soviet retreat. At a Politburo meeting in early November 1986, it was decided to begin exploring a means to pull back Soviet forces. It was the first defeat in Cold War Soviet military history. At the beginning of December, Pakistan's permanent foreign secretary, Abdul Sattar, was invited to Moscow by Deputy Foreign Minister Yuli Vorontsov. The Soviet minister was very candid, speaking of the war as a "bleeding wound" and stating categorically, "We are leaving." Vorontsov said emphatically that the price of the war had simply become too high for the Kremlin. He wanted Sattar's help in ensuring that a Soviet withdrawal would not lead to a bloodbath. Sattar said that Islamabad would do what was necessary to ensure the orderly withdrawal of Soviet forces.[20]

A few weeks after Sattar flew home, Mohammad Najibullah, the new president of Afghanistan and the former head of the secret police, was summoned to the Kremlin by Gorbachev. A number of other members of the Afghan Politburo joined Najibullah in Moscow. The invitation characterized the meeting as a routine consultation, but the real purpose was much more grave. On December 12, the visitors filed into St. Catherine's Hall in the great Kremlin Palace, an elegant room and an ironic choice, full of icons and images of the Russian imperial past. As Najibullah and his cohorts were seated, they were joined by Mikhail Gorbachev, Foreign Minister Eduard Shevardnadze, Defense Minister Sergei Sokolov, KGB Chief Viktor Chebrikov, and the elder diplomat Anatoly Dobrynin.

Gorbachev pushed aside formalities and began speaking in no uncertain terms. Soviet forces would be withdrawn from Afghanistan within two years, the general secretary flatly told his guests. Moscow could no longer sustain the war effort. Gorbachev told the assembled that he was still committed to a communist victory in Afghanistan, and that he would do everything in his power to give the Najibullah government a fighting chance. Soviet forces would continue to fight aggressively until their withdrawal, and vast quantities of advanced arms and equipment would be given to the government. But you will have to fight alone, Gorbachev told the Afghan Politburo.[21]

The bleeding was by now costing the Kremlin $4 billion per year and thousands of young lives. The escalation of the war by the Reagan administration had simply made it impossible to win. And the Kremlin was too tired to fight simply to avoid losing. The only complete military defeat in Cold War Soviet history, it would have revolutionary consequences for Soviet Russia, just as losses in 1905 and 1917 had for its imperial predecessors.

But while the Kremlin planned its orderly retreat from Afghanistan, the capital of Kazakhstan (Alma-Ata) erupted in violence when hundreds of citizens took to the streets in an anti-Russian rampage. It was becoming very clear that the tempest begun in Afghanistan did not respect international borders. Ostensibly the violence was sparked by the ouster of Dinmukhamed Akhmedovich Kunayevand, the Kazakh Communist Party leader, and his replacement with an ethnic Russian, Gennadi Kolbin. But the growing tide of nationalistic and religious rebellion was so great that the reshuffling was only a convenient excuse.

The rioting was nationalistic and widespread. The rioters were well organized and had clearly prepared for an outburst. Kazakhstan had been the focus of the joint American-Pakistani anti-Soviet propaganda push in Soviet Central Asia. Radio broadcasts, literature, and other materials were being sent into the region. China was doing much the same. The effect of such campaigns is impossible to gauge, but what became very clear during the riots were the sentiments of the antigovernment crowds. Protesters carried banners that read, "We want to join China" and "America is our friend," a blunt and frightening message for Moscow.[22]

As Soviet power was on the retreat in Poland and Afghanistan, the specter of the American Strategic Defense Initiative continued to haunt the Kremlin. By late 1986, the project was beginning to show some notable technical successes. Funding had more than doubled since fiscal year 1985 to almost $3.3 billion in fiscal year 1987. Several foreign governments had concluded collaborative research agreements with the Reagan administration, a particularly troublesome development for Gorbachev because it further legitimized the research program in addition to giving more brainpower to it.

The Kremlin was running a vitriolic public campaign against American allies, warning against cooperation with the SDI research program and stressing that the system represented a Reagan administration attempt to achieve world strategic superiority. But on a different track, Marxist-Leninist and Soviet-backed terrorist organizations were launching military-style strikes against SDI research facilities and scientists across Europe. Between July 1986 and March 1987, three senior advisers to their governments who had participated in the secret cooperation talks were assassinated. On July 6, 1986, Karl-Heinz Beckhurts and his driver were killed by a remote-control bomb outside Munich. Beckhurts was the director of research at the Siemens Company, an SDI contractor. In June 1985, he had met with U.S. government officials to discuss the possibility of conducting SDI research. In late 1985 and early 1986, Beckhurts served as an adviser to the Bonn government during the SDI cooperation talks with Washington. A letter left by the Red Army Faction (RAF) at the scene of the crime indicated that Beckhurts was assassinated because of his involvement in these "secret negotiations."

On October 10, Gerald von Braunmuhl, a West German Foreign Ministry official, was shot dead by a masked gunman while leaving a taxi outside his Bonn home. Von Braunmuhl had been a principal adviser to West German Foreign Minister Hans-Dietrich Genscher during the SDI cooperation talks, in which he had "great responsibility," according to the *Frankfurter Allgemeine Zeitung.* The RAF claimed responsibility for this hit too, proclaiming in an apparent reference to the SDI talks, "Today we have, through the Ingrid Schubert Commando, shot dead the secret diplomat von Braunmuhl." Kurt Rebmann, Germany's federal prosecutor who investigated these attacks, called them "a coordinated offensive" against the West in general and SDI in particular.

The third senior official to pay with his life for negotiating the SDI cooperation agreement was Gen. Licio Giorgieri of the Italian Defense Ministry. The director general of the Department of Space and Armaments Procurement at the ministry was gunned down by two assassins on March 20, 1987. Like Beckhurts and von Braunmuhl, the general served as a principal adviser to his government during the SDI cooperation talks. The Union of Fighting Communists, a faction of the Italian Red Brigades, claimed responsibility for the attack. In a rambling fourteen-page communiqué, the group said Giorgieri "was struck down exclusively for his responsibility exercised following the Italian adhesion to the Star Wars project." The letter closed with the words "No to Star Wars."

West European scientists and companies that conducted SDI research were also targets. On July 24, 1986, the offices of the Fraunhofer Research Institute in Aachen, West Germany, were rocked by a bomb blast. The institute was conducting SDI-related research on a high-energy laser project known as Eurolaser. On July 25, a fifteen-pound bomb caused heavy damage at the headquarters of the Dornier Company in Inimenstaad. Dornier was working with the Sperry Corporation on the Instrument Pointing System, a device to target objects in space. In August 1986, barely two months after it had been awarded an SDI research contract, CSF Thomson had its Paris office bombed. The firm was working on free-electron lasers, a technology that, according to SDI director Gen. James Abrahamson, would make "a dramatic difference" in the SDI system. Thomson was also reportedly working on gallium-arsenide integrated circuits for SDI. The circuits would reduce the reaction time of the defense system. The IBM Research Center in Heidelberg was damaged on November 16, 1986, when a bomb exploded inside. The RAF claimed responsibility for the attack; IBM had four SDI contracts.

That a number of otherwise independent terrorist organizations began hitting SDI targets at the same time was curious, particularly since left-wing terrorist groups traditionally confined their attacks to largely political targets, or symbols of capitalism and "Western imperialism." Moscow, which at the time was granting safe harbor to terrorists in East Berlin and elsewhere in the Soviet bloc, no doubt saw the attacks as something of benefit.[23]

On the diplomatic front, Gorbachev figured his best hope for finishing off SDI was providing President Reagan with an offer he could not refuse. The Reykjavik Summit in October 1986 offered such an occasion.

Gorbachev was looking for two things from the Reagan administration. As he had told Soviet diplomats during a speech in early 1986, Soviet diplomacy "must contribute to the domestic development of the country." His highest foreign policy goal, he told the assembled, was to "create the best possible external conditions" for his reforms.[24] That meant gaining access to Western technology and credits and ending the technological challenge posed by SDI and the Reagan defense buildup.

The Reykjavik Summit proved a watershed meeting in many ways. In it the superpowers moved to the brink of eliminating all nuclear weapons, but Soviet hopes of eliminating the SDI research program were dashed once and for all. Reykjavik was the second meeting of these superpower leaders. If Geneva had been a chance to feel each other out, Reykjavik was a battleground for two visionaries, radically different in goals and values but equally committed to prevailing.

Some weeks before the summit, there had been leaks that the general secretary was planning to spring something big on President Reagan at the meeting. An Indian official had learned from former Ambassador Dobrynin, by then a senior secretary of the Communist Party Central Committee, that Gorbachev was planning to make an offer that might trap the president. In the White House there was the clear perception that Gorbachev was looking for relief and help. "They were desperate for an agreement on SDI," recalls Don Regan. "They were in trouble, we could see that. And the president did not bend."[25]

The elimination of all nuclear weapons, a dramatic proposal Gorbachev had advanced in January 1986, was his stalking horse. Reagan's abhorrence of nuclear weapons and his idealistic nature were well known in the Kremlin. The Gorbachev proposal played to these impulses, and it was hoped that it would prove too tempting for Reagan to reject.

Reykjavik was the least planned of all the summits. What began as another of several summit meetings quickly descended into a game of high-stakes political poker, with both making offers and counteroffers in search of a winning hand. Both Reagan and Gorbachev arrived not knowing what to expect but hopeful that each might set the agenda early and push the other to meet his demands. The venue for the summit was Hofdi House, isolated along the seaside. It was widely reported to be haunted but suited its purpose nicely.

The first session opened on October 11, at 10:30 A.M. Reagan and Gorbachev, along with their interpreters, met around the small dining room table. The general secretary announced almost immediately that he had ambitious proposals in every area of the relationship, particularly arms control. After a few remarks, Secretary of State George Shultz and Foreign Minister Eduard Shevardnadze joined them to present initiatives. The Soviet proposals zeroed in on three areas— strategic nuclear weapons, intermediate nuclear forces, and space weapons. The proposals were indeed radical—50 percent cuts across the board in strategic nuclear weapons and cuts in intermediate forces on both sides. But on space weapons Gorbachev was insisting that SDI be confined to the laboratory.

After the first session, Reagan huddled with his senior aides, including Shultz, John Poindexter, Paul Nitze, Kenneth Adelman, and Richard Perle. The president, his uncommonly good instincts intact, listened to his aides and mulled over the Gorbachev proposals. Nitze was very excited by what the general secretary had brought. But Reagan said, "He's brought a whole lot of proposals, but I'm afraid he's going after SDI."[26]

Talks resumed at 2:00 P.M., and Reagan, Gorbachev, Shultz, and Shevardnadze sat facing one another. Reagan responded to Gorbachev's proposals, outlining the U.S. offers on arms control. On the second floor of Hofdi House, members of both delegations milled around talking informally. John Poindexter spoke with Marshal Sergei Akhromeyev on a sofa in the corner. To Poindexter it became clear almost immediately that the marshal was sincere about arms control but that he also had an abject fear of SDI. "It is an attempt to shift the correlation of forces in your favor," he warned. By the time Poindexter left the nearly hourlong conversation, two strategic themes were etched firmly in his mind: "He was sincere in wanting an agreement, of that I am sure. They needed an agreement. But it was also very clear that he was extremely concerned about SDI and the challenge it presented to Moscow. They were prepared to do whatever they could to stop it."[27]

Day two of the summit offered the same sort of roller-coaster ride. Tremendous Soviet concessions were made in the strategic and intermediate nuclear force portions of the talks. But it all hinged on SDI, said Gorbachev. With his country a superpower largely because of its military capability, Gorbachev's willingness to agree to dramatic cuts and link them to strategic defense was further evidence of just how desperate Moscow was for relief from the West.

Reagan clung stubbornly to his vision of a strategic defense system. He left Iceland angry and deeply disappointed, but one month later, says John Poindexter, "the president understood just what we had in the SDI system, and that it posed a grave challenge to the Kremlin."[28]

1. State Department memo, January 1986.
2. Interview with the author.
3. U.S. official, interview with the author.
4. *Pravda*, August 15, 1985.
5. *Kommunist*, no. 4, March 1986, pp. 81–98.
6. "The 27th Congress of the CPPSU and Its International Significance," *International Affairs* (Moscow), June 1986.
7. Senior administration officials, interview with the author; Bush comments and White House response, Daniel Yergin, *The Prize: The Epic Quest for Oil, Money and Power* (New York: Simon and Schuster, 1991), p. 756.
8. U.S. official, interview with the author.
9. "USSR: Facing the Dilemma of Hard Currency Shortages," Central Intelligence Agency: Directorate of Intelligence, May 1986.
10. Joseph Persico, *Casey: The Lives and Secrets of William J. Casey* (New York: Penguin, 1991); interview with U.S. official.
11. Interview with the author.
12. John Poindexter, interview with the author.
13. Vincent Cannistraro, interview with the author.
14. Mohammad Yousaf, interview with the author; Vincent Cannistraro, interview with the author.

15. Vincent Cannistraro, interview with the author.
16. Mohammad Yousaf, interview with the author.
17. Sergei Tarasenko, comments at Princeton University conference "A Retrospective on the End of the Cold War," February 27, 1993.
18. Fred Ikle, interview with the author.
19. Mohammad Yousaf, interview with the author.
20. Senior Pakistani official, interview with the author.
21. See Don Oberdorfer, *The Turn* (New York: Poseidon, 1991), pp. 239–43.
22. See S. Enders Wimbush, "The Muslim Ferment in Soviet Central Asia," *Global Affairs*, Summer 1987, pp. 106–18.
23. For more on these SDI attacks see James Denton and Peter Schweizer, "Murdering SDI," *National Review*, July 31, 1987, pp. 37–39.
24. Quoted in Don Oberdorfer, *The Turn* (New York: Poseidon, 1991), p. 162.
25. Donald Regan, interview with the author.
26. John Poindexter, interview with the author.
27. John Poindexter, interview with the author.
28. John Poindexter, interview with the author.

Epilogue

By late 1986, the Reagan administration faced a political maelstrom as allegations arose in what came to be known as the Iran-Contra affair. The National Security Council was immediately plunged into disarray. At the same time, CIA Director William Casey became seriously ill and died in early 1987. The resignation of Defense Secretary Caspar Weinberger soon followed. The team that had so skillfully crafted the strategic offensive against the Soviet Union was largely gone. Those who remained, or others who might want to persevere, were soon in a defensive posture, hunkering down in the face of the Iran-Contra storm. However, critical elements of the strategy did remain in place.

United States financial and logistical support for Solidarity in Poland continued up until the national elections of 1989.[1] This aid made a fundamental contribution to the survival and effectiveness of the Solidarity underground. Military assistance and intelligence continued to flow to the Afghan mujahedin, even after the Soviet withdrawal began in May 1988. Restrictions on technology exports to the Soviet bloc remained largely in place even after the collapse of the Soviet Union in 1991. The specter of lower energy prices and reduced hard currency earnings haunts Moscow even today. And the defense buildup, which effectively reached a budget plateau in the middle of the decade, continued to be characterized by a commitment to advanced new weapons research projects, including the Strategic Defense Initiative. The strategic and resource parameters of the superpower competition established during the early Reagan years remained intact up until the collapse of the Soviet Union.

The Soviet Union did not collapse by osmosis, nor because time was somehow on our side. Had the Kremlin not faced the cumulative effects of SDI and the defense buildup, geopolitical setbacks in Poland and Afghanistan, the loss of tens of billions of dollars in hard currency earnings from energy exports, and reduced access to technology, it is reasonable to believe that it could have weathered the storm. Soviet communism was not an organism doomed to self-destruct in any international environment. American policies could and did alter the course of Soviet history. It is ironic that many Western observers who once insisted that the Soviet economy was comparable to that of the United States, and that a policy of confrontation would be fruitless given the relative strength of the Soviet position, now suddenly contend that the decline and fall of the Soviet empire was somehow inevitable.

The early Reagan era marked the beginning of the end for the Soviet Union. Although the vital signals at the time did not indicate that death was approaching, the period brought unprecedented stress to an already ill body. It was forced to expend precious lifeblood to run a race against a more athletic foe. Unable to gain access to external medicines that might revive it, or at least deal with some of the symptoms, the body saw its vital members attacked. It was during the early 1980s that the Soviet Union took the first steps in what would become its death march.

At the time no one in the administration (with the exception of Ronald Reagan) ever articulated a vision of a collapsing Soviet edifice. The goal was to weaken and strain the Soviet system. But policies designed to weaken the Soviet system became life-threatening. The first blows to the nails of the Soviet coffin came in the early 1980s and were driven home at the end of the decade.

In 1989, Solidarity won a significant victory when national elections were held in Poland. According to Sergei Tarasenko, principal foreign policy assistant to Foreign Minister Eduard Shevardnadze between 1985 and 1991, that momentous event convinced Mikhail Gorbachev that the Soviet system would break up.[2] But it is highly unlikely that Solidarity would have even survived the decade had it not been for the overt and covert policies of the Reagan administration. If the administration had taken the European line on Poland and not pressed for Western sanctions; had balked at providing covert financial, logistical, and intelligence support to the underground; and had not negotiated for the survival of the opposition by using American sanctions, the crackdown in Poland might very well have succeeded.

The Soviet defeat in Afghanistan sent shock waves throughout the communist bloc. It was evidence that the so-called Brezhnev Doctrine, which held that no socialist countries would ever be "lost" to the West, was in effect null and void. But without an aggressive American policy, it is doubtful that the Soviet reversal would have come at all. The mujahedin, brave as they were, faced an opponent that outgunned them and demonstrated no qualms about ruthlessness. They would most certainly have lost without American assistance. "CIA aid was necessary and critical in the eventual defeat of the Russians," says Brigadier Mohammad Yousaf.[3] The U.S. covert aid program, launched tentatively by the Carter administration in 1980, grew throughout the decade. But the quality and sophistication of weapons also increased, and detailed intelligence was shared with the resistance. The goal of harassing Soviet forces was changed in 1985 to working for victory, and the war was even expanded into the Soviet Union itself. The cumulative effect of these initiatives was a dramatic jump in Soviet casualties, which ultimately ushered in the Soviet exit from Afghanistan.

At the same time that the administration was working to exploit the geopolitical cracks in the Soviet bloc, it was effectively exacerbating the Soviet resource crisis. The American defense buildup is a case in point. The immediate purpose was to enhance deterrence, but the administration also had a much more fundamental objective. As spelled out in the Department of Defense Five-Year Planning Directive, the buildup was designed not only to raise the relative military strength of the United States vis-à-vis the Soviet Union but also to contribute to the absolute decline in Soviet economic power. It was a form of economic warfare.

The buildup was not simply about larger budgets. How the funds were spent was equally important. The commitment to high-tech advanced weapons systems (including SDI) suddenly injected what for Moscow was a dangerous dynamic into the arms competition. The Kremlin favored a largely quantitative race, because it would cap the American technological advantage. But when the race assumed largely qualitative parameters, Moscow was at a dramatic disadvantage and proved to be not up to the task. It was for this reason that Gorbachev possessed such an overarching fear of SDI and other American high-tech defense programs.

At the same time, the Reagan administration worked to hit the Kremlin's pocketbook. The completion of the Siberian natural gas pipeline half its planned size and two years behind schedule was a big financial blow, along with a constant American campaign to drive down international energy prices. Tens of billions of dollars in critical hard currency earnings were lost when they were most needed. Tighter restrictions on technology exports also retarded Soviet economic performance.

But assume for a moment that the American defense buildup begun by Jimmy Carter in 1980 had petered out by 1983, or that SDI had never seen the light of day; that Soviet access to Western technologies had remained constant; and that a natural gas pipeline had generated hard currency with energy prices relatively high. The Soviet resource crisis would have been much more manageable.

No singular event or policy pushed the Kremlin over the brink. The power of the Reagan administration's overall strategy is measured by the cumulative effect of the policies that were adopted. They came as a flurry of hard blows to a weakened Soviet system. The death of Soviet communism killed off the Cold War. The irony of course is that current historiography has given Mikhail Gorbachev the lion's share of the credit for the dawning of the post–Cold War era. This is a most curious development, giving the vanquished more credit than the victor.

1. John Poindexter, interview with the author.
2. Sergei Tarasenko, comments at Princeton University conference "A Retrospective on the End of the Cold War," May 3, 1993.
3. Mohammad Yousaf, interview with the author.